A Short Life of
Kierkegaard

A SHORT LIFE OF
Kierkegaard

BY

WALTER LOWRIE

With Lowrie's essay "How Kierkegaard
Got into English" and a new introduction
by Alastair Hannay

PRINCETON UNIVERSITY PRESS

PRINCETON AND OXFORD

First printing of *A Short Life of Kierkegaard*, 1942
Fifth paperback printing, 1974
Paperback reissue, with "How Kierkegaard Got into
English" and an introduction by Alastair Hannay, 2013

Library of Congress Control Number 2012952482
ISBN 978-0-691-15777-1

British Library Cataloging-in-Publication
Data is available

Printed on acid-free paper.∞

Printed in the United States of America

1 3 5 7 9 10 8 6 4 2

TO

JOHN A. MACKAY

DOCTOR OF THEOLOGY

PRESIDENT OF PRINCETON THEOLOGICAL SEMINARY

AT HOME ON BOTH AMERICAN CONTINENTS

AND BEFORE BECOMING AMERICAN

A KIERKEGAARDIAN

THIS LITTLE BOOK IS AFFECTIONATELY

DEDICATED

CONTENTS

INTRODUCTION

WALTER LOWRIE was ninety-one years old when he died at Princeton Hospital on August 12, 1959, the recent translator of twelve works of Kierkegaard, author of this *Short Life* and of its more than six-hundred-page predecessor. Although Lowrie's engagement with Kierkegaard had begun earlier in the century, it is staggering to realize that it was not until he had reached the age of sixty-four that he began studying Danish with a view to translation. The energy and enthusiasm with which he plunged into this enormously influential undertaking is still tangible in the retrospective essay accompanying this reissue of the *Short Life*. The reissue itself, apart from providing a welcome opportunity to renew our appreciation of Lowrie, also offers a chance to look at the motivation behind such prodigious effort and at its effect on the ways in which the English-speaking world has taken, or not taken, to Kierkegaard.

For a present generation of scholars young enough to have been directed to the sometimes forbidding, fearsomely annotated, but formidably "established" Hong translations, the fact that the Danish thinker's name was hardly known in Anglophone circles in the 1940s may be hard to believe. For my own generation it was through the eminently readable renderings by Alexander Dru, David F. Swenson, and Walter Lowrie that we first met Kierkegaard, so to speak, face to face. As with many others still today, my first contact was with *Fear and Trembling*, the book Kierkegaard believed would make him famous. Although Lowrie modestly describes his translations as more "literal" than "literary," I think most readers will agree that the latter is largely false, while on the other hand many will have discovered that the former is not always true. To me, with its iconic narrative and the stark alternatives drawn from it, *Fear and Trembling* came through loud and clear, the louder and clearer for not being read through a now ever-thickening prism of textual commentary and explanation. From that provocative beginning it was natural to proceed to the invitingly entitled *Either/Or*, a translation left unfinished by David Swenson and completed by Lowrie. Still energized, I proceeded, though at times flaggingly, through the outwardly ramshackle and seemingly endlessly concluding *Postscript*, this being Lowrie's completion of yet another unfinished Swenson translation. That work, *Concluding Unscientific Postscript: A Mimic-Pathetic-Dialectic Composition, An Existential Contribution*, had already appeared in 1941, and by this time the firm "Swenson and Lowrie" had all but become synonymous with at least the first part of its long title. Packing in, as it does, most of Kierkegaard's thought up to the time it was written, Swenson and Lowrie's *Postscript* became the Anglophone Kierkegaard scholar's bible, just as Lowrie's *Kierkegaard* from 1938 was the original source of all those iconic anecdotes that were the stock-in-trade of the Kierkegaard *cognoscenti*: the strict father who as a child had cursed God, the rebellious young man, the broken engagement, the spat with *The Corsair*, the all-out attack on the church, the terminal sickness when his money had just run out.

There are by now several English-language biographies of Kierkegaard. None, however, shows the near devotional respect for its subject that we find in Lowrie's *Kierkegaard*. Nor does *A Short Life* contain any noticeable revision in this respect, its brevity made possible, as Lowrie explains in the essay, because there was no longer "a necessity for such abundant quotation." In what is generally taken to be an antidote to Lowrie's glowing portrayal, Josiah Thompson has portrayed Kierkegaard, with considerable scenic skill, as a somewhat elusive anti-hero.[1] Thompson, an academic with literary rather than theological interests who later wrote on the Kennedy assassination before turning his talents to private detection in San Francisco, presents Kierkegaard as an intriguing but shadowy figure, furtive even, and with few redeeming

---

[1] Josiah Thompson, *Kierkegaard* (New York: Alfred A. Knopf, 1973).

features beyond those prized by literary theorists. Another biographer, Danish, has more recently made his fellow countryman into a figure we might just meet, if fleetingly, on Copenhagen's streets, imagine in the night behind his glowing apartment window, or even hear speaking to one of his few friends.[2] In spite of his theological background, Joakim Garff tones down even to the point of ignoring those aspects from which Lowrie extracts what his English-speaking readers came to understand as Kierkegaard's "message." In yet another biography, my own, and no doubt typically of the foreigner whose cultural genes, or memes, are from another place, the man is seen first of all through his published works and *Nachlass*, and thus as a thinking writer. The biography attempts a narrative of what drove Kierkegaard to write the books he did and in such a way as to give them *their* life history.[3]

Walter Lowrie's biographies are sometimes described as hagiography. What truth there is in this can be left to his readers. But it is as well to sketch in those features of Lowrie's own life that would lead one to expect a fairly saintly portrait from his hand. If there has been a tendency in some quarters, and particularly in the United States, to canonize Kierkegaard, something that a fair knowledge of what Kierkegaard wrote about himself tells us is misguided, then some of the blame must indeed be placed on Lowrie. Not that saintliness is out of the question; it is well known that Ludwig Wittgenstein found some. But the latter's background and atheistic leanings lead one to suppose that he saw it in some quality other than the staunch upholding of Christian faith. In a Faroese novel (translated as *The Lost Musicians*) Kierkegaard is described as the "tragic satan," one who, by attacking reason with its own weapons and then turning them mercilessly on himself, upstages even Mephistophe-

---

[2] Joakim Garff, *Søren Kierkegaard: A Biography*, trans. Bruce H. Kirmmse (Princeton, N.J.: Princeton University Press, 2004).

[3] Alastair Hannay, *Kierkegaard, A Biography* (Cambridge: Cambridge University Press, 2001).

les.[4] In general, we should probably accept as a twofold truth that Kierkegaard was a complex person as well as a complex writer, and that a biography cannot help but be to some extent a reflection of the biographer's own background. When a good portrait painter chooses the sitter for the portrait he or she is about to paint, the attraction that led to that choice is almost certain to be visible in the result.

Lowrie, and we might well call him a man of his time, could have overlapped Kierkegaard had not the latter died an early death at forty-two just thirteen years before Lowrie was born on April 26, 1868, the son of a clergyman. He attended Lawrenceville School in New Jersey and then, in the fall of 1886, entered the freshman class at Princeton College. On graduating in 1890 he continued to Princeton Theological Seminary, taking a master's degree in divinity in 1893. Between then and 1899, between assorted clerical positions including several years as summer minister in New York State, Lowrie spent three periods of study abroad, which took him to Germany, Switzerland, and Italy. Rome was on the last two itineraries, and it was there, after further study at Princeton and some pastoral work elsewhere, that he was to settle for twenty-three years as rector of St. Paul's American Church in Rome. Appointed in 1907 at the age of thirty-nine, he remained in that post until he was sixty-two, at which point "having lived, off and on, for twenty-seven years on the Continent of Europe," he returned home, in his own words, as "a superannuated clergyman."[5]

From Lowrie's first real encounter with Kierkegaard, through the Swiss theologian Karl Barth, to the completion of his Kierkegaard saga—the working part, so to speak, for

[4] William Heinesen, *De fortabte Spillemænd* (Copenhagen: Gyldendal, 1965), p. 144.

[5] From "How Kierkegaard Got into English," published here. Quotations from Lowrie *not* signaled as from this source or another are from the preface and the introduction to his *Kierkegaard* (Oxford and New York: Oxford University Press, 1938), much of which the essay recapitulates.

those interested in Kierkegaard—the reader is referred here to Lowrie's own account in "How Kierkegaard Got into English." In his own characteristically unforced style we read there of the varied results of an extended tour in 1933–34 to China and Japan, where as the introduction to the earlier *Kierkegaard* had put it: "China is not inclined to attach any importance to subjects which have not yet emerged in America," while the Japanese demonstrated to him their "just pride" in "learning also from the continent of Europe." We read also how, once back home, Lowrie set about removing the root cause of Chinese disinterest in Kierkegaard. Now studying Danish in earnest, he began work on the extensive biography that appeared five years later, and also on the first translations, the first of which appeared in 1939 and the twelfth, and last, only five years later.

Lowrie begins by noting the initiative taken by Charles Williams (1886–1945) at Oxford University Press. What he doesn't mention is that Williams was a poet, novelist, theologian, and literary critic, and also a member of the Inklings, that group of literary enthusiasts that included J.R. Tolkien, C. S. Lewis, and Owen Barfield. Kierkegaard had come to Williams's attention as a religious writer with qualities congenial to the group's dedication to literary forms, and in particular fantasy, as ways of mediating aspects of life that philosophy failed to embrace. Williams had persuaded Alexander Dru to translate selections from Kierkegaard's journals, then quite unknown to an English-speaking reading public. As Lowrie says, "While Dru held the door open I walked in." Dru's *The Journals of Kierkegaard 1834–1855* appeared in 1938, the same year as Lowrie's biography, both of them published from Oxford University Press's New York office, as were Lowrie's first translations.

Lowrie lists the first English translations in the order in which Kierkegaard produced them, but the order of translation reveals his mission more clearly. The earliest were (in 1939) *Christian Discourses* and *The Point of View for My Work as an Author*; then (in 1940) *The Present Age* and *Two Minor Ethico-*

Religious Treatises, and *Stages on Life's Way*; then (in 1941) *Training in Christianity*, *For Self-Examination* and *Judge For Yourselves*, *Repetition*, *Fear and Trembling*, *The Sickness Unto Death*, and the completion of Swenson's *Concluding Unscientific Postscript*; and finally (in 1944) *The Concept of Dread*, *Either/Or*, and *Attack upon "Christendom" 1854–1855*.

Lowrie's speed was in contrast to the painfully slow progress made by David Ferdinand Swenson, the first to bring Kierkegaard to the notice of Americans, though in very small numbers. Only a handful of academics will have come across Swenson's "The Anti-Intellectualism of Kierkegaard" in the 1916 volume of the *Philosophical Review*. To the frustration of those seeking further enlightenment, Swenson's articles were "hidden away in the back numbers of specialist reviews." The contrast was reflected in the styles of their engagement. For Swenson it was first of all a private affair, and although Lowrie says that what drew him to Kierkegaard was "the presentiment that what he had to say was what I personally was in need of," there was also this more immediate urge to make Kierkegaard known. In a foreword to the Swenson and Lowrie *Postscript*, Lillian Marvin Swenson describes how the chance discovery of the Danish text by her husband, then "a young graduate student in philosophy not wholly oriented in his thought," had "marked a crisis in his intellectual and spiritual development," and says that for the rest of his life Swenson remained "saturated" in Kierkegaard's thought. Anxious not to let Kierkegaard's style invade his renderings, he was a slow translator: "For many years," says his wife and by now widow, "his was a lone voice crying in the wilderness, for though Kierkegaard's works had long been known in Germany and France, even his name was practically unknown to English-speaking people." But then,

> some eight years ago Dr. Walter Lowrie of Princeton, burning with a dynamic enthusiasm for the Kierkegaard literature, returned to this country, and began his crusade for an English edition of Kierkegaard's works. Under this stimulus, and encour-

aged by the co-operation of one more aggressively active than himself, Mr. Swenson completed his translation of *Philosophical Fragments*, and then took up in earnest the translation of the *Postscript*.[6]

Unfortunately, Swenson, who had taught at Minnesota throughout the 1920s and 1930s, was unable through illness to complete the task. Eight years Lowrie's junior, he died in 1940.

Lowrie's dynamism spills over into his characteristically informal prefaces and introductions, the easy, not to say companionable, style of which happily infects both the essay published here and the *Short Life*. In "How Kierkegaard Got into English" he quotes Mrs. Swenson saying that he was more "aggressive" than her husband and, without taking offense, concedes that "in the proper sense of the word" he might be called that. He then tells a story in which he introduces the notion of providence, to Lowrie's unstrained dealings with which we shall return.

The easy familiarity with which not only his readers are treated, but also his subject, deserves our attention. Lowrie's constant reference to "S.K.," a practice that endures to this day in Kierkegaard circles, might have been a way of resolving difficulties of pronunciation or just a convenient abbreviation. Neither seems enough, nor both in combination; these two conveniences are more obviously byproducts of the special rapport that Lowrie feels with Kierkegaard, a rapport so close that it almost seems as though Kierkegaard had found *him*. To use a profane parallel, there is some hint in Lowrie's "S.K." of the satisfaction of a regional representative promoting a foreign import. Indeed Lowrie describes himself as a "promoter" and seems not averse to some association with "traveling salesmen." But there is something more: a familiarity not just with the goods but with the manufacturer.

[6] *Kierkegaard's Concluding Unscientific Postscript*, trans. David F. Swenson and Walter Lowrie (Princeton, N.J.: Princeton University Press, 1941), pp. vii–viii.

In the closing pages of *The Point of View for My Work as Author* Kierkegaard quotes a hypothetical "poet" whose words more or less summarize the account Kierkegaard has just given there of his suffering and of the role played by providence in its productive exploitation. The point of the lyrical version seems to be that it comes from someone abstracted from a society that condemns and ridicules Kierkegaard, someone therefore better able to see that he had "completed the task of reflection—that of casting Christianity, becoming a Christian, wholly and fully into reflection."[7] Lowrie, apparently aware that readers may suspect him of assuming that poet's role, says:

> I am not deluded by the notion that I might faintly resemble such a figure. But S.K. also spoke of the time when "my lover" will come—and the reader will easily discern that this book is written by a lover.

In *Works of Love*, first translated by David Swenson and Lillian Marvin Swenson (1946), love is said to bring out a person's positive sides and give conciliatory explanations of whatever sins may be visible. It can be true of biography: lives presented by aficianodos are inevitably seen through rose-tinted glasses. But then why should they not be? What life is seen as it is, or was, through plain glass? What one biographer sees escapes the eagle eye of another. In dealing with the ghost still haunting the streets of Copenhagen, on which he continues to be portrayed in *The Corsair*'s caricature and one suspects not only for the sake of tourists, Garff makes no attempt to elicit affection. He does however raise questions of honesty and even mental stability, questions that a lover who knows Kierkegaard first through his texts and a suitable selection from the journals may see little or no reason to raise, to say nothing of other closer-to-home matters true of most lives and lifetimes: envy, jealousy, even sexual repression.

---

[7] *The Point of View*, trans. Howard V. Hong and Edna H. Hong (Princeton, N.J.: Princeton University Press, 1998), p. 97.

How far a biographer can go in this direction without loss of perspective is a matter of judgment and taste, but the choice is there just as motivations differ. According to Garff, his biography too is a labor of love, but not so much for his subject as for the opportunity to bring the writer behind the writings to account at last, and the opportunity to put the life into eminently readable words. With the evidence at his fingertips Garff can offer a vast palette of facts, hints, and conjectures out of which readers may piece together their own likenesses of a Kierkegaard living a life in something like the way we all do, bringing him to heel, as it were. There is a certain kind of familiarity in that too. Its nature is indicated by the Danish title's use of Kierkegaard's initials, this time in full, "SAK," hinting at the Danish *sik-sak* (zig-zag) and *saks* (scissors). The result is a far cry from the candidate for canonization that in some quarters emerged from Lowrie's "S.K."

Lowrie admits that "getting to know" Kierkegaard was impossible from the texts alone. For that he needed the journals and papers. To some, however, the texts themselves proved difficult enough. A sociologist asked to review *The Concept of Dread* was left "puzzled."[8] On seeking some guidance and finding the copies of Lowrie's *Kierkegaard* on loan, for background he resorted to E. L. Allen's *Kierkegaard, His Life and Thought*.[9] Allen, however, had been unable to place Kierkegaard's polemic in the wider development of modern European culture. In comparing Kierkegaard with his most enduring Danish theological opponent, N.F.S. Grundtvig, Allen came out in favor of the latter. His conclusion was that Kierkegaard had no real understanding of the wider issues and polemics to which his works might be thought to contribute. In the essay Lowrie refers to both Allen and John A. Bain as having written "their little books" in an "incredibly

---

[8] Ellsworth Faris, "Review of *The Concept of Dread* by Søren Kierkegaard," *American Journal of Sociology* 50 (1945): 401–4.

[9] E. L. Allen, *Kierkegaard, His Life and Thought* (London: Stanley Watt, 1935).

short time" but then having "washed their hands of Kierke-gaard." Whatever assistance or otherwise the reviewer received from Allen, the result demonstrated how easy it was in 1940 to caricature the thought—as easy as it had been in the 1840s for *The Corsair* to caricature the person.

> The enthusiastic Kierkegaardians of our day do not, obviously, base their allegiance on [the] teachings of the master. Among the acceptable doctrines which appeal to our contemporaries are: original sin, the supremacy of faith over reason, and the value of "existential truth." [Kierkegaard's] "teleological suspension of the ethical" receives less emphasis. In this "moral form of evil" faith takes precedence over the ethical. Abraham knew it was wrong to sacrifice Isaac, but he was willing to do it if God said so. This revelation seems to have come to our author after he had done wrong to the woman to whom he had been pledged.[10]

With the extensive background available today, both in the chronologically ordered translation of *Kierkegaard's Journals and Notebooks* and with the historical information available in informative works such as Kirmmse's *Encounters*,[11] distortion of this kind should be a thing of the past.

Whether the reviewer would show a better grasp and more appreciation with the benefit of Lowrie's positive portrait is hard to say. Lowrie's promotional zeal might put off those who did not share his belief in Kierkegaard. Lowrie himself admits that "a great many persons, especially in America, if they were to become acquainted with S.K., would indignantly reject him." But the example does point to a problem that time deepens rather than resolves. Translation means both displacement and transplantation. The reviewer Ellsworth Faris plausibly suggests that interest in Kierkegaard in the early 1940s was part of a "current reaction against the scientific method and all it implies." In some places that is no

---

[10] Faris, ibid.
[11] Bruce H. Kirmmse, ed., *Encounters with Kierkegaard: A Life as Seen by His Contemporaries*, trans. Bruce H. Kirmmse and Virginia R. Laursen (Princeton, N.J.: Princeton University Press, 1996).

doubt true also today. Scientism, however, was not Kierkegaard's own target. His concern was with matters that occupy people in an open confrontation with life, matters wrongly assumed to be in the hands of the masters of metaphysics and theology. Kierkegaard was wary of scientists, but science itself was something he held in considerable respect, though typically enough mocking popular expectations.[12] Lowrie was the first to tell us that in his university entrance examination, besides philosophy, Kierkegaard passed in both mathematics and physics with the highest distinction.[13] We have *The Concept of Dread*'s clear restrictions on what psychology can say in the context of "spirit," but what Kierkegaard's attitude to sociology would be is harder to guess. In any case, a better formula for his critical engagement than "the supremacy of faith over reason" would be "the primacy of the engaged first-personal point of view."

Lowrie's campaign was fueled by fear of an English-language repetition of the German and French receptions. Knowing from his European experience how selective translation had favored the secular readings for which Kierkegaard's compatriot Georg Brandes had prepared the way, Lowrie's first translations, as we saw, were from Kierkegaard's decidedly religious post-*Postscript* writings. *Either/Or*, along with its "Seducer's Diary," came at the end. As he admits, Lowrie's plan at first had been to translate no more than *The Point of View*, along with two religious works from the same late period. He accepts Kierkegaard's account in the former of his own authorship without demur, and some will say he fails to penetrate to the reason for Kierkegaard's withholding of this work from publication until after his death, that the book itself was part of a continuing struggle to measure up to the implications of its invocation of divine

[12] *Kierkegaard's Journals and Notebooks*, ed. Niels Jørgen Cappelørn et al. (Princeton, N.J.: Princeton University Press, 2007–), vol. 4, NB:76. "[Y]ear after year, something that once caused astonishment becomes commonplace."

[13] Walter Lowrie, *Kierkegaard* (Oxford and New York: Oxford University Press, 1938), p. 67.

assistance. Lowrie, who is prone to invoke providence openly and more casually than Kierkegaard, seems impervious to such scruples. In general he writes as if he and Kierkegaard both shared a "result" that Kierkegaard kept under his hat only so that readers less perceptive than Lowrie could come to the same result on their own. Lowrie has no such Socratic plans for his own readers, and we find, in his enthusiastic vocational exercise, little reflection on Kierkegaard's Socratic side, little hint of the impression a reader may receive of a latter-day Socrates who was his own Meno.

Readers today are in a better position to know where Lowrie himself stands, and consequently, if they follow him, where they stand. They can see why some claim that the Kierkegaard emerging from Lowrie's eminently readable translations is scarcely distinguishable from an "orthodox Christian believer."[14] Those who have embraced Kierkegaard as a resource for renewal *within* the established church and have heard of his wish not to receive the sacraments from the hands of a cleric[15] may ask themselves whether an ordained minister is the right person to restore him, figuratively speaking, to life.

Lowrie is aware of the problem. He admits having had to shake off the limitation of being a parson, one of Kierkegaard's two most savaged targets, luckily escaping the other through not having become a university "don." Here too we should perhaps take account of time. The Kierkegaard who changed the young David Swenson's life, and whose works Walter Lowrie D.D. felt could speak to his personal needs, sounds quite unlike the Kierkegaard who said very little to his contemporaries' taste, contemporaries who resented the dismissal of their faith as a sham and their preachers as theatrical showmen. And who knows? Today Kierkegaard might

[14] See Roger Poole, "The Unknown Kierkegaard: Twentieth-century Receptions," in Alastair Hannay and Gordon D. Marino, eds., *The Cambridge Companion to Kierkegaard* (Cambridge: Cambridge University Press, 1998), p. 59.

[15] Søren Kierkegaard, *Papers and Journals: A Selection*, trans. Alastair Hannay (London: Penguin Books, 1996), pp. 654–55.

have found it more important to question militant atheists about the sincerity of their *dis*belief. Starting a new campaign against congregational interference with individual faith might seem the wrong way to go when so many individuals have stopped being congregational.

We can assume one thing: that Kierkegaard, who, having seen things from "the very core of Christianity,"[16] refused the last rites, would not allow that his scruples in this matter were better appreciated by "followers" who found it expedient to phase out the Christian frame than by those who held it fast. In view of the situation in Europe at the time it might occur to him that Walter Lowrie's arrival on the scene was most opportune. It might even have struck him that providence had a hand in it. He would be more likely than Lowrie to keep that to himself.

Lowrie, who is more "upfront" than Kierkegaard in all respects, is also open and lyrical enough in his writing for us to consider his biography in the light of what Kierkegaard would call "the poetic"—perhaps not sufficiently so to have become that hypothetical poet whom Kierkegaard spoke both for and of, but, and to the pleasure of his readers, enough to qualify Lowrie as his own poet.

A Short Life says as much about Lowrie himself indirectly as the accompanying essay says about his historical mission directly. We should be grateful for this welcome renewal of *their* lives, very appropriately occasioned by the two-hundredth anniversary of the beginning of Kierkegaard's own.

ALASTAIR HANNAY
University of Oslo

[16] Søren Kierkegaard, *Papers and Journals: A Selection*, p. 654.

PREFACE

THE Princeton University Press about eight months ago asked me to write "a relatively short" life of Kierkegaard. I did not at once decide to take up the task; for though I agreed that a small book is needed, it seemed to me strange for one man to write two biographies of the same person. But then again, if such a distinction is more unique than rare, why not seek it? One must be distinguished for something. I reflected then that I had already written two biographies of Kierkegaard, the first of which was nearly half as large again as the book which actually was published. In a truly Kierkegaardian manner it was ascribed to two pseudonyms—becoming thereby so complicated that no publisher could be expected to touch it. So why not a third?

This book is barely a quarter the size of the *Kierkegaard* which was published by the Oxford University Press in 1938. This in itself is no commendation, except to those who would spend less money and less time in learning about Kierkegaard. And it is obviously no disparagement of the bigger book to say that it is big. At the time when it was written, before a single book by Kierkegaard had been published in English, a big wedge was necessary to make a hole large enough for all the works to follow. Besides being a biography, it had to provide samples of S.K.'s literary production, which is not only voluminous but exceedingly various. It sought to cultivate a taste for this. For this reason two fifths of the book consisted of quotations, and they, of course, are the best part of it. It is, therefore, even now the best introduction to S.K.'s works.

But now the situation is different; now all S.K.'s works

are available in English, or will be, I hope, within the year. For the orientation of the reader I append to this Preface a list of the twenty-three volumes of translations published in the course of six years. At the present time a shorter life is desirable, and now for the first time it is possible. It would not be possible to me, however, had I not written the bigger book first and disfigured it, if you will, with references to authorities and sources and with every sort of pedantic apparatus, such as this book, which aims to be popular, can now dispense with.

This little book, being simply a biography, may perhaps be more lucid than the other, in which it was sometimes difficult to see the forest for the trees. Having devoted myself for a month last year to the unaccustomed task of writing a mystery story, I may perhaps have learned to make the big events in S.K.'s life appear more thrilling than before—but never more thrilling than they were. And perhaps after spending the last six years translating the greater part of S.K.'s works I have learned to know him better than I did at first. At all events, this little book is not merely an abstract or condensation of the bigger one. It has been written afresh from beginning to end, and barely half a page here and there has been copied—except, of course, the quotations from S.K., and they have been carefully revised.

I have added this to my labors in behalf of Kierkegaard, with the ardent hope that it may make him more widely known, and may make him better known by prompting many people to read his works. To those who really desire to know him well I cannot say too emphatically that they should begin with the last and most definitely religious works, which I have translated in *The Point of View,* the *Christian Discourses, Training in Christianity,* and *For Self-*

Examination, which in four volumes unite twelve works which were originally separate.

WALTER LOWRIE

Princeton
November 9, 1942

A Short Life of
Kierkegaard

BACKGROUND

O NE must have at least some slight notion of the Copenhagen of a hundred years ago in order to follow feelingly the story of S.K. and imagine him in his proper setting. It is a setting which remained the same throughout his whole life. For in this drama there is little action and no change of scene.

In Copenhagen Søren Aabye Kierkegaard was born on the fifth of May 1813, in the great house his father had recently bought alongside the City Hall, facing one of the greatest squares of the city, called the New Market (*Nytorv*). In Copenhagen his whole life was spent; there he died, in Frederik's Hospital, on November 4, 1855; and there he was buried (with a popular demonstration which almost degenerated into riot) in the family lot, where a marble slab bearing his name now leans against his father's monument, though owing to the crazy jealousy of his elder brother, Peter Kierkegaard, subsequently Bishop of Aalborg, there is no sign to indicate where his body lies.

Denmark was and is a little land. At that time Copenhagen was a city of two hundred thousand inhabitants, but it was the capital of this little land, the residence of an absolute monarch. The great medieval monuments, whether cathedrals or castles, are to be found elsewhere; for Copenhagen was not always the residence of the King. But in the elegance of its modern buildings it outstripped every other city in the land. Beside the King's palaces and parks it possessed the one university (at that time) in Denmark; Frue Kirke was the cathedral of the bishop primate of the Danish Church and

3

was already adorned with Thorwaldsen's celebrated statues of Christ and the Twelve Apostles; it had a Royal Opera House, of course, and the Royal Theater, and the Royal Library, in front of which is now to be seen the bronze statue of S.K. by Aarsleff, which has only the defect of being much too big for "little Kierkegaard," and hence is not nearly so good as the little statuette by Hasselriis from which it was copied. With all this elegance Copenhagen still enjoyed the amenities of a small town which had not yet become an industrial center—a town which was refreshed by the salt water of the Sounds which nearly encircled it, and by the forests which crept close to it on the other side.

Of course all the artistic and literary talent of Denmark flowed toward the capital, S.K. being one of the few great men who was born there. Almost all the conspicuous men of the time figure prominently in S.K.'s life and must be enumerated here as the most important feature of the background against which we are to see him. I mention first of all the Most Reverend J. P. Mynster, Bishop Primate of the Church of Denmark. He comes first, not merely because of his ecclesiastical rank, nor because he was, in fact, a man of genuine piety, persuasive eloquence, and altogether a great churchman, who, as S.K. said, "had carried a whole generation," but also because he figured so largely in S.K.'s life. He had been his father's pastor, had confirmed S.K. as a child, and became the object of his most enthusiastic admiration—until he was confronted by the bitter necessity of denouncing his bishop as the most conspicuous symbol of the worldly degeneration of the Church which he died combating. S.K. always aimed his shafts at shining marks. The other man involved in the same attack was Professor Martensen, who succeeded Mynster in the bishopric. Him

Kierkegaard had known from his university days and had never liked, though he did not grudge to recognize publicly his eminent learning and talents. In fact Martensen was a figure known throughout the world when S.K. was unknown; his works were promptly translated into English, and I knew them when I was a youth, fifty years before I had heard of S.K.

Next in order, both for his own importance and for the role he played in S.K.'s life, is J. L. Heiberg, playwright, professor in the university, editor of an important review, enough of a philosopher to unite with Martensen in making the philosophy of Hegel the vogue in Denmark, and above all the acknowledged literary arbiter of Copenhagen. His house was the center of intellectual society; for not only was his mother a woman of great distinction (still known by the name of Fru Gullembourg which she had made famous as an actress and as a writer), but his wife too was a distinguished actress. Into this charmed circle S.K. was admitted even while he was a student in the university, and it was chiefly there he displayed his talent as a wit—sometimes to the discomfiture of his fellow guests. In one way or another he kept up these associations even when he had ceased to appear in any society but such as he encountered in the streets. Though he had no substantial beliefs in common with Heiberg he managed to maintain a friendship which on his part was chiefly expressed by good-humored banter. His little book called *Two Ages* was principally an appreciation of a serious novel by Fru Gullembourg; and his last "aesthetic" work, *A Crisis and the Crisis in the Life of an Actress,* was an appreciation of Fru Heiberg, which in turn was much appreciated in those high quarters.

Christianity in Denmark bears today very distinctly the

stamp of the great religious leader Grundtvig, who not only wrote the hymns which are now sung with the greatest fervor, but established the Folk Schools which are an enviable distinction of that land. S.K., perhaps, would have been willing to concede that he was a "religious genius," but he would not have meant this as flattery, and he said of him, "Even in eternity he will be distasteful to me." In most of his works he found or took occasion to express his distaste pungently and wittily; but for all that he kept up, as he expressed it, "a sort of jolly intercourse" with this "inspired yodeler," much to the mystification of the devout followers of this apostle, among whom his brother Peter was numbered. Poul Martin Møller, professor in the University of Copenhagen and a poet in his own right, was the teacher to whom S.K. owed most. He undoubtedly owed to him his profound appreciation of Greek tragedy and Greek philosophy; but he owed to him also the "trumpet note" which aroused him from the moral nihilism into which he was sinking. For this, as well as for his sterling character and parts, he rightly regarded him with affectionate veneration.

Another admired teacher was F. C. Sibbern, professor of philosophy, with whom he always remained on familiar terms. There were other professors of philosophy with whom he was intimate, but they were his coevals, not his teachers. First of all there was Hans Brøchner, who was perhaps the only man who at that time understood what S.K. was aiming at, and for whom, though he candidly dissociated himself from Christianity, S.K. had a great respect. There was also Rasmus Nielsen, who, although he was a professor, sought and obtained permission to sit at S.K.'s feet as a pupil—or rather to walk with him in the street. It was, however, a relationship which ultimately caused S.K. considerable embarrassment. In spite of his fierce contempt for journalists in general he was on very friendly terms with Giødwad, associate editor of "The Fatherland" (*Fædrelandet*); and although with Meïr Aaron Goldschmidt, as editor of the *Corsair* he finally collided in a conflict which was exceedingly discomfiting to both, he had appreciated this young man's talent more generously than did any other illustrious citizen of Copenhagen.

During a period of his university life when S.K. was at war with his father and took his meals away from home he was thrown into intimate contact with a group of young men who sat at the same boarding-house table, and in a separate sittingroom in the same house jestingly constituted a club which they called "The Holy Alliance." Professor Frithiof Brandt has with prodigious acumen made out that "The Banquet" in the *Stages* was a real event, a banquet actually given by S.K., though of course it was embellished by the author, and that the guests were made up of this group. Accordingly, J. V. Jacobson, who held the office of judge assessor, and was the oldest and most worthy member in the group, suggested the character of "Judge William" who in *Either/Or* and in the *Stages* writes about marriage with moral enthusiasm. The least reputable member of the group, P. S. Møller, a young man of some talent and great literary ambition, with whom at a later time S.K. came into destructive collision on account of his relation to the *Corsair,* is supposed to figure as "the Seducer" in both of these books. A man of depraved character but a noted wit, Jørgen Jørgensen, became acquainted with S.K. about the same time, and it is surmised that he and P. S. Møller were the two men who seduced him into "the path of perdition." Hans Christian Andersen, an awkward giant, was the member of the group who suffered most from the shafts of S.K.'s wit—who later had to bear the brunt of a devastating review of a novel he ought not to have written, and in one of his charming tales got even with S.K. by presenting him in the character of a parrot, with evident allusion to his rasping voice. The last member of the group I have to mention is the poet Hertz— not a great poet, but one who gives us in his *Stemninger og Tilstande* the only account we have of this coterie and of S.K.'s not very amiable part in it. The only other character I need mention is Emil Boesen, who became dean of Aarhus, who had been a friend of S.K.'s in his youth, the only confidant he ever had, to whom he clung with a faithful memory of their old affection even to the day of his death, though it was evident then that there was little common ground between them and still less understanding.

A tiresome list of the *dramatis personae?* Well, at all events it is a relief that we are done with them, that no others, as I hope, need be referred to in this book, except S.K.'s own kindred and the kindred of his fiancée. But S.K. knew everybody that was worth knowing—and many more. The circle of interesting people in Copenhagen was fairly large, but not too large for them all to know one another; and S.K. was to learn to his discomfiture that no distinguished man in Copenhagen was unknown to the populace he encountered in the street. After he became an author and was so constantly engrossed in his writing that he rarely admitted any one to his house, his social life was lived in the street, where he took the frequent promenades which were his sole recreation, and where he discoursed amicably with everybody, with simple market-women as understandingly as with university dons, not only giving out his sympathy but getting from all of them something he could turn to account.

Copenhagen

S.K. sometimes complained petulantly that Copenhagen was a provincial town—literally a "market town," a word-play on the name Kjøbenhavn or Merchants' Harbor. He complained that he was a poet in a market town. But he loved his birthplace dearly, and in the *Stages* evidently expresses his own feelings when he says through the mouth of a pseudonym (pp. 138-142):

"I rejoice in existence, rejoice in the small world which is my environment. Some of my countrymen are perhaps of the opinion that Copenhagen is a tiresome town and a small town. To me, on the contrary, it seems that, refreshed as it is by the sea on which it is situated, and without being able even in winter to dismiss the recollection of its beech forests, it is as favorable a place as I could desire to dwell in. Big enough to be a great city, small enough to have no market price set upon men, where the tabulated consolation one has in Paris that there are so and so many suicides, where the tabulated joy one has in Paris that there are so and so many persons of distinction, cannot penetrate disturbingly and whirl away the individual like foam, so that life acquires no significance, consolation lacks its day of rest and joy its holy day, because everything dashes off into space without content—or too full of it.—Some of my countrymen find the people in this town not vivacious enough. It does not seem so to me. The speed with which in Paris thousands form a mob around one person may indeed be flattering to the man about whom they collect, but I wonder if that makes up for the loss of the quiet mind which permits the individual to feel that he too has some importance. Precisely because the individuals have not totally fallen in price, as though it took a dozen to make one man, and because the people are too indocile to comprehend the half-hour erudition which only flatters the despairing and the blind, precisely for this reason is life in this capital so entertaining to him who knows how to find in human beings a delight which is more enduring and yields bigger returns than getting a thousand men to acclaim one for half an hour. Its defect is perhaps rather that one individual dreams of foreign lands, another is absorbed in himself, a third is narrow-minded and separatist etc., and so all these individuals prevent themselves from taking what is bountifully offered, from finding what exists in abundance when it is sought. He who is unwilling to undertake any enterprise might, nevertheless, if he had an open eye, lead a life rich in enjoyment, merely by paying attention to others; and he who has also his own work to do, would do well to take heed not to be too much imprisoned by it. But how pitiful if there were many who miss what costs nothing, no entrance fee, no expense for banquets, no dues to one's society, no inconvenience and trouble, what costs the rich and the poor equally little and yet is the richest enjoyment, who miss an instruction which is not obtained from a particular teacher but *en passant* from any person whatsoever, from conversation with someone unknown, from every accidental contact. That upon which one has in vain sought enlightenment from books is suddenly illuminated by a flash of light on hearing one serving-maid conversing with another; an expression which one has tried in vain to torture out of one's own brain, in vain has sought in dictionaries, even in the 'Dictionary of the Society of the Sciences,' one hears in passing—a raw soldier utters it, and does not dream what a rich man he is. And as he who walks in a great forest, amazed at it all, sometimes snatches a branch, sometimes a leaf, sometimes stoops to pick a flower, sometimes a leaf, now listens to the note of a bird—so does one walk in the midst of the human throng, amazed at the marvelous gift of speech, snatches now one and now another expression from a passerby, rejoices in it and is not ungrateful enough to forget to whom he owes it; so one walks in the midst of the human throng, sees now one expression of a mental state, now another, learns and learns and becomes only more avid of learning. So let no one be deceived by books, as though the humane were of such rare occurrence, so let no one read of this sort of thing in the newspapers, where the best part of the saying, the most lovable, is sometimes not preserved.

"Some of my countrymen are of the opinion that their mother tongue is hardly capable of expressing difficult thoughts. This seems to me a strange and ungrateful thought, as it also seems to me strange and exaggerated to be so zealous for one's language that one almost forgets to rejoice in it, to assert so zealously its independence that the zeal almost seems to indicate that one already feels one's dependence, and that in the end excitement is derived from the strife of words rather than refreshment from the joy of the language. I feel myself fortunate in being bound to my mother tongue, bound perhaps as few are, bound as Adam was to Eve because there was no other woman, bound because it has been impossible for me to learn any other tongue, and hence impossible to look down proudly and haughtily upon the tongue to which I was born. But I am also glad to be bound to a mother tongue which is rich in original idioms, which expands the soul and delights the ear with its softer sounds; a mother tongue which does not puff and groan when it is held in the toils of a difficult thought (for which reason some think it is incapable of expressing it), for it makes the difficult easy by uttering it; a mother tongue which does not sound strained and panting when it is confronted with the unutterable, but employs itself with it in jest and earnest until it manages to utter it; a language which does not find at a remote distance what is near, nor seek in a profound abyss what is close at hand, because it is on such good terms with the subject that it passes in and out like a fairy, and like a child comes out with the happiest expression without quite knowing it; a language which is vehement and emotional when the right lover knows how to incite manfully the feminine passion of the language, is self-confident and victorious in the strife of thought when the right ruler knows how to lead it, is supple as a wrestler when the right thinker will not let go of it and will not let go of thought; a language which, if it seems poor in a single instance, is nevertheless not so, but is disdained as a false lover disdains an unassuming maiden who possesses in reality the greatest worth and above all is not sophisticated; a language which is not lacking in expressions for the great, the decisive, the conspicuous, yet has a charming, a winning, a genial preference for the nuances of thought, for the qualifying term and the small talk of humor and the thrill of transition and the subtlety of inflection and the concealed luxuriousness of modest affluence; a language which understands jest quite as well as earnest—a mother tongue which binds its children with a chain, 'easy to bear—yes—but hard to break.'

"Some of my countrymen are of the opinion that Denmark lives by the consumption of the memory of its ancient greatness. This seems to me a strange and ungrateful opinion to which no one can assent who would prefer to be friendly and joyful rather than sullen and refractory—the only thing which wastes and consumes. Others are of the opinion that a peerless future awaits Denmark; some also who think themselves undervalued and unappreciated comfort themselves with the thought of a better generation to come. But he who is happy in the present generation, and is quick in inventiveness when the point is to be satisfied with this, has not many moments free for peerless expectations and is no more inclined to be disturbed by them than he is to grasp at them. And he who thinks that he is unappreciated by his contemporaries uses a wondrous argument in predicting a better generation to come. Even if it is true that he is unappreciated, and even if it is true that he would be recognized in a better age which would praise him, it is nevertheless unjust and a proof of prejudice to say of this later age that it is better because it thinks better of him. There is no such great difference between one generation and another; precisely the generation he censors finds itself in the position of praising what an earlier generation of contemporaries failed to appreciate.

"Some of my contemporaries are of the opinion that to be an author in Denmark affords a poor livelihood. They do not merely mean that this is the case with such a questionable author as I am, who have not a single reader, and only a few who get so far as the middle of the book, and of whom therefore they are not thinking in passing this judgment; but they mean that it is the case even with distinguished authors. Now this land is only a little land. But in Greece was it so mean a position to be a magistrate, even though it cost money to be one? Suppose it were so, suppose it were to continue to be so, and in the end it were the lot of an author in Denmark to pay a certain sum yearly for the labor of being an author. Well then, what if it were possible for foreigners to say, 'In Denmark it is a costly thing to be an author, hence there are mighty few of them; but then again they have not what we foreigners call catch-pennies, a thing so utterly unknown in the realm of Denmark that the language does not even possess an expression for it.'"

In the preface to one of his last works he saluted his mother tongue for the last time and proudly: "Expressing thanks for such sympathy and good will as have been showed me, I could wish that I might, as it were, present these works (as I now take the liberty of doing) and commend them to the nation whose language I am proud to have the honor of writing, feeling for it a filial devotion and an almost womanly tenderness, yet comforting myself also with the thought that it will not be disgraced for the fact that I have used it."

How careful S.K. was in the use of his mother tongue we learn from a passage in the Journal which was written near the end of his life:

". . . Thus I sometimes could sit for hours, in love with the sound of speech—when it resounds, that is, with the pregnancy of thought—thus I could sit for whole hours, ah! like a flute-player entertaining himself with his flute. What I have written was most of it many times, perhaps a dozen times, spoken aloud before it was written down. In another sense, most of it was written *corrente calamo,* as they say; but this was owing to the fact that I make everything ready while I am walking. The construction of my periods might for me be called a world of recollections, so much have I lived through and enjoyed and experienced in the genesis of these thoughts, and in their searching until they found the form. And even though in a certain sense they had it almost at the first instant, one may say, until (in what was properly the later labor, the business of perfecting the style; for everyone who really has thoughts has also style immediately) every insignificant detail was adjusted so that the thought could find itself, as they say, completely at its ease in the form."

This passage would be absolutely deterrent to a modest translator—if it were not so absolutely necessary to have S.K.'s works translated. In any case it is a serious admonition.

The best proof of S.K.'s love for Copenhagen is the fact that he rarely left it except for carriage drives in the environs, in which he took the keenest pleasure. Once he stayed in Berlin for nearly five months. The occasion for this long absence was the wish to escape from the gossip aroused by his broken engagement, but he was also eager to hear Schelling who had begun to lecture there against the philosophy of Hegel. In that he was disappointed—but he wrote the greater part of *Either/Or*. Again, when he was agitated by the suspicion that his late fiancée had nodded to him in church he took refuge a second time in Berlin and stayed nearly two months, during which he wrote *Repetition* and *Fear and Trembling*. Twice again he was in Berlin, but for less than a fortnight. The path had become familiar to him and hence relatively easy, in spite of sickness on the short voyage and the dreadful journey by diligence from Stralsund to Berlin which he describes feelingly in *Repetition* (pp. 36ff.). But he made no visit to any other foreign city. This is the more significant because he had the means for foreign travel. He once exclaimed in his Journal, "I am a poet, I must travel," but nothing came of it. I have often speculated what might have been the effect upon S.K. if he had gone to Italy, as Andersen did with such exuberant delight, as Thorwaldsen had done with such good effect, as so many of his countrymen did then and still do. Would Italy have cured his melancholy?—and perhaps quenched his peculiar talent! I recall that he was intolerant of heat, that he disliked bright sunlight and carried his famous umbrella as a protection against it; also that he preferred the autumn to every other season of the year, and the late afternoon to every other time of day. Perhaps he would not have loved Italy.

Even in his own land S.K. made only one journey beyond the island of Seeland. It was a pious pilgrimage across to Jutland and the heath country where his father was born and as a boy had suffered desperately from hunger, cold and loneliness. He made the trip, not immediately after his father's death, but as soon as he was free to do it, as soon as he had fulfilled his father's first wish by passing his theological examination. His father, Michael Pedersen Kierkegaard, was born at Sæding, which was not a village, not even a hamlet, but a scattered parish in the heath country where only shepherds and peat-diggers could eke out a scanty existence. Although in recent times this country has been reclaimed for cultivation by the labors of Enrico Dalgas and the Heath Society, yet even now the little stone church at Sæding suggests the utmost poverty and desolation. Now there is no dwelling near it, it is too poor to have a belfry, and within, except for the altar, a brightly painted pulpit, and a great crucifix, the only ornaments are two wooden tablets on the wall of the nave, both bearing inscriptions in gilt lettering upon a black ground. One was placed there in 1821 by S.K.'s father and records the gift he made to the parish in honor of his mother's brother, Niels Andersen Seding, who when he was a boy of twelve delivered him from his bitter lot, took him to Copenhagen, and started him on the path to wealth. This gift provided for the support of a fit schoolteacher, for aid to needy pupils (who were required to serve as choristers in the parish church), and for the purchase of suitable text books.

The other records a gift made in behalf of the school and the poor of the parish in honor of S.K.'s father by the nephew, Michael Andersen Kierkegaard, to whom he had turned over his business. He describes his uncle as "the guide and support of my youth, the benefactor of Sæding school." Not long after I saw this church the Bishop of Ribe dedicated there in 1935, the eightieth anniversary of S.K.'s death, a marble tablet in memory of him, and at the same time dedicated a monument which now marks the site where his father was born. For no trace is left of the old parsonage in which this poor peasant family lived and from which they took their name. As this church was too poor to have a minister of its own, the parsonage with its glebe (which as well as the cemetery was known as the churchyard or *Kirkegaard*) was rented, and the family which occupied it was called by this name. Surnames were still so new and so unstable in Denmark that the next family which moved in took the same name. S.K.'s father, when he was settled in Copenhagen, added an "e" to distinguish the cognomen from the common noun, just as Taylors and Smythes and many others did in England. Nor is anything left of the "Red House" which the elder Kierkegaard built for his mother and two sisters, providing that after their demise it should be used as a schoolhouse. It was, like all the other houses, roofed with thatch, but because it was built of brick and timber it was much admired in that region, where all the other houses were of clay.

In the Red House S.K. spent three days with his one surviving aunt; but even there the conditions of life must have been primitive, to say the least, for he made the following entry in his Journal: "It seems as though I must experience the sharpest contrasts. After living for three days with my

17

poor old aunt, pretty much like Ulysses and his companions [literally, stable-brothers] the next place I came to was so chock full of counts and barons that it was frightful."

The profound impression made upon S.K. by the desolate heath was intensified by the thought of his father's desperate suffering as a boy, and by the knowledge he then had, of the guilty secret which had darkened the man's whole life. At his last stopping-place before reaching Sæding he wrote: "Here I sit entirely alone (I have, it is true, often been just as much alone but was never so conscious of it) and I count the hours till I shall see Sæding. I never can remember any change in my father, and now I shall see the places for which I have often felt nostalgia on account of his descriptions. Suppose I were to fall ill and be buried in Sæding cemetery! Uncanny thought. His last wish for me is fulfilled [i.e. in the fact that he had taken his theological examination]—might my whole earthly destiny come to no more than this? Good Lord! My task cannot be so lowly, considering all I owe to him. From him I learned what father-love is, and I got a conception of the divine father-love, the one unshakable thing in life, the true archimedean point."

The next entry is: "Would that I knew what a young girl—" At this one might well be astonished if one did not know that on this pilgrimage he was thinking not only of his deceased father but of his prospective bride, to whom many of his disconsolate entries obscurely refer. This was an anxious thought, perhaps made more gloomy by his surroundings; and when we read in the Journal, *Nulla dies sine lachryma* (no day without a tear), we cannot tell for which loved one the tears were shed. But this story must be reserved for another place.

The gloomy impressions predominated: "It is related here

in Sæding that there is a house hereabouts where once there lived a man who in time of the pest outlived all the others and buried them. He plowed long furrows in the peat and buried his neighbors in long rows." This melancholy impression was lasting, for many years later he wrote: "I sat the other day self-absorbed, in a strange mood, and read an old folk song which tells of a maiden who expected her lover of a Saturday night, but he did not come, and she went to bed and 'wept so bitterly'; again she arose and wept so bitterly. Suddenly the scene widened before me; I saw the Jutland heath with its indescribable loneliness and its single larch-tree; and now there rose up before me one generation after another, whose maidens all sang for me and wept so bitterly, and sank back into their graves, and I wept with them."

Yet he was not indifferent to the idyllic impressions provided even by the little Red House: "Standing before the door of this little place, with the aroma which hay always emits, in the light of the late afternoon; the sheep drifting home constitute the foreground; dark clouds broken by strong beams of light such as indicate a gale—the heath rising in the background—if only I might remember clearly the impression of the evening." And he remarked: "The heath must be particularly fitted to develop strong minds. Here everything lies naked and unveiled before God; and here is no place for the many distractions, the many nooks and crannies wherein consciousness can hide and from which seriousness so often has trouble in recovering the dispersed thoughts. Here consciousness must definitely and precisely hedge itself in. Truly here upon the heath one well may say, 'Whither shall I flee from thy presence?'"

A few days before reaching his destination S.K. wrote: "I

had thought of preaching for the first time in Sæding church
—and now that must be next Sunday—and hence I see with
no little wonder that the text [i.e. the Gospel for the seventh
Sunday after Trinity] is Mark viii. 1–10 (the feeding of the
four thousand), and I was struck by these words: 'From
whence can one satisfy these men with bread *here in the
wilderness?*' for I am to speak precisely in the poorest parish
in Jutland, in the heath country." There is no record that
S.K. preached at Sæding; but in the next volume of his
Journal there are four entries which refer expressly to the
passage above cited and outline an impressive sermon on this
text.

I cannot now go on consecutively from this point and tell
of S.K.'s engagement; for we have not yet come to *his* story;
this is his remote background, but it is the immediate background of the father as seen through his eyes. About Michael
Pedersen Kierkegaard we must now speak.

THE FATHER

David, when he was still a boy, the youngest of eight
brethren, was summoned from the fields where he tended
the sheep and was anointed by Samuel to be king over Israel.
Little Michael Kierkegaard, one of a family of nine children,
who at only twelve years of age had already, as a shepherd
lad on the desolate heath of West Jutland, suffered cold and
hunger and loneliness, and who in spite of the consciousness
of mental gifts which only exasperated his discontent, was
seemingly condemned to a life of poverty and obscurity,
suddenly found himself chosen by his mother's brother, Niels
Andersen Seding, to go with him to Copenhagen where he
had established a small business as a hosier. To us this reads

like a fairy story, and how much more marvelous it must have seemed to the small boy who just when he had reached the climax of his discontent found himself started upon the road to opulence. But to him it was no fairy story; being religiously brought up, he saw in it the hand of God—and trembled.

Since wool was produced principally in Jutland, it is natural that the Jutlanders were prominent in this trade. S.K., who dedicated to his father each new installment of the *Edifying Discourses,* described him regularly as "sometime hosier here in this city." He modestly used a humble title. But a "hosier" was more than a dealer in stockings; he dealt also in ready-made clothing. The English would say that he dealt in slops, but we in America hardly know this invidious distinction because most of us hardly conceive the possibility that a man might have his clothes made to order—and often enough when they are supposed to be so they are not. S.K.'s father was undoubtedly a very able man. Though he was content with being registered as a hosier, he developed a considerable business in cloth, and on December 4, 1780, when he was only twenty-four years of age, he obtained a license to deal also in food stuffs, while on September 19, 1788, he was licensed by royal patent to deal also in Chinese and East India wares, as well as merchandise from the Danish West Indies, "such as sugar (refined as well as unrefined), syrup and coffee beans, and to sell the same at wholesale and retail to all and sundry." When he was barely thirty years old he had become a wholesale grocer on a big scale. He was thus amassing a considerable fortune—when suddenly, in his fortieth year, he retired from active life and left his business to a nephew, Michael Andersen Kierkegaard.

We cannot but wonder at this decision, for it is seldom a

merchant retires from a successful business in middle life when his vigor is unimpaired. In fact he had not quite reached the middle of his days, for he was to live forty-two years longer. His retirement followed immediately upon the death of his wife, which without doubt was in some sense the cause of it. She died after two years of married life without leaving him any children. One might think that the childless widower would have felt the need of immersing himself more thoroughly in business.

But this is not the only mystery. Before the year of mourning was up he was married, on April 26, 1797, to Ane Søren-datter Lund, a distant kinswoman from Jutland who before his wife's death was living as a servant in the house—or as "help," if we would employ the New England euphemism. The first child, Maren Kirsten, was born on September 7, 1797, exactly four months and eleven days after the marriage. Two more daughters, Nicoline Christine and Petrea Seve-rine, and the eldest son, Peter Christian, were born in the course of the next eight years in the suburban town of Hil-lerød, before Michael Kierkegaard moved his family to Co-penhagen, where Søren Michael was born in 1807, and where two years later, after he had bought the great house on the Nytorv alongside of the City Hall, Niels Andreas was born to him. Then, after an interval of four years, when no such blessing was expected, the father being fifty-six years old and the mother forty-five, Søren Aabye Kierkegaard was born, the last of seven children.

One can hardly fail to remark upon the fact that two children in this family bore the same name. Perhaps this was not so unusual in Denmark, for the mother was one of three sis-ters who were all of them named Ane. Here we have two Sørens. Or should we say three? For Severine was the fem-

inine form of this name, Søren being a corruption of Seve-
rinus. I do not know why this saint, who died towards the
end of the fifth century in Noricum and is buried near Na-
ples, attained such celebrity in Denmark that at one time his
name was bestowed in baptism more frequently than any
other. How frequently it was used we can infer from the
fact that Sørensen is still one of the commonest surnames.
But no boys are named Søren any more. S.K. was the last
Søren, or rather it was he who spoiled this name for future
use. The popular ridicule heaped upon the greatest writer in
Denmark made this name so ridiculous that "don't be a
Søren" was said as a warning to children.

About his birth S.K. once remarked with somber wit that
"it occurred in that year when so many worthless [literally,
mad] notes were put in circulation." He had in mind the
great inflation which only two months before his birth
brought financial ruin upon most of the well-to-do families
in Denmark. To provide for its part in the Napoleonic Wars
the Government had issued a prodigious number of bank
notes, which resulted, of course, in a complete collapse of
credit. The only security which did not shrink to a small
fraction of its nominal value was the so-called "Royal Loan."
Upon that, because the bonds were held chiefly by foreign
governments, Denmark was obliged to pay the stipulated
interest in gold. The elder Kierkegaard had invested his
whole fortune in this security, and, therefore, from the general crumble of values he emerged not only as rich as he was
before but relatively richer than ever.

This rich man lived in his great house with patriarchal
simplicity and ruled his numerous family with old-fashioned
severity. He was profoundly religious and brought up his
children in the fear of God. Though he was loyal to the

State Church and devoted to his pastor, J. L. Mynster, who afterwards became Bishop of Seeland, there was a time when he frequented the meetings of the Moravian Brethren, where he found many of the friends who became intimate with the family. His own profound melancholy impressed upon his religion a character of severity and gloom which was disastrous to his children, to Søren especially, as will be evident in the sequel.

Not many merchants on retiring from business contrive to employ their leisure as well as he did. He had evidently a powerful mind which in spite of the total lack of academic training was able to deal with the most abstruse problems of philosophy and theology. Much of his time was spent in pondering over the German philosophers, and he found his keenest pleasure in disputing upon such lofty themes with men of similar tastes who were frequent visitors in his house. In these discussions, according to S.K., his father was indomitable.

The mother is described by her granddaughter, Henriette Lund, as "a nice little woman of an even and cheerful disposition. The intellectual development of her children was rather over her head, their high flight seemed to her troubled heart like a flight away from the place where she felt at home and where she would fain have kept them. Hence she was never in such high spirits as when a transitory illness forced them back for a while under her rule. She was especially content when she could put them to bed, for then she wielded her scepter with joy and kept them as snug as a hen does her chickens."

It is amazing and it is ominous that whereas in his Journal and in his works S.K. has so much to say of his father, there is nowhere a single reference to his mother. It is evident that morally she had no influence upon him, or only a negative influence. S.K. seems to have divined in early childhood, perhaps as an inference from his father's treatment of the mother of his seven children, that she was not in the highest sense a wife. A recollection recorded by Bishop Mynster, referring back to the time when he was the pastor of Michael Kierkegaard, seems to indicate that he continued to regard his first wife as his real wife. He relates that when this man was already married to his second wife he came to him one day in great agitation and said, "Good God, I have been thinking so much today of my blessed wife, . . . I thought of her so long, . . . here are two hundred dollars. Will you give them to the poor?" It is certain that the mother did not count for much in that family—not even as housekeeper, for the father attended to everything, even to buying the food. The fact that there was something which impeded S.K. from honoring his mother and from loving her as a son ought, was certainly a principal cause of his tragedy, and perhaps it accounts in part for the particular misfortune that he was not able to "realize the universal" by marrying the woman he loved. He who wrote so much about woman, and so beautifully, though at the end so spitefully, was able to think of her only as the counterpart of man, and except when he wrote about "Mary the Mother of God" he rarely dwelt upon the noblest and tenderest aspect of woman as a mother.

And yet, if S.K.'s disposition to melancholy was in part a physical inheritance from his father, whom he describes as "the most melancholy man I have ever known," it may be that from his mother he derived the opposite quality of merriment. In the testimonial which he took up to the University from the rector of his school he is described as *juvenem carum et jocundum.* "He has a good intelligence," says the Rector, "open to everything which promises unusual interest, but for a long time he was childish in a high degree and totally lacking in seriousness. . . . He has a desire for freedom and independence, which also shows itself in his conduct by a good-natured, sometimes comical sauciness." Here I am anticipating the story of S.K.'s childhood, but still with a view to the background, and in order to suggest the possibility that his inheritance included, if not an antidote to melancholy, at least a counterbalancing trait. S.K., naturally enough, was more keenly conscious of his melancholy, and even believed that the merriment he assumed for the sake of hiding it was no more than a clever disguise. But perhaps he might not have been able from his very childhood to deceive everybody in this way if there had not been a merry S.K. beneath the somber one. It seems to me that there was a childlike quality in S.K. to the very end, and this is a characteristic which especially endears him to me. He was as sensitive as a child and as tender, he was always humorous and often whimsical; as a child he was accustomed to play with his thoughts, and he continued to play with them even in his serious works—to the scandal of many of his readers. This is the more observable because it stands in striking contrast to the grimness of his fate and the sternness of his purpose. So even if his mother had no personal influence upon him, he may well have owed to her this inheritance.

Although S.K. came of a sturdy race, both of the parents being peasants from West Jutland, the most purely Danish stock in Denmark, yet the early death of most of the children of this family suggests that they were physically frail. Certainly S.K., the child of old age, had a body deplorably unequal to his mind. But beside this there was in this family a taint of psychic instability which partly accounts for the father's melancholy and wholly for the melancholy of his elder brother Peter Christian, which was so close to insanity that it compelled him to resign his office as bishop. He who had sought with all his learning to combat his father's illusion that he had committed the unforgivable sin, himself fell a victim to the same delusion. His son was insane enough to be confined in an asylum—and yet witty enough to say, "My uncle was Either/Or, my father is Both-And, and I am Neither/Nor." Another of S.K.'s nephews had several attacks of insanity and in one of them committed suicide.

Naturally enough, the question has been raised whether S.K. was entirely sane. He would have said no—but he would have added that no man is entirely sane. He recognized that in the period of his youthful revolt against his father and against God he was several times "on the verge" of insanity and was fearful of becoming actually insane. He several times meditated suicide. It seems marvelous that in such a time as that he succeeded in keeping his balance, but nothing can be clearer than the fact that he did succeed, and evidently what saved him was his power of mind and the habit of straight thinking. That saved him so completely that he never had reason in later life to fear insanity. In later life too he had the comfort of a Christian faith.

In *Fear and Trembling* the pseudonymous author, Johannes de silentio, quotes from Seneca a saying which he in turn derived from Aristotle: *nullum unquam exstetit magnum ingenium sine aliqua dementia* (there never was great genius without some madness). Then he goes on to say:

"For this *dementia* is the suffering allotted to genius in existence, it is the expression if I may say so, of the divine jealousy, whereas the gift of genius is the expression of the divine favor. So from the start the genius is disoriented in relation to the universal and is brought into relation with the paradox—whether it be that in despair at his limitation (which in his eyes transforms his omnipotence into impotence) he seeks a demoniacal reassurance and therefore will not admit such limitation either before God or men, or else he reassures himself religiously by love to the Deity. Here are implied psychological topics to which, it seems to me, one might gladly sacrifice a whole life—and yet one so seldom hears a word about them. What relation has madness to genius? Can we construct the one out of the other? In what sense and how far is the genius master of his madness? For it goes without saying that to a certain degree he is master of it, since otherwise he would be actually a madman. For such observations, however, ingenuity in a high degree is requisite, and love; for to make observation upon a superior mind is very difficult. If with due attention to this difficulty one were to read through the works of particular authors most celebrated for their genius, it might in barely a single instance perhaps be possible, though with much pains, to discover a little."

If this may be regarded as S.K.'s invitation to study his case, it is hardly an enticing one. Several Freudians have rashly undertaken to psychoanalyze S.K. without observing these very exacting conditions. Hjalmar Helweg, Director of the Hospital for the Insane at Oringe, Denmark, has taken the pains to read every word S.K. wrote and studied them with sympathy. He modestly concludes his preface with these words: "However well one may think one has managed to say a thing, he will always discover that S.K. has said it better." I have no fault to find with the verdict he renders except that it is not very illuminating. He concludes that

S.K. suffered from a condition of depression alternating with, or more commonly blended with, maniacal exaltation. It is to be noted that "maniacal" is a technical word: S.K. was not pronounced insane. In my opinion S.K. "said it better."

Having sought help in vain from physicians, he became the physician of his own soul. He became a psychologist by analysing his own symptoms, both the normal and the pathological, and thereby he anticipated much which now goes by the name of "deep psychology." When we normal common-sense people busy ourselves about the question of S.K.'s sanity, he is quite capable of turning the tables on us. In *Repetition* (p. 98, cf. p. 11) the "young man," who seemed to the perfectly common-sense Constantine Constantius a little mad, writes to his mentor as follows: "I admire you, and yet at times it seems to me as if you were deranged. Or is it not a sort of mental derangement that you subject to such a degree every passion, every emotion of the heart, every mood, to the cold discipline of reflection? Is it not mental derangement to be so normal, to be a mere idea, not a human being like the rest of us, pliant and yielding, capable of being lost and of losing ourselves? Is it not mental derangement to be always awake, always sure, never obscure and dreaming?"

So much for the background. It is dark enough, but a more lurid light will be shed upon it later.

At this point I ought perhaps to say that no one is less inclined than I to believe that the character of Kierkegaard was fixed, his fate determined and his life explained by inheritance and environment. These factors, of course, exerted a prodigious influence, which to a certain extent we can trace; S.K. attained an understanding of himself by reviewing his life from early childhood, and he had an unusually vivid feeling of solidarity with "the family, the clan, the race"; but on the other hand, the freedom and responsibility of the individual was his most ardent conviction, and therefore he accounted "the individual higher than the race." I know that I should encounter his scathing disapproval if in the manner of materialistic historians I were to endeavor to account for him by this background of inheritance and environment.

CHILDHOOD

Halb Kinderspiele,
Halb Gott im Herzen.
—GOETHE

On September 9, 1839, S.K. inscribed in his Journal the above lines from *Faust,* remarking that he could find no better motto to characterize his childhood. Dates are so rare in this Journal that one learns to be on the alert to detect a special significance in even so brief an entry as this. The next entry too is dated (September 10), and it registers the reflection that foresight is really hind-sight, a reflection of the future which is revealed to the eye when it looks back upon the past. From this one might guess that S.K. was at that moment intent upon reviewing his past life with the expectation of catching a glimpse of his future. In fact he made such a review of the first twenty-six years of his life and inscribed it carefully in an undated document which we cannot hesitate to ascribe to this time, inasmuch as it begins with these very lines from Goethe and ends with an expression of doleful impatience with "the great parenthesis" in the midst of which he then found himself. It was not inscribed in the Journal but "written upon three sheets of fine letter-paper, small octavo, with gilt edges." Thus it is described by Barfod, to whom old Bishop Peter Kierkegaard tardily (twelve years after his brother's death) confided the publication of the journals and papers. But, alas, the original document exists no more. Barfod had it printed—and then with incredible negligence suffered it to disappear. He was as careless about all the manuscripts confided to him when once they were printed. But this was the only tragic loss. It was tragic because in the printing he garbled it. He also occasioned a

good deal of confusion by assigning it to the period between
S.K.'s twenty-fifth birthday in May 1838 and his father's
death on the eighth of the following August. Fortunately,
Gottsched, a German lover of Kierkegaard, took up the task
of editing his papers when Barfod, because of failing health,
dropped it ten years later. Gottsched was responsible for five
volumes out of the eight, performing his task admirably and
expeditiously in less than two years. But the editors of the
latest edition accepted without question Barfod's date for the
gilt-edged document, and naturally the English translator
followed them. It is a strange thing that Barfod, though he
confessed that he did not understand the significance of
this document, was nevertheless obscurely aware of its importance and assigned to it the most conspicuous place, at
the very beginning of his first volume, before the earliest
entries of the Journal. And there, in a garbled form, it has
stood on the very threshold, an initial stumbling-block to
every student of S.K.'s life. There is hardly one of them that
has not been tripped by it.

As a consequence of these misapprehensions the document
which might have been the most precious help for the understanding of S.K.'s early life has been the greatest hindrance.
The Danish students of S.K., if they have not been led completely astray, have been hopelessly puzzled. And this perhaps accounts for the astonishing fact that in spite of all
that has been written about S.K., in spite of the ingenious
studies of the Danes, which throw light upon particular episodes and furnish abundant material for a biographer, no
biography in the strictest sense, that is, no genetic study of
the first thirty years of S.K.'s life, was written before my
Kierkegaard—or, as Hohlenberg affirms, before his book,
which was published in 1940, when he knew nothing of

mine. Like me he had learned from Professor Emanuel Hirsch of Göttingen to appraise justly the significance of the gilt-edged document, of which Hirsch says that "in spite of its brevity it is a mature and deeply pondered religious auto-biography in small compass, composed with prodigious dialectical subtilty, in short, a little masterpiece which we cannot sufficiently admire." The clues which this document furnishes I have followed assiduously, as may be seen in the fact that at the head of this chapter, and at the beginning of all but two of the following seven (i.e. on pp. 67, 79, 92, 118, 128), I have placed one after another the six sections into which this document is divided.

Because I have made so much of this document I am obliged to justify my appraisal of it. For me this is a dolorous necessity, far more trying than it can be to the reader to puzzle over the dry details I am about to insist upon. For I had set out to write a popular life of S.K., without footnotes, without any reference to authorities, without the least appearance of pedantry; and here at the outset I am confronted by this terrible snag, the necessity of writing a scholium—or giving the whole thing up. Before this problem I halted for five days, staring at it despairingly, unable to put pen to paper.

But the thing must be done! I summon the reader to sharpen his wits and prepare himself to deal for a few minutes with a problem as intricate as a good crossword puzzle. I am somewhat consoled by the reflection that many people like puzzles, that detective stories cannot be too intricate for them. S.K. has maliciously provided many a puzzle for his biographers. He boasted of possessing as a psychological observer precisely the talents needed by a police detective, and so careful he was to cover his own tracks that he was assured no one would be able to discover his secret. But this boast has been provocative to ingenious students, and I believe that in the whole history of literature there has never been so much acumen displayed in ferreting out the secrets of an author—except perhaps in the case of the rather inconclusive efforts to discover to whom Shakespeare referred as "the onlie Begetter of these insuing Sonnets." In the main these puzzlers, especially P. A. Heiberg and Frithiof Brandt, have been highly successful. But the gilt-edged document, as we shall see, furnishes the clue to the discovery of S.K.'s deepest secret, and because of the common misapprehension of its significance this clue has not been followed up fruitfully.

I must give here a brief account of the contents of this document, though the reader will find each of the six sections translated in full at the head of the appropriate chapters. On three sheets of gilt-edged letter paper S.K. essayed to give a brief appraisal of his life under three headings: "Childhood," "Youth," and "Twenty-Five Years of Age." Under each heading there stood a poetical motto which characterized that particular period of his life. We are almost compelled to suppose that a document drawn up with such unusual elegance was symmetrical, in the sense that each sheet was devoted exclusively to one particular period. This implies that the three prose comments, which now are lumped together after the poems, were originally placed each of them under the motto to which it was related. This in fact is affirmed by Barfod in a prefatory note, for he says (though no one has noticed it) that each prose piece, "as can be seen," follows its appropriate motto. Alas, this can no longer be seen—that is the tragedy!—for, as they are printed, the three mottoes with their respective headings follow one another consecutively, and after them the three prose comments are lumped together at the end, as if they were all of them relevant to the last period exclusively, which is called "Twenty-Five Years of Age." Consequently, the first prose comment, which begins with a definite indication of time ("Then occurred the Great Earthquake"), is supposed to refer to a discovery which S.K. made on his twenty-fifth birthday, when according to Danish law he came of age. The father is supposed to have chosen that moment to confide to him his dreadful secret. Nothing could be further from the truth. We shall see subsequently that on this solemn occasion the father did reveal something to his son, but something so different from the earthquake that it was rather an atonement for it. That was the occasion when S.K. was reconciled with his father. But what then accounted for his revolt? We shall see in due time that it was precisely the Great Earthquake, which occurred in his twenty-second year, perhaps on his twenty-second birthday, an experience which put an end to his childish innocence and his childish faith.

Professor Hirsch, in attempting to reconstruct the development of S.K.'s early life resolved to leave this document entirely out of account, feeling that as it was then interpreted it afforded no secure foundation. But when from the Journal alone he had reached solid conclusions he saw how this document ought to be understood, that is, in what order it ought to be read; and he perceived that it afforded a short cut to the conclusions he had reached by a more laborious path. In my bigger biography I required the reader to follow the more laborious path; in this small book I must take the short cut, and to justify it I must require the reader to give attention for a moment to this laborious disquisition.

Hirsch did not suspect that all the trouble had been caused by the careless printing of this document. He did not notice Barfod's admission that it was not printed in the original order. Neither did he notice Barfod's confession that he did not understand the document: "Except for the last prose piece, if I have understood him aright, none has any connection with the motto written above it." Because Barfod perceived no connection, he was indifferent to the order in which the pieces were printed. Hirsch too remarks upon the apparent irrelevance of the prose pieces to the mottoes, but he sees that they are more than irrelevant, that they are contradictory, and therefore stand in a dialectical relation to the mottoes, exhibiting S.K. as "a man with his contradictions" (illustrated by the "real I" and the "reflective I" in the last passage, p. 128), but also as one who by his fate was involved in contradiction, so that he must construe his life in terms of the three-fold Hegelian formula: position (childlike faith); contradiction (revolt against God); reconciliation (with God and with his father). Hirsch lays stress upon the fact that this is a religious autobiography. For this reason "childhood" is made to reach as far as his twenty-second year, so as to include the whole period characterized by immediate religiousness under the dominance of his father. "Youth" is then the period of his revolt against the penitential religiousness of his father. On coming of age he finds himself cordially united with his father in penitence—and after the father's death doing penance in the "great parenthesis."

I confess that I cherished the hope of being able for once to achieve such elegant simplicity that this little book might rank among the great biographies, seeing that it deals with so great and interesting a figure. I profess to be his admirer and for a moment I was vain enough to think that perhaps I might become his poet. That proud hope has now vanished.

Evidently I am only a pedant. And perhaps after all S.K. is not an apt subject for simple treatment. I have an uneasy presentiment that perhaps in such a task as this I may not be able in the sequel to avoid entirely similar digressions. But no future emergency of the sort can give me so much pain as this. This snag stuck in my throat, reminding me of what an illustrious Chinese exponent of the Zen sect said of the doctrine of the Buddha: "It is like a red-hot ball of ice which has got stuck in one's throat; you cannot get it up, and you cannot get it down." At last I have "expectorated" it—to use S.K.'s expression, meaning that I have got it off my chest. Commonly, hard writing makes easy reading, and the possibility of "reading without tears" implies that some one has shed them abundantly.

Now we can return to the motto:

> Half child-play,
> Half God in the heart.

This signifies that S.K.'s childhood was a normally happy one, as the report of his schoolmaster and his nearest kindred indicates, that at all events it was not by any means so unhappy as he saw it and described it in a more remote perspective after melancholy had so clouded his vision that even his earliest days seemed to be tinged with it. We have reason to believe that during his childhood he did not suffer from melancholy in the strictest sense, but that this malady emerged after the Great Earthquake. And "half God in the heart" confirms the suspicion he often suggests, that the religious education he received from his father, however perverse it may have been, however inappropriate to childhood, and however deep were the scars it left upon him, had nevertheless the effect of planting God indelibly "in the heart." And in spite of everything that was grim about his religious education, we hear him say that "the a priori apprehension the child receives of God as the God of love is the principal thing," and he means us to understand that this was the apprehension he got from his father.

A year earlier, in 1838, he noted in his Journal the memory of happy childhood which was revived in him on one of his country excursions by the sight of the farmyard where as a child he had run about in his "little green jacket and gray breeches," and he added, "Alas, I now cannot catch up with myself; the only thing that remains to me of childhood is to weep."

Many accounts agree in representing that as the Benjamin of the family S.K. was petted by his older sisters, and that the stern father was inclined to be indulgent with him. Although S.K. has transmitted to us no criticism of his father which was not in the same breath revoked by an observation which condoned the fault, we have indications from other sources which suggest how intolerable the old man must have been. For example, there was the occasion when little Søren accidentally upset the salt and the father flew into a violent passion, apostrophizing him as "a prodigal son"—and worse things than that. Generally, however, though he required unquestioning obedience, the father was just, and to the youngest son he was evidently partial, putting up with his pertness, and encouraging an intimacy which was rare if not unique between an old man and his little son. That Søren was a pert child is implied by the name by which he was commonly known in the family. He was called Fork—after an episode when he was rebuked at table for shoveling the food greedily upon his plate with the fork and rejoined, "I *am* a fork, and I will stick you." This is significant of the polemical temper which, as we shall see, was a dominant trait throughout his whole life. In childhood it took the form of pertness, which cost him solemn rebukes from his teachers and sometimes a bloody nose from a bigger playmate, for he was never deterred by fear from directing his stinging wit against companions who were physically stronger than he. His schoolmates, who subsequently contributed their reminiscences of the great man as a boy, do not give a pleasing picture of him. One of them describes him as "a regular little wild cat." Welding, Dean of Viborg, wrote: "To the rest of us who led a genuinely boyish life S.K. was a stranger and an object of compassion, especially on account of his dress, always the same, made of rough cloth of a dark mixed color and a peculiar cut, the coat having short skirts. He wore heavy woolen stockings and shoes, never boots. [It is the distinction between low shoes and high shoes, as we say in America.] This procured him the nickname of Choirboy [because it resembled the costume in charity schools], a name which alternated with Søren Sock, in allusion to his father's previous business as hosier. S.K. was regarded by us all as one whose home was wrapped in a mysterious half-darkness of severity and oddity."

He goes on to tell of S.K.'s characteristic retort to one of his teachers: "Professor Mathiessen [teacher in German] was an exceedingly weak man who never had any authority over us. Once when the horseplay in class had gone very far—it was quite wild in all his classes—when the pupils had made a complete meal with butter-bread, sandwiches and beer, and had toasted one another with formal prosits, Professor Mathiessen was about to go out and report the affair to Professor Nielsen [the Headmaster]. The rest of us surrounded Mathiessen with prayers and fair promises, but S.K. said only, 'Please tell the Headmaster that this is what always goes on in your class'—whereupon Mathiessen sat down and made no report."

It was a dreadful cruelty to the little boy that his father compelled him to dress as no other boys did. Nothing can be more excruciating to a child. The other boys had no skirts to their coats, and they commonly wore boots. Perhaps it was reaction from this suffering which prompted S.K. to dress foppishly as soon as he was at liberty to select his own clothes. When he was in the university he ran up enormous bills with the tailor, which his father eventually was obliged to pay. In his childhood S.K. was keenly aware that there was something strange, even uncanny, about his home, perhaps too about his unusual intimacy with his father, and for this reason he never invited a schoolmate to visit it.

Pastor Anger, recalling proudly that he himself had always stood number one in the class, excluded the possibility that S.K. had ever stood higher than number two. He speaks of the "single combats" in which S.K. was often engaged, and remarks that "in spite of this it was always a question which of us two was the weakest in the class and the poorest in gymnastics." We shall see later that his father in sending him to school had required of him only that he was to stand third in the class.

There can be no doubt that Søren was a very frail child, and whatever his malady may have been, it pursued him to the end, probably occasioning his early death. It is perhaps most plausibly attributed to a marked curvature of the spine, occasioned, as he believed, by a fall from a tree in early childhood. Some sort of spinal trouble was the vague diagnosis of the hospital, whither he was carried from the street after a fall which was the result of paralysis, and where he died in a few weeks. We have several accounts of similar attacks which were not permanent. For example, at a social gathering he once fell from the sofa and lay impotent upon the floor—beseeching his friends not to pick "it" up but to "leave it there till the maid comes in the morning to sweep." But it is not necessary to discover the particular malady which troubled S.K., seeing that all his brothers and sisters were frail. Two of them died before Søren was nine years old, and a few years later three died in quick succession.

The sense of his physical inferiority was an acute distress throughout his whole life. He commonly spoke of it as "a disproportion between my soul and my body." Of course it was most painful to him in childhood not to be like other boys. Even if we suppose that the melancholy which he projected back into the years of childhood was in reality a later development, this sense of unlikeness is enough to belie the effort of his nephew Trols Lund to depict his childhood as idyllically happy. S.K. says in the *Point of View:*

"In the two ages of immediacy (childhood and youth), with the dexterity reflection always possesses, I helped myself out, as I was compelled to do, with some sort of counterfeit, and not being quite clear about myself and the talents bestowed upon me, I suffered the pain of not being like the others—which naturally at that period I would have given everything to be able to be, if only for a short time. A spirit can very well put up with not being like the others—indeed that is precisely the negative definition of spirit. But childhood and youth stand in a close relation to the generic qualification expressed in the species, the race, and just for this reason it is the greatest torment of that period not to be like the others, or as in my case, to be so strangely topsy-turvy as to begin at the point where a few in every generation end, whereas the majority, who live merely in the factors of the soulish-bodily synthesis, never reach it—that is, the qualification spirit. . . . But when one is a child—and the other children play or jest or whatever else they do; ah! and when one is a youth—and the other young people make love and dance or whatever else they do—and then, in spite of the fact that one is a child or a youth, then to be spirit! Frightful torture! Even more frightful if by the help of imagination one knows how to perform the trick of appearing to be the youngest of all."

"I was already an old man when I was born," says S.K. elsewhere, and in the Journal he describes himself as follows: "Delicate, slender, and weak, deprived of almost every condition for holding my own with other boys, or even for passing as a complete human being in comparison with others; melancholy, sick in soul, in many ways profoundly unfortunate, one thing I had: an eminently shrewd wit, given me presumably in order that I might not be defenseless. Even as a boy I was aware of my power of wit and knew that it was my strength in conflict with far stronger comrades."

In another entry he says: "I am in the deepest sense an unfortunate individual who has from the earliest age been nailed fast to one suffering or another, to the very verge of insanity, which may have its deeper ground in a disproportion between my soul and my body; for (and this is the remarkable thing in conjunction with my infinite cheerfulness) this is entirely out of proportion to my spirit, which anomalously, and perhaps because of the strain and stress between soul and body, has acquired a tensile strength which is very rare."

S.K. has described his childhood in several of his anonymous works, ascribing his experiences, of course, to the pseudonym. For example in the second part of *Either/Or* he describes through the mask of Judge William his first impressions of school.

"When I was five years old I was sent to school. Such an event always makes an impression upon a child, but the question is, what impression. Childish curiosity is engrossed by the various confusing conceptions as to what significance this may properly have. That such was the case with me too is quite likely; however, the chief impression I got was an entirely different one. I made my appearance at the school, was introduced to the teacher, and then was given as my lesson for the following day the first ten lines of Balle's *Lesson-Book*, which I was to learn by heart. Every other impression was then obliterated from my soul, only my task stood out vividly before it. As a child I had a very good memory, so I had soon learned my lesson. My sister heard me recite it several times and affirmed that I knew it. I went to bed, and before I fell asleep I catechized myself once more; I fell asleep with the firm purpose of reading my lesson over the following morning. I awoke at five o'clock, got dressed, got hold of my lesson-book and read it again. At this moment everything stands out before my eyes as vividly as if it had occurred yesterday. To me it was as if heaven and earth might collapse if I did not learn my lesson; and on the other hand, as though even if heaven and earth were to collapse, this would not exempt me from doing the task assigned to me, from learning my lesson. At that age I knew so little about duties; I had not yet, as you see, learned to know them from Balle's *Lesson-Book* [which was a primer of morals], I had only one duty, that of learning my lesson, and yet I can trace my whole ethical view of life to this impression. . . . When I was two years older I was sent to the Latin School. Here began a new life, but here again the principal impression was the ethical, although I enjoyed the greatest freedom. . . . I knew only one duty, that of attending to my school, and in this respect I was left entirely to my own responsibility. When I was sent to this school and the prescribed school books had been bought, my father handed them to me with the words, 'William, when the month is up you are the third in your class.' I was exempted from all parental twaddle: he never asked me about my lessons, never heard me recite them, never looked at my exercise book, never reminded me that now it was time to read, now time to leave off. . . . I got a thoroughly deep impression of the fact that there was something called duty and that it had eternal validity. In my time we studied grammar with a thoroughness which in this age is unknown. Through this instruction I received an impression which had a singular influence upon my soul. The unconditional respect with which I regarded the rule, the reverence I cherished for it, the contempt with which I looked down upon the miserable life the exception led, the righteous way, so it seemed to me, in which it was tracked down in my exercise book and always stigmatized—what else is this but the distinction which lies at the bottom of every philosophical way of thinking? When under this influence I regarded my father, he appeared to me an incarnation of the rule; what came from any other source was

44

the exception, in so far as it was not in agreement with his commandment."

In a work which was never finished and now is to be found among his *Papers,* S.K. allows the pseudonymous author Johannes Climacus to tell of the still more important education he received from his father at home.

"His home did not offer many diversions, and as he almost never went out, he early became accustomed to occupy himself alone and with his own thoughts. His father was a very severe man, apparently dry and prosaic, but under this rough coat he concealed a glowing imagination which even old age could not quench. When Johannes occasionally asked permission to go out, he generally refused to give it, though once in a while he proposed instead that Johannes should take his hand and walk back and forth in the room. At first glance this might seem a poor substitute, and yet, as in the case of the rough coat, there was something totally different concealed under it. The proposition was accepted, and it was left entirely to Johannes to determine where they should go. So they went out of doors to a nearby castle in Spain, or out to the seashore, or about the streets, wherever Johannes wished to go, for the father was equal to anything. While they walked back and forth in the room the father described everything they saw; they greeted passers-by, carriages rattled past them and drowned the father's voice; the cake-woman's goodies were more enticing than ever. The father described so accurately, so vividly, so explicitly even to the least details everything that was known to Johannes, and described so fully and perspicuously what was unknown to him, that after half an hour of such a walk with his father he was as much overwhelmed and fatigued as if he had been a whole day out of doors. Johannes soon learnt from his father how to exercise this magic power. What first had been an epic now became a drama; they conversed in turn. If they were walking along well known paths they watched one another sharply to make sure that nothing was overlooked; if the way was strange to Johannes, he invented something, whereas the father's almighty imagination was capable of shaping everything, of using every childish whim as an ingredient of the drama which was being enacted. To Johannes it seemed as if the world were coming into existence during the conversation, as if the father were the Lord God and he was his favorite, who was allowed to interpose his foolish conceits as merrily as he would; for he was never repulsed, the father was never put out but agreed to everything, and always to Johannes's contentment. While life in the father's house continued thus to develop his imagination, teaching him to like the taste of ambrosia, the education which fell to his lot in school was entirely in harmony with this. The lofty authority of Latin grammar, the dignity of the rules developed a new enthusiasm. It was Greek grammar, however, which especially appealed to him. Absorbed in this, he forgot to read Homer aloud as commonly he was wont to do for the sake of the beauty of the rhythm. The Greek master taught the grammar in a rather philosophical way. When it was explained to Johannes, for example, that the accusative signifies extension in time and space, that the preposition does not govern the case, but it is the relationship which does that, then everything widened out before him. The preposition vanished, extension in time and space remained as an enormous empty picture for the intuition. His imagination was again employed, but in a different way than heretofore.

What delighted him on the walking tours was filled space, he could not get it thick enough round about him. His imagination was so productive that it was able to get along with very little. Outside the window of the sitting-room there grew some ten blades of grass. Here he sometimes discovered a little creature which ran between the stems. These straws became an immense forest which yet had the same denseness and darkness as the bunch of grass. Now, instead of filled space he got empty space, he gazed again but saw nothing except enormous extension."

The same narrative tells how Johannes, when he grew older, was permitted to listen in upon his father's philosophical discussions.

"The father always allowed the opponent to state his whole case, and then as a precaution asked him if he had nothing more to say before he began his reply. Johannes had followed the opponent's speech with strained attention, and in his way shared an interest in its outcome. A pause intervened. The father's rejoinder followed, and, lo, in a trice the tables were turned. How that came about was a riddle to Johannes, but his soul delighted in the show. The opponent spoke again. Johannes could almost hear his heart beat, so impatiently did he await what was to occur. It occurred; in the twinkling of an eye all was inverted, the explicable became inexplicable, the certain doubtful, the contrary evident. When the shark would seize its prey it must turn over upon its back, for its mouth is on the side of the belly; it is dark on the back, silver-white on the belly. It must be a magnificent sight to witness this alternation of color; it must sometimes glitter so brightly as to hurt the eyes, and yet it must be a delight to look upon it. Johannes was witness of a similar alteration when he heard his father engage in disputation. . . . The older he grew, and the more the father engaged him in conversation, the more attentive he became to this inexplicable power; it was as though the father had a mysterious intuition of what Johannes was about to say, and so with a single word could confound it all. When the father was not merely confuting him but expounding his own view, it was possible for Johannes to perceive how he went about it, how he approached by successive steps the position he wished to reach. Johannes surmised now that the reason why the father, by a single word, was able to turn everything upside down must be that he himself had forgotten something in the succession in which his thoughts were marshaled. What other children get through the fascination of poetry and the surprise of fairy tales, he got through the calmness of intuition and the alternations of dialectic. This was the child's joy; it became the youth's delight. So his life had a rare continuity; it did not know the various transitions which commonly mark the different periods of growth. When Johannes grew older he had no toys to lay aside, for he had learnt to play with that which was to be the serious business of his life, and yet it lost thereby nothing of its allurement."

In spite of his natural independence of character, Søren was absorbed in his father to an extraordinary degree. But the father's dominance over the child was more complete and more profound than we have yet seen, for he undertook more especially the religious education of his son and thus influenced him in the deepest way one person can influence another. We shall see later why the father was so intent upon instilling in his children, especially in his youngest son, the most decisive concepts of Christianity.

The Crucifixion

One of his devices for educating Søren is described in *Training in Christianity:*

"Imagine then a child [who has never before heard of Christ's suffering and death], and give this child delight by showing it some of those pictures which one buys on the stalls, which are so trivial artistically, but so dear to children. This one here on the snorting steed, with a tossing feather in his hat, with a lordly mien, riding at the head of thousands upon thousands which you do not see, with hand outstretched to command, 'Forward!' forward to the summits of the mountains which you see in front of you, forward to victory—this is the Emperor, the one and only Napoleon. So now you tell the child a little about Napoleon. This one here is dressed as a huntsman; he stands leaning upon his bow and gazes straight before him with a glance so piercing, so self-confident, and yet so anxious. This is William Tell. You now relate to the child something about him and about that extraordinary glance of his, explaining that with this same glance he has at once an eye for the beloved child, that he may not harm him, and for the apple, that he may not miss it. And thus you show the child many pictures, to the child's unspeakable delight. Then you come to one which intentionally was laid among the others. It represents a man crucified. The child will not at once nor quite directly understand this picture, and will ask what it means, why he hangs like that on a tree. So you explain to the child that this is a cross, that to hang on it means to be crucified, and that in that land crucifixion was not only the most painful death penalty but also an ignominious mode of execution employed only for the grossest malefactors. What impression will that make upon the child?

49

The child will be in a strange state of mind, it will surely wonder that it could occur to you to put such an ugly picture among all the other lovely ones, the picture of a gross malefactor among all these heroes and glorious figures. For just as "The King of the Jews" was written above His cross as a reproach to the Jews, so this picture which is published regularly every year as a reproach to the human race is a remembrance which the race never can and never should be rid of. . . . However, we have not yet reached the decisive point, the child has not yet learned who this gross malefactor was. With the curiosity characteristic of children the child will doubtless ask, 'Who is it? What did he do? Tell me.' Then tell the child that this crucified man was the Saviour of the world. Yet to this he will not be able to attach any clear conceptions; so tell him merely that this crucified man was the most loving person that ever lived. . . . Now what impression do you think it will make upon the child, who naturally will ask, 'But why were people so bad to him then?' "

In one of the *Two Ethico-Religious Treatises* (translated in the little volume entitled *The Present Age*) there is a similar passage: "Once upon a time there was a man. As a boy, he was strictly brought up in the Christian religion. He had not heard much about that which other children commonly hear, about the little child Jesus, about the angels, and such-like. On the other hand they showed him all the more frequently the Crucified, so that this picture was the only one he had, the only impression he had of the Saviour. Although only a child, he was already as old as an old man."

No wonder S.K. in the *Point of View* stigmatized this as a "crazy" way to bring up a child: "As a child I was strictly and austerely brought up in Christianity; humanly speaking, crazily brought up. A child crazily travestied as a melancholy old man. Terrible! What wonder then that there were times when Christianity appeared to me the most inhuman cruelty, although I never, even when I was furthest from it, lost my reverence for Christianity, being firmly resolved (especially in case I might not choose to become a Christian) that I would never initiate any one into the difficulties which I experienced, and which I have never heard tell of nor read about."

No wonder that he remarks in his Journal upon the dangers of such an education: "The most dangerous case is not when the father is a free thinker, and not even when he is a hypocrite. No, the danger is when he is a pious and godfearing man, when the child is inwardly and deeply convinced of it, and yet in spite of all this observes that a profound unrest is deeply hidden in his soul, so that not even piety and the fear of God can bestow peace. The danger lies just here, that the child in this relationship is almost compelled to draw a conclusion about God, that after all God is not infinite love."

His own experience led him to think a great deal about the religious education which is appropriate in the age of childhood. Johannes Climacus says in the *Postscript* (pp. 523, 530): "To cram Christianity into a child is a thing that cannot be done; for it is a general rule that everyone comprehends only what he has use for, and the child has no decisive use for Christianity. . . . When one talks to a child about Christianity, and the child is not violently maltreated (in a figurative sense), the child will appropriate everything that is gentle, childish, lovable, heavenly; he will live in companionship with the little child Jesus, and with the

51

angels, and with the Three Kings of Orient, he sees their star in the dark night, he travels the long road, now he is in the stable, one amazement after another, he is always seeing the heavens opened, with all the fervor of imagination he longs for these pictures—and now . . . let us not forget the ginger-nuts and all the other splendid things which are the perquisites of this festival."

I do not forget that it is a pseudonym who says this, but S.K. happens to refer to this passage in his Journal and affirms that "Climacus was right."

We shall subsequently find reason to suspect that the father regarded his youngest son not only as his Benjamin but as his Isaac, the son who is to be sacrificed as his atonement, or at least for his guilt, and that principally for this reason (as S.K. himself says) he sought to prepare him for another world.

We find in the Journal a strange entry dated two years before his death (i.e. on October 13, 1853): "There are two thoughts which arose in my soul so early that I really cannot indicate their origin. The first is that there are men whose destiny it is to be sacrificed in one way or another for others in order to bring the idea out—and that I with my peculiar cross was one of them. The other thought is that I should never be tried by having to work for my living—partly because I thought that I should die very young, and partly because I thought that in consideration of my peculiar cross God would spare me this suffering and problem. Whence come such thoughts? I do not know. But this I know, that I have not got them from reading, nor have I derived them from another person."

This was a thought which was often in S.K.'s mind. In 1848 he remembered with amazement that eight years earlier he had confided this gloomy thought to his fiancée "in one of my first conversations with her." He was almost ready to believe that such thoughts were innate, but it is plausible to suppose that he derived them from his father in early childhood, that his father's behavior toward him made him obscurely conscious that he was regarded as one who was doomed to be a sacrifice.

This brings us to the point where it does not seem incredible that the strange story entitled "The Quiet Despair" (one of the autobiographical sketches inserted in Quidam's Diary in the *Stages*) might really represent what occurred between an old man and his little son. I quote it here.

January 5, Midnight.

THE QUIET DESPAIR

When Dean Swift was old he was taken to the madhouse he himself had founded in his youth. There, it is related, he often stood before a mirror with the persistence of a vain and wanton woman, though not exactly with her thoughts. He looked at himself and said: "Poor old man!"

There was a father and a son. A son is like a mirror in which the father beholds himself, and for the son the father too is like a mirror in which he beholds himself in time to come. However, they rarely regarded one another in this way, for their daily intercourse was characterized by gay and lively conversation. It happened only a few times that the father came to a stop, stood before the son with a sorrowful countenance, looked at him steadily and said: "Poor child, you are going into a quiet despair." True as this saying was, nothing was ever said to indicate how it was to be understood. And the father believed that he was to blame for the son's melancholy, and the son believed that he was the occasion of the father's sorrow—but they never exchanged a word on this subject.

Then the father died, and the son saw much, experienced much, and was tried in manifold temptations; but infinitely inventive as love is, longing and the sense of loss taught him, not indeed to wrest from the silence of eternity a communication, but to imitate the father's voice so perfectly that he was content with the likeness. So he did not look at himself in a mirror like the aged Swift, for the mirror was no longer there; but in loneliness he comforted himself by hearing the father's voice: "Poor child, you are going into a quiet despair." For the father was the only one who understood him, and yet in fact he did not know whether he had really understood him; and the father was the only confidant he had, but the confidence was of such a sort that it remained the same whether the father lived or died.

Two-thirds of this story has been told in S.K.'s words. I cannot think that too much has been said here about S.K.'s childhood, for if ever the child was father of the man, it was in this instance.

EARLY YOUTH

1830 TO 1834

"THERE was a rare continuity in my life," said S.K. To his mind the period of childhood was not definitely brought to an end by putting on long trousers, nor even by entering the University in the year 1830 at the age of seventeen. I see no reason to doubt the affirmation of his schoolmaster, that though he had grown more serious, there was something unusually childish about him. In an unfinished book he describes himself under the name of Johannes Climacus.

"It is true, however, that he was in love, fanatically in love...with thoughts. No young lover can be more deeply moved by the incomprehensible transition through which love awakens in his breast, by the lightning flash in which reciprocal affection awakens in the beloved, than was he by the comprehensible transition through which the one thought fits into the other, a transition which for him was the happy instant which he had surmised and awaited in quietness of soul. So when his head was heavy with thought and bowed like a ripe ear of wheat, this was not because he heard the voice of the beloved, but because he was listening to the secret whisperings of the thoughts; when his look was dreamy, this was not because her picture was in his mind's eye, but because the movements of the thoughts were coming into vision. It was his delight to begin with a single thought, from which to climb up step by step along the path of logical consequence to a higher thought; for the logical consequence was for him a *scala paradisi,* and his blessedness seemed to him even more glorious than that of the angels. Then when he had arrived at the higher thought he found an indescribable joy, a passionate rapture, in plunging headlong down along the line of the same consequences until he reached the point from which he had set out. In this, however, he did not always succeed according to his wish. If he did not perform exactly as many motions as there were links in the chain of consequences, he became distressed, for then the movement was imperfect. Then he began over again. Then, if he succeeded, his soul shuddered with delight; for sheer joy he could not sleep at night, but continued for hours making the same movement; for this up-and-down and down-and-up of thought was a joy beyond compare. In his happy hours his gait was light, almost a glide; at other times it was anxious and uncertain. That is, so long as he was laboring to climb up, so long as the consequence had not yet proved able to make a way for itself, he was oppressed; for he was fearful of losing track of the many consequences he had ready, without being yet perfectly clear about their necessity. When one sees a man carrying a great number of fragile objects stacked one above the other, one is not inclined to wonder that he walks uncertainly and is every moment clutching after equilibrium; whereas if one does not see the stack, one may smile, as many smiled at Johannes Climacus without suspecting that he was carrying a higher stack than that which amazed them in the other case, that his soul was anxious lest a single consequence might drop out, for then the whole would fall to pieces."

This is doubtless an idealized picture; it leaves out a less attractive side of his character, but it does not exaggerate his interest in thoughts. During his first years in the University he was as diligent as ever in studying his lessons, and that not only because it was a duty but because he rejoiced in the opportunity for broader culture which was there offered to him, or which the free life of a university student made possible. Now for the first time he was able to transcend the narrow bourgeois interests of his strange home in which there was no place for the beautiful, and while he still pursued the philosophical interests his father had encouraged he grasped avidly after the pleasures of literature and music. There was music in his soul, though he had never known it in the home, and he became an opera enthusiast. He had a dramatic instinct which led him to become a habitué of the theater. He appropriated passionately the aesthetic side of life; and these were interests which he never condemned and never relinquished; for in later years he affirmed that the religious "does not abolish the aesthetical but dethrones it." By these interests he was separated from his elder brother Peter, who, though he had the advantage of studying in Germany for his doctorate and was already a lecturer in the University when Søren was a student, never acquired an appreciation of such things and disapproved of Søren's interest in them.

We may surmise that the son's broader interests made him inexplicable to his aged father, and that the home seemed narrow and stuffy to the boy, but there is no evidence that his affection and admiration for the father was diminished. He had followed dutifully his father's wish by inscribing himself as a theological student. But it was not expected that he would begin with theological studies; on the contrary it was required that during their first years, or at least until what was called the Second Examination, the students in every faculty should devote themselves to liberal studies, and Søren seized this opportunity with enthusiasm. He took the Second Examination within the first year and passed it brilliantly. It is noteworthy that while he got *laudabilis* for history, Latin, Greek, and Hebrew (which he had already studied in school), he received *laudabilis praeter caeteris* for philosophy, physics and mathematics. We see therefore that it was not because of a lack of aptitude for scientific studies that he resolved three years later not to devote his life to them. Doubtless he did not begin his theological studies as promptly or as seriously as his father might have wished, and it is likely that his father was profoundly disquieted—not perhaps so much by his lack of interest in theology as by his interest in everything else, whether it was offered in the liberal curriculum of the University or available to him in books, whether it was to be found in the student debating club, or in student life in the cafés, or in the theater, or by way of observing the life of the streets. For it seems that during his first year in the University he was a familiar figure in the streets and found his keenest diversion there, as he did to the end of his life. Evidently this was a continuation of the fictitious promenades upon which his father led him in the sitting room. As no one guessed that he was observing life to good purpose, he was regarded as a *flaneur* who was merely killing time.

During the first four years in the University he showed no signs of the melancholy which he later attributed to his childhood but hardly to this period of his youth. At this time life beckoned him hopefully forward, neither was there any trace at this time of scrupulous indecision and vacillation which a few years later was so evident and so painful, and which tormented him until almost the end of his life. Accordingly we must recognize that this trait was a symptom of his subsequent malady. At this period it was Peter who exhibited the symptoms of melancholy, as we can see now from the scraps of his diary which have lately been published by Weltzer. At this time Peter could not make up his mind whether to separate from the Moravian Brethren or to return to their meetings. He did both—and regretted both. This entry is parallel to one of the *Diapsalmata* in *Either/Or:* "Do it, or don't do it—you'll regret both," except that in Peter's diary there is neither wit nor humor. Peter could not make up his mind whether to follow an academic career or to seek a parish and be ordained. He made application for a country parish, and after some delay he was nominated to one...but not to the one he wanted. Thereupon he was distressed by the fear that he was unworthy to be a clergyman, and he had to go to the King to beg permission to withdraw his application. The King rebuked him but granted his request. This was a case so unusual that it aroused a good deal of scandal. And all this time Peter could not decide whether to join openly the party of Grundtvig, which was so much in disfavor with the authorities that he might well fear to jeopardize his chance of a position either in the Church or in the University. Later, when the cause of Grundtvig prevailed he became an open disciple, and he was made a bishop, but ultimately resigned from this office, obsessed by the notion that he had committed the sin against the Holy Ghost, the unforgivable sin. Between the two brothers there was always discord, and all this time their study-chambers were side by side on an upper floor of the big house. It was a marked case of incompatibility of temper, and we can see now from Peter's diary that the fault was not altogether on Søren's side. In several entries Peter expresses regret he has not been able for some time to take the Holy Communion, "because I could not be reconciled with my brother."

It argues some seriousness on the part of the young student that in his third year in the University (1833), when he was twenty years old, he began the Journal which was to become one of the most famous documents of the sort the world has ever known. It was begun tentatively and not with the sort of entries one expects in a diary, for the first (dated December 3, 1833) is a translation into Latin of a part of St. Paul's Epistle to the Galatians, the second (March 10, 1834) is likewise an exegetical study, and all have to do with questions of theology until we reach the eleventh (September 12, 1834), which is the first of several entries dealing with "The Master Thief," which he thought a good theme for a book. All this does not indicate, however, a deliberate resolution to write a journal, for the sixty-two entries which compose the first book were originally written on loose sheets of paper and subsequently transcribed. The first entries made in a book were his impression of North Seeland during the vacation he enjoyed during the summer of 1835, when he made his headquarters at Gilleleje. The period following this, which was the period of rebellion, dissolute living and despair ("the path of perdition"), the book-entries were relatively few.

That he began to take the Journal more seriously a year later is shown by an entry which is pompously described in the margin as "Resolution of July 13, 1837, given in our chamber at 6 o'clock P.M." From this we are surprised to learn that S.K. felt "a strong indisposition to record occasional observations." He too had "often wondered" at this, and thinking of several great men who by precept and example had recommended the practice of keeping a journal, he came to the conclusion that the reason why this was "disagreeable and even loathsome" to him was that in each case

he thought of the possibility of publicity, which would require a more elaborate development than he cared to give;
"and under the incubus of such an abstract possibility (a
literary hiccough or nausea) the aroma of the thought and
of the mood evaporated. For this reason the entries I have
are so crunched together that I now no longer understand
them, or they are quite accidental, so I can see that there
are commonly a lot of entries on the same day, which indicates that there has been a sort of day of reckoning—but
that is crazy. The apparent wealth of thoughts and ideas
one is sensible of in the abstract possibility must be just as
uncomfortable and evoke the same sort of unrest as the
cows suffer from when they are not milked at the proper
time. One had better therefore milk oneself when outward
circumstances do not come to one's aid." With these con-
siderations in view he formed the resolution "by more frequent entries to let the thoughts come forth with the um-
bilical cord of the first mood, without any reference to their
possible use (which in any case I should never have from
them by thumbing the pages of my book), but as if I were
unbosoming myself to a friend, thereby to gain first of all
a possibility of knowledge of myself at a later moment, as
well as a pliability in writing, articulation in written expression, which I have to a certain degree in speaking. . . . Such
practice behind the scenes is certainly necessary to every man
whose development is not in a way public."

To this program S.K. adhered throughout his life, but of
course his notion of what a journal might be and might
accomplish became more definite as time went on. It was
only in 1842 he began to call his note books journals. They
are not properly called diaries, for though at the head of
one of them he wrote, *nulla dies sine linea,* S.K. rarely dated

his entries. For the most part they were timeless thoughts. The earlier journals were certainly addressed to himself alone, and over them might have been written the rubric he used for the *Diapsalmata: Ad se ipsum*. But in 1846, while he continued to jot down the customary aphoristic entries in the book he had marked JJ, and continued to write many entries on loose sheets, as he did for the rest of his life, he began on March 9 a new book designated NB, the first of the long series of NB Journals which ended with NB[36]. From this time on, occasional attempts to sum up the experiences of his life were entitled "Report," "Report—Result," or "Accounting." This evidently indicated an expectation that after his death these journals would be published. With this in view he began in 1847 a revision of his earlier journals, and was careful thenceforth to use only such abbreviations as would be commonly understood. He even suggested the name under which they might be published: "The Judge's Book." He said once in his Journal, "After my death not only my works but my life will be studied and studied." This expectation has certainly not been disappointed.

Because no consecutive account of the origin and development of S.K.'s Journal has (so far as I know) ever been written, I have introduced it here at the point where this stupendous work was begun.

The inception of such a work is a proof that this young man was not the frivolous idler he appeared to be, in the eyes especially of his father and elder brother. In an entry of November 22, 1834, he remarks upon the tragedy of being misunderstood. In large part he was himself to blame for this, for he liked to pretend to be more frivolous than he was. But he several times found reason to complain that

Peter behaved like "the elder brother" in the parable, and Peter confirms this in his diary when several times he reveals that he was petulant because the younger brother, who was not so deserving as he, was treated more generously by the father. In fact, the Journal itself shows that Søren was pretty diligent about his theological studies, and in the spring of 1834 he took Martensen as his tutor (in preference to his brother Peter, who had the fame of being the best tutor in the University). They were to study Schleiermacher together, but S.K. soon insisted upon a general discussion of theological themes. Martensen recognized at once the unusual talents of his pupil but thought him too "sophistical." S.K.'s judgment was that Martensen never got to the bottom of any subject. It was a strange fate which thus brought together so early these two men who in the end were to clash so dreadfully. Martensen says of S.K. that "at that time he was very much devoted to me." But this was rather a misunderstanding.

In view of the free life S.K. had begun to enjoy and the wider interests which were opening before him, the home must have seemed very narrow and its religious atmosphere very stuffy. "All that I had to suffer from at home," he complained, "and especially from Peter after he had become morbidly religious." That sounds petulant, but it must be remembered that Søren was at that time a religious youth. Until some time in 1835 he went regularly to the Holy Communion with his father and brother. From S.K.'s Journal we get no idea of how morbid and unintelligent was the religiousness which prevailed in that household, but now when we can read Peter's diary it is enough to suffocate one. The whole environment of the family, as we see from the letters of Peter's most intimate friends, was disagreeably redolent of the same sort of religiosity, partly sentimental and partly conventional.

But worse things were in store for that family, which for a long time had seemed to be particularly favored by God, and which was in its way an ideal bourgeois home. A good while earlier, in 1819, little Søren Michael died at the age of twelve as a result of bumping his head against another boy's head. In 1822 Maren Kirsten died of cramps at the age of twenty-four. But in 1832 calamities began to fall upon this house in quick succession. One might think that it was a nemesis upon a family the gods had devoted to destruction. The melancholy father saw in them the hand of an angry God. First Nicoline Christine died on September 10, 1832, when she was thirty-three years of age, in giving birth to a still-born baby. A year later, on September 21, 1833, Niels Andreas died in his twenty-fifth year at Paterson, N.J. This was a loss which Søren felt keenly, for Niels was the brother nearest to him in age. To the father it was not only a cause of sorrow but of sharp pangs of conscience. He had treated this son harshly, forcing him against his will to go into business, and finally sending him to America to make his fortune. There the young man spent many anxious months seeking in vain for a position. He found America "a feast for simple laborers, but not for clerks strange to the language and without sufficient money to begin with." At last he found some sort of a post in Paterson, but there he soon fell sick and died. The only relief to this sad picture is the parental kindness of a Mr. and Mrs. Rogers in whose house he died, and the pastoral solicitude of the Reverend Ralph Williston, rector of St. Paul's Episcopal Church. This loss was the more poignantly felt by the father for the fact that in the messages the dying boy sent to his family his mother was remembered affectionately but his father was not mentioned, so that the clergyman who transmitted them assumed that the father must be dead. The old man could make no other atonement than to provide a stone to mark his son's grave. Alas, the grave can no longer be found, for the cemetery has been engulfed by the city. Ten months later, on July 31, 1834, the old man lost his wife after a painful illness of many weeks; and five months after that, on December 29, the most brilliant of his daughters, Petrea Severine, who had married Henrik Ferdinand Lund, a director of the State Bank, died in her thirty-third year in giving birth to a son.

Thus in the space of two years the old man had lost three of his children and his wife; there were only two left of the seven children with whom God had seemed to bless this home—only Peter and Søren, the eldest son and the youngest. It is to be remembered that not one of them had lived to be thirty-four years old. Not without plausibility the old man inferred that none of his children would live longer than that. Indeed to Peter and Søren (who then were respectively twenty-nine and twenty-one years of age) he allotted no more than this span of life, which was indeed nine years longer than the average at which his other children had died; and the two sons did not doubt that the father's prophecy was true. Søren remarked in his Journal upon the striking fact that Christ at His death was only thirty-three years old, an age, as he says, which corresponds to one generation of mankind. Moreover, since he came of a long-lived family, the father was convinced that it would be his sad lot to outlive all of his children—and his sons had no doubt of it.

It did not require a melancholy mind to see tragedy in these many deaths which followed one another so swiftly, but by this experience the father's melancholy was prodigiously increased. The home must have been intolerably gloomy for the two young men, and especially for Søren, who had to suffer from the increasing melancholy of Peter. Although the old man uttered sincerely the words of Job which are so often uttered with conventional pretense at resignation, and uttered them so impressively that Søren could never forget them, "The Lord gave, the Lord hath taken away, blessed be the name of the Lord," he thought secretly that the Lord had given him children only to be able to punish him by taking them away. He knew himself to be a sinner in the hands of an angry God. Søren, on the other hand, thought of the themes of Greek tragedy. He remembered the passionate response a tragedian had put in the mouth of a peasant in reply to the question whether he had any reason for believing in the gods—"Because the gods hate me." He was soon to discover a deeper analogy with the Greek conception of tragedy.

THE GREAT EARTHQUAKE

Then it was that the great earthquake occurred, the frightful upheaval which suddenly forced upon me a new infallible rule for interpreting the phenomena one and all. Then I surmised that my father's great age was not a divine blessing, but rather a curse; that the distinguished talents of our family existed only to create mutual friction; then I felt the silence of death increasing around me, when in my father I beheld an unfortunate man who must outlive us all, a sepulchral cross upon the grave of all his own hopes. Guilt must rest upon the whole family, a divine punishment must be impending over it; it must disappear, be stricken out by God's mighty hand, be wiped out as an unsuccessful experiment. And only now and then did I find a little relief in the thought that my father had the heavy duty of consoling us with the comfort of religion, of preparing us all, so that a better world would be open to us if we were to lose all in this, even if there were to fall upon us that punishment which the Jews devoutly wished for their foes, that our remembrance would be cut off from the earth and our name *blotted out."*

Thus does S.K. describe (in the gilt-edged document we began to study on p. 33) the overwhelming experience which in his twenty-second year brought to an end the period of childhood, or rather the period which was continuous with his childhood, inasmuch as he was still affectionately subservient to his father and had not yet thought of striking out with the independence of youth upon new paths, or of forming his own plans in conformity with his personal inclinations and talents.

But what was this "earthquake"? Before we seek to answer this question it would be well to have in mind another account which S.K. gives of the same experience. It is one of the autobiographical insertions which occur on the fifth of every month in Quidam's Diary. This entry is dated March 5, midnight. I quote it in full.

SOLOMON'S DREAM

Solomon's judgment is well known. It availed to discriminate between truth and deceit and to make the judge famous as a wise prince. His dream is not so well known.

If there is any pang of sympathy, it is that of having to be ashamed of one's father, of him whom one loves above all, to whom one is most indebted—to have to approach him backwards with averted face in order not to behold his dishonor. But what greater bliss of sympathy can be imagined than to dare to love as the son's wish prompts him, and to dare to be proud of the father, moreover, because he is the only elect, the singularly distinguished man, a nation's strength, a country's pride, God's friend, a promise for the future, extolled in his lifetime, held by memory in the highest esteem! Happy Solomon, this was thy lot! Among the chosen people (how glorious it was even to belong to them!) he was the King's son (enviable lot!), son of that king who was the elect among kings.

Thus Solomon lived happily with the prophet Nathan. The father's strength and the father's achievements did not inspire him to deeds of valor, for indeed no opportunity was left for that, but it inspired him with admiration, and admiration made him a poet. But if the poet was almost jealous of his hero, the son was blissful in his devotion to the father.

Then one time the son made a visit to his royal father. In the night he awoke at hearing movement where the father slept. Horror seizes him, he fears it is a villain who would murder David. He steals nearer—he beholds David with a crushed and contrite heart, he hears a cry of despair from the soul of the penitent.

Faint at the sight he returns to his couch, he falls asleep, but he does not rest, he dreams, he dreams that David is an ungodly man, rejected by God, that the royal majesty is a sign of God's wrath upon him, that he must wear the purple as a punishment, that he is condemned to rule, condemned to hear the benediction of the people, whereas the justice of the Lord secretly and hiddenly pronounces judgment upon the guilty one; and the dream suggests the surmise that God is not the God of the pious but of the ungodly, and that one must be an ungodly man to be God's elect—and the horror of the dream is this contradiction.

While David lay upon the ground with crushed and contrite heart, Solomon arose from his couch, but his understanding was crushed. Horror seized him when he thought of what it is to be God's elect. He surmised that holy intimacy with God, the sincerity of the pure man before the Lord, was not the explanation, but that a private guilt was the secret which explained everything.

And Solomon became wise, but he did not become a hero; and he became a thinker, but he did not become a man of prayer; and he became a preacher, but he did not become a believer; and he was able to help many, but he was not able to help himself; and he became sensual, but not repentant;

and he became contrite and downcast, but not again erect, for the power of the will had been strained by what surpassed the strength of youth. And he tossed through life, tossed about by life—strong, supernaturally strong (that is womanishly weak) in the stirring infatuations and marvelous inventions of imagination, ingenious in expounding thoughts. But there was a rift in his nature, and Solomon was like the paralytic who is unable to support his own body. In his harem he sat like a disillusioned old man, until desire for pleasure awoke, and he shouted, "Strike the timbrels, dance before me, ye women." But when the Queen of the South came to visit him, attracted by his wisdom, then was his soul rich, and the wise answer flowed from his lips like the precious myrrh which flows from the trees in Arabia.

On or about the date of his birthday, May 5, 1843, S.K. made the following entry in his Journal: "After my death no one will find in my papers (this is my comfort) a single explanation of what it was that really filled my life, the secret writing in my inmost parts which explains everything and often transforms what the world would call bagatelles into events of prodigious importance for me, which I too regard as insignificant apart from the secret gloss which explains them." But has he not divulged his secret in the two passages quoted above? Yes, in a way—but without revealing it. He remarks that a murderer feels a constant urge to tell his secret, and so did he; but his imagination furnished him with the means of telling his secrets again and again without disclosing them. Another entry of about the same date deals with "Abraham's collision" which he was depicting in *Fear and Trembling,* and of this he says, "He who has explained this riddle has explained my life. But who among my contemporaries has understood this?"

In August of the same year he wrote: "I might perhaps reproduce the tragedy of my childhood, the appalling private explanation of the religious which fearful presentiment suggested to me, which my imagination hammered out, my offense at the religious—I might reproduce it in a novel entitled 'The Enigmatic Family.' It ought to begin entirely in a patriarchal idyllic tone, so that no one would suspect the tragedy before this word would ring out and transform everything to destruction."

Ah, if only he had told this story! His biographers would not then have been put to such straits. We learn hardly more than that this secret was his father's guilt and therefore was inviolable. We are left to surmise what this guilty secret was. There is one indubitable indication. In February 1846 S.K. made this brief entry in his Journal: "The dreadful case of a man who when he was a little boy suffered much hardship, was hungry, benumbed with cold, stood upon a hummock and cursed God—the man was not able to forget this when he was eighty-two years old."

S.K. may well have thought that there was nothing in this to betray his secret; but eighty-two was the age of his father when he died, and this probably prompted Barfod, the first editor of S.K.'s *Papers*, to show the passage to Bishop Peter Kierkegaard when he was an old man. As soon as the old Bishop saw it he exclaimed, "This is our father's story *and ours*." According to Barfod, the old man went on to say that his father as a boy of about eleven years tended sheep on the Jutland heath, where he suffered much from hunger, cold and loneliness. Once in his desperation he stood upon a hummock, lifted up his hands to heaven and cursed the

Lord God, who, if he did exist could be so hard-hearted as to let a helpless, innocent child suffer so much without coming to his aid. "But the memory of this curse in his childhood never left the boy, the man, the patriarch—and seeing that God's grace from that very moment showered temporal blessings upon him, so that instead of tasting the divine wrath he was overwhelmed with riches, marvelously gifted children, universal esteem—then solemn anxiousness and dread gripped his soul most deeply. God *did* exist, and *he* had cursed this God—was not this the sin against the Holy Ghost which never can be forgiven? It was for this cause the old man's soul continued in anxious dread, for this reason he beheld his children condemned to 'the silent despair,' for this reason he laid upon their shoulders in tender years the sternest requirements of Christianity—for this cause he was a prey to temptation and in constant conflict of soul."

It seems likely to me that the father did not tell the story of the curse till a short while before he died, and it may be that for Søren the great earthquake was the revelation of his father's sensuality. That was the fault which Solomon discovered in David. We do not know how much he learned at that moment. In the passages quoted above the words "presentiment" and "surmise" occur, and it was "imagination" which "hammered" these suspicions into more or less definite shape. Yet an earthquake, or even a dream, occurs at a definite moment of time. S.K.'s overwhelming experience may have been due to something he casually overheard, or to something the father felt compelled against his will to disclose. We must remember that at this period, in consequence of so many deaths, the father had fallen into the profoundest melancholy. I am inclined to suppose that the father may have made some sort of confession to Søren alone on the occasion of his twenty-second birthday on May 5, 1835. The birthday of his Benjamin—or his Isaac!—was at that period one of the rare occasions when the father could have intimate converse with his son. Three years later Søren's twenty-fifth birthday was the occasion of the father's last and most complete confession.

The following passages which I quote from the Journal may seem irrelevant to our present interest, and they are, in fact, composed of many casual observations registered at random, the first paragraph being written on "a scrap of paper," the second in the body of the Journal, the others on the margin. But remember that we are seeking to detect a crime, and in such a pursuit the most trivial details, a mere finger-print, may be of the utmost importance. In fact, if S.K. ever revealed his secret, we might expect to find the clue in such casual observations, which are not far removed from automatic writing. Observe that we are on the lookout here for three things: the time of the earthquake; the character of the crime; and, last but not least, an explanation of the prodigious effect this experience had upon S.K. It will be seen eventually that most of the items here have a bearing on the last point, which will be more particularly investigated in a subsequent chapter.

"If something is to become thoroughly depressing, there must first develop in the midst of the most favorable circumstances a suspicion whether things are all right, one is not clearly conscious of anything so very wrong, it must lie in family relations, there the consuming power of original sin shows itself, which may rise to the point of despair and affect one more terribly than does the fact which confirms the truth of the presentiment.

The Great Earthquake

"A sort of presentiment commonly precedes everything that is to happen (cf. a scrap of paper); but just as this may have a deterrent effect, so also it may have a tempting effect, for the fact that it awakens in a person the thought that he is predestinated, as it were, he sees himself carried on through a chain of consequences, but consequences over which he has no control. Hence one must be so cautious with children, never believe the worst, never by an untimely suspicion or a chance remark (a firebrand from hell which kindles the tinder there is in every soul) to arouse an alarmed consciousness whereby souls innocent but not strong are easily tempted to believe themselves guilty, fall into despair and thereby take the first step towards the goal which the alarming presentiment foreboded—an utterance which gives occasion for the kingdom of evil with its snaky benumbing eye to reduce them to a sort of spiritual impotence. To this case also the saying applies: 'Woe unto him through whom the offense cometh.'

"Here it is in point to observe the effect often produced by reading about the symptoms of sickness. . . . There is a certain susceptibility which is so strong that it is almost productive. . . . All sin begins with fear.

"It made a most horrible impression upon me the first time I heard that indulgences contained the statement that they compensate for all sins, *etiam se matrem virginem violasset*. I still remember the impression it made on me when several years ago in youthful romantic enthusiasm for a master thief I let fall the remark that it was after all only a misuse of powers, that such a man might well be able to reform, and Father then said with great seriousness, 'There are crimes which one can contend against only by God's constant help.' I hastened down to my room and looked at myself in the mirror. Or when Father often remarked that it would be a good thing if one had such a venerable old man as a confessor to whom one could open oneself.'"

First, for the light this throws upon the date of the earthquake. It appears that S.K.'s suspicions that something was wrong were most alert at the time when he was thinking of the master thief, to which scattered references in the Journal occur from September 12, 1834, to March 15, 1835. This brings us sufficiently near to his twenty-second birthday. Remember that we are here dealing with the early part of the Journal, and with entries which, as S.K. said, are so "crunched together" that even he sometimes could not understand them. The father's irrelevant reply to an innocent remark about the master thief made Søren realize that he "thought the worst" of him—hence he rushed off to look in the mirror to see if he appeared as depraved as his father thought him. What he thought of his father appears with startling clearness in the words, *etiam se matrem virginem violasset*. This man who was his father had violated his mother when she was a virgin! His mother! Horrible! His father had seduced a servant-maid who was entirely dependent upon him. S.K., who boasted in later years of his prowess as a police detective, likely enough began to exercise this talent in his youth, and this was surely the first fact he would ferret out. But doubtless he learned more than this. This was likely not the first transgression of the sort his father was guilty of, for he married rather late in life, and the extreme moral severity of his later years may well have been a reaction from the dissoluteness and sensuality of an earlier period.

In a subsequent chapter we shall see reason to believe that like Søren he was precipitated into guilt by dread. Dreadful things might have been surmised by his son if he had over-heard his father's prayers, and from the prayer of a crushed and contrite heart he would have learned explicitly that the father (as Bishop Peter's communication to Barfod shows) was haunted all his life by the thought that the benefits showered upon him were a sign of God's wrath and an indication of his doom. Especially when so many of his family had died and he looked forward to the gloomy fate of outliving them all he must have felt that the Hound of Heaven was close upon his heels. The son was still so much under the dominance of the father that his gloomy prognostications were accepted without question. The sudden confirmation of his father's guilt was the "frightful upheaval" which imposed upon Søren a new infallible rule for interpreting all the "phenomena" which had aroused his suspicion. The story of Solomon's Dream and the entry about the earthquake both imply a radical breach with the father—but also with God ("offense at the religious"). The breach with the father is expressed more sharply in "Periander," another of the autobiographical insertions in Quidam's Diary, this being dated May 5, which was Søren's birthday. Unfortunately, it is too long to quote here, but it may be found in the *Stages* (pp. 298*ff*.). Periander, Tyrant of Corinth, was a man whose wise words were belied by his foolish actions. He had killed his wife "with a kick." Only the younger brother was sensitive enough to resent with mortal hatred the treatment of his mother. Unlike Søren he never became reconciled to his father.

S.K. found still another way of telling his secret without revealing it. He hid it more securely by ascribing his own experience to a female character, Antigone, and feeling secure under this disguise he ventured to incorporate this story in his first literary work, *Either/Or*. Later, in the course of the year 1843, he wrote in his Journal a short passage which shows how his Antigone was related to Solomon's Dream: "I must again occupy myself with my 'Antigone.' The task will be to develop and explain the presentiment of guilt. It was with this in view I reflected upon Solomon and David, Solomon's youthful relationship to David; for it is perfectly certain that both Solomon's intelligence (the paramount note in him) and his sensuality were consequences of the greatness of David. He has early come to suspect the prodigious perturbation in David, he did not know what guilt might weigh upon him, but saw this profoundly godfearing man give to his penitence so ethical an expression—for it would have been another matter if David had been a mystic. These apprehensions, these presentiments, stifle the energetic qualities (except in the form of imagination) and awaken the intellectual qualities; and this combination of the imaginative and the intellectual, where the factor of will is lacking, is properly what constitutes the sensual."

I can quote only a brief passage from *Either/Or:* "So the race of Labdakos is the object of the fury of the angry gods; Oedipus has killed the Sphinx, liberated Thebes, murdered his father, married his mother, and Antigone is the fruit of this marriage. So it is in the Greek tragedy. Here I diverge. In my version everything remains the same and yet all is different. Oedipus has killed the Sphinx and liberated Thebes, so much is known to all, and Oedipus lives honored and admired, happy in his love for Jocasta. The rest is hidden from men's eyes and no suspicion has recalled that horrible dream to reality. Only Antigone knows it. How she came to know it lies outside the tragic interest, and every one is free in that respect to make his own surmise. At an early age, when she was not yet fully mature, dark hints of that horrible secret had at moments gripped her soul, until at last certainty at one blow cast her into the arms of anguished dread."

The rest of the story of Antigone, as S.K. reconstructs it in conformity with the modern ideal of tragedy, I must abbreviate. He supposes that after a time Oedipus dies and his memory is held in the highest honor. Antigone then feels bound more solemnly than ever to keep secret the crime which would damn her father's memory if it were to become known. The most serious collision occurs when she falls in love with a man who is also deeply in love with her, and being aware of her love for him, cannot understand why she persists in holding aloof. Here S.K. in a book which was meant for Regina explains his own case, and yet disguises it by assigning to a woman the role which he had played. He stresses the fact that Antigone cannot divulge the secret which would bring shame upon her father's memory, and that therefore she cannot marry him, for she will not enter into a marriage which is not perfectly openhearted. The grim secret is her undoing.

ᴀᴛ ᴛʜᴇ ᴄʀᴏss ʀᴏᴀᴅs

1835

Begging—that's not our resource.
Youth on the highway of life
Seizes the treasure by force.
CHRISTIAN WINTHER

IN THE gilt-edged document the above is the motto chosen to characterize the manly period of youth upon which S.K. entered when on May 5, 1835, he had completed his twenty-second year. Up to this time, according to his way of reckoning, he had been essentially a child, inasmuch as he was completely under the dominance of his father. Essentially the Great Earthquake crushed him, the effect was precisely like that which, according to his account, the discovery of David's guilt had upon Solomon; but at the same time it liberated him—it liberated him immediately from the dominance of his father, made him a free man, and prodigiously aroused the intellectual side of his nature, as he affirms in the prose passage which follows this motto, and is cited at the beginning of the next chapter. There he describes himself as "inwardly rent asunder." That is what we might expect, and in fact that was the ultimate effect; but at first an exuberant sense of freedom prevailed. It was profoundly characteristic of S.K. that he did not feel at once the full effect of a woe, but felt it long. By his imaginative and reflective craft the shock was diffused throughout his life. I have used here the phrases which Tennyson used of himself in view of Arthur Hallam's death. For indeed S.K. made in his Journal the same psychological observation when he heard of his brother Niel's death in America, which occurred a year before the death of Hallam. He remarked that he would feel it more and more as years went by. And

79

in the *Concept of Dread,* having in view the experience of the Earthquake, he says that "Dread [*Angst*] is not sudden like a dart, but slowly bores its way into the heart."

The sense of independence was enhanced by the fact that at this moment the father provided him with ample means for a summer vacation of two months in North Seeland. Having been prepared to "believe the worst" of his youngest son, the father, we may suppose, was immensely relieved on discovering that things were not so bad after all, that his son had fallen into no serious vice, indeed that this "prodigal" had preserved an extraordinary purity of mind. He was moved, therefore, to treat him generously, thinking perhaps that a short absence from Copenhagen would separate him from companions whose ways and interests were strange to the sober but narrow traditions of the paternal home. Peter still regarded Søren as the Prodigal Son, and in the character of the "elder brother" of the parable he remarked in his diary that he would have enjoyed such a vacation but was obliged to continue his studies in the sweltering heat of Copenhagen.

This vacation was a precious boon to S.K. This city youth with the soul of a poet had then, for the first time, an opportunity of living in the country, where he first, so far as we can judge, became keenly awake to its beauties. He began then the long carriage drives which were to be the principal diversion of his adult years; and he discovered Gribskov, the great forest, and its "Nook of Eight Paths," which later was to be his favorite resort. He was interested also in the historical monuments of the region, and in the personalities he encountered, whether they were peasants or parsons. This was his first opportunity of complete freedom, and perhaps this was the first moment when he was inwardly at liberty to enjoy freedom. At the moment his sense of emancipation was exhilarating. He was sovereignly free to choose among the infinite possibilities which his imagination presented to him. The fact that he was a student of theology did not hamper him. He weighed deliberately the advantages of all the liberal professions—except, strangely enough, that of philosophy—though it may be that this was contemplated in the part of a letter which he omitted with the note: *Non nulla desunt.* He was very much attracted to the natural sciences—but perhaps this was accentuated by the fact that he was writing to a scientist, Peter Wilhelm Lund, the brother-in-law of his favorite sister Petrea, a botanist who had lived long in Brazil and now made his home there. He is also described as a palaeontologist and as a zoologist—science was not narrow in those days. He must have been a remarkable man to have drawn from this reticent youth a frank exposition of his state of mind, though perhaps the letter was never sent, or perhaps he was chosen as the recipient of such a confidential communication because he lived in a remote part of the world. The letter was written on June 1, 1835, that is, a month before the vacation began, but it was transcribed in the book which records the experiences in North Seeland, and was inscribed there for the sake of the contrast it afforded with a very long entry made on August 1 at Gilleleje, the small town which he had chosen as his headquarters. In this entry he recognizes that the choice of a profession (that of barrister was one for which he had a predilection) was after all a rather formal matter which did not solve the deeper questions which he now raises. At the very beginning of this entry he refers to the above-mentioned letter dated one month earlier.

"The situation actually appeared to be as I have tried to present it in the foregoing pages. Now, on the contrary, when I try to attain a clear view of my life I think differently. . . . I believed then that I might reach a certain repose by entering a different faculty, by directing my powers towards another goal. And for a time indeed I might likely have succeeded in dispelling a certain disquietude, but undoubtedly it would have returned, as a fever does after the enjoyment of cold water. [It was a common belief that a drink of cold water was all but fatal to a patient with fever.] What I really need is to become clear in my own mind *what I must do,* not what I must know—except in so far as a knowing must precede every action. The important thing is to understand what I am destined for, to perceive what the Deity wants *me* to do; the point is to find the truth which is truth *for me,* to find *that idea for which I am ready to live and die.* What good would it do me to discover a so-called objective truth, though I were to work my way through the systems of the philosophers and were able, if need be, to pass them in review? . . . What good would it do me that I were able to develop a theory of the State [like Hegel] and out of particulars fetched from many quarters put together a totality, construct a world wherein again I did not live but which I merely held up to the gaze of others? What good would it do me if I were able to expound the significance of Christianity, to explain many individual phenomena, if *for me* and *for my life* it did *not* have any really profound importance? . . . What good would it do me that truth stood before me cold and naked, indifferent as to whether I recognized it or not, producing rather a fearful shudder than a trustful devotion? To be sure, I am willing to recognize an *imperative of the understanding* and to admit that persons may be influenced through this; *but then it must be livingly embodied in me*—and *this it is* I now recognize as the principal thing. It is for this my soul thirsts as the deserts of Africa thirst after water. . . . It was this that I lacked, the experience of leading a *complete human life* and not merely a life of understanding, so that with this I should not be basing the development of my thought—well, upon something that is called objective, something which at all events is not my own, but I should be basing it upon something connected with the deepest roots of my soul, through which, so to speak, I have grown into the divine nature and cling fast to it even though the whole world collapses. This is what I *lack,* and *towards it I am striving*. . . . The thing that counts is this inward action, this godward side of man, not a mass of recognized facts, for they will come of themselves and will not then appear as accidental aggregates, or as a row of particulars, the one alongside of the other, without a system, without a focal point in which all the radii meet. Such a focal point I too indeed have sought. On the unfathomable sea of amusement as well as in the profundity of the understanding I have in vain sought an anchorage; I have felt the almost irresistible power with which one amusement grasps the hand of another; I have felt the sort of spurious enthusiasm which this is capable of producing; I have also felt the boredom, the laceration which succeeds it. I have tasted the fruits of the tree of knowledge and have often enjoyed their savor. But this joy was only in the moment of apprehension and left in me no deeper mark. It appears to me that I have not drunk from the chalice of wisdom but rather have fallen into it."

Fortunately, this long entry and the long letter which

precedes it can be read in Dru's translation of the Journal (pp. 16–22). Hardly ever has a young man taken stock of himself so deliberately, so completely and so wisely. Any one who is acquainted with S.K.'s works will recognize that the words he has emphasized in the passage here quoted indicate the direction of his subsequent thought, which later was expressed by such phrases as "subjectivity is truth," "appropriation," "reduplication of truth." In another passage he expresses his task in the Socratic maxim, "Know thyself." With this he made a good beginning here—but, alas, this is a task not soon accomplished.

In his letter to Lund S.K. said, "Here I stand, a great question mark. Here I stand like Hercules—but not at the cross roads, no, here there appears to be a far greater multiplicity of paths, and it is all the more difficult, therefore, to apprehend the right one. This perhaps is precisely the misfortune in my case, that I am interested in too much, and not in anything decisively; my interests do not all stand in a unity of subordination but are all coordinate." He was attracted by the thought of the "eight paths" radiating from one point in Gribskov, but at this moment his imagination presented him with more possibilities. He knew, no one better than he, what it means "to live in possibility," and for the greater part of his life he continued to live in it, his imagination furnishing him abundantly with the materials for such a life. But he knew too, and was to experience again and again, the despair which results from possibility unchecked by necessity—as he expresses the situation in *The Sickness unto Death*. At this moment his exuberant sense of freedom was unchecked by necessity—and despair was soon to follow.

The long, deliberative entry written at Gilleleje in the

midst of his vacation, on August 1, ends unexpectedly with a passionate resolution: "So let the die be cast—I cross the Rubicon! This path, to be sure, leads me into battle, but I will not lose heart, will not sorrow over the past—for what use is there in sorrow? With vigor I will push on and not waste time by sorrowing—like the man in the quicksand who wanted first to calculate how deep he had sunk, without taking into account that during the time he is employed upon this calculation he is sinking still deeper. I will hasten on along the path I have found and will call to every one I meet, not to look back like Lot's wife, but to remember that it is a hill up which we are struggling."

This sounds like a real choice and a noble resolution—perhaps a determination—to prepare diligently for his theological examination, both for the reason that it would please his father and because this was the ostensible reason for being in the University. But we learn from the sequel that crossing the Rubicon meant anything but this, and that the battle he was prepared to face with so much courage was conflict with his father. There was to be no more "begging"; it was more becoming for a spirited youth to "seize the treasure by force." There is no indication that he made choice of any one path among the many which were visible to him. He perceived later that he had not faced the decisive *either/or*, which, as Judge William put it, is not the choice of good or evil, but the recognition that there is such a choice to be made. He perceived too late that when no real choice is made by the will, it is made for one by one's baser inclinations, that "while the helmsman delays to put the ship about it is all the time drifting upon the rocks." He was blinded to these facts by an exhilarating sense of emancipation from his father . . . and from God. He was later to understand that his attitude was one of defiance and that his doubt was rebellion. "It is so difficult to believe," he said, "because it is so difficult to obey."

In *The Point of View* (p. 78) S.K. clearly characterized this moment as a period of joyful independence: "So I set out in life, favored in every way with respect to intellectual gifts and outward circumstances. Everything was done and continued to be done to develop my mind as richly as possible. . . . In a certain sense I may say that I set out in life with a proud and almost foolhardy bearing. I have never at any moment of my life been deserted by the faith that one can do what one will—only one thing excepted, all else unconditionally, but one thing not, to throw off the melancholy in whose power I was. What I am saying will seem to others a vain conceit, but so it was with me in truth, as truly as what I tell next, which to others again will seem a conceit. I say that it never remotely occurred to me that in my generation there lived or was to be born a man who had the upper hand of me—and in my inmost self I was the most wretched of all men. It never remotely occurred to me that, even if I were to attempt the most foolhardy enterprise, I should not be victorious—only one thing excepted, all else absolutely, but one thing not, to throw off the melancholy from which and from its attendant sufferings I was never entirely free even for a day. . . . When this is given (i.e. such a pain and such a close reserve), it depends upon the personal characteristics of the individual whether this lonesome inward torment finds its expression and satisfaction in hating men and cursing God, or in the very opposite."

S.K. asserts in *The Point of View* that he "never gave up Christianity," but at this time he was moving very rapidly away from it. In his letter to Lund he said that its "fundamental positions must for the time being be left *in dubio*"; but hardly had he got home from his vacation when the entries in his Journal begin to speak of Christianity and "the Christians" with a critical detachment and proud aloofness which appears strange in a theological student. On October 17 he states roundly the conclusion he had come to: "*Philosophy and Christianity, however, can never be united.*" This is what S.K. often asserted in later years, meaning to say, Away from speculation!—Christianity remains, but philosophy must go by the board. Here, however, he means to say that Christianity must be rejected because it cannot be reconciled with philosophy. This is made only too clear by what follows, especially in an entry made a few days later which I quote in part.

"I have sought to show why Christianity and philosophy cannot be united. In order to justify this separation I have considered how Christianity, or rather the Christian life, must appear from the standpoint of reason. I shall now confirm this by showing how man as such outside of Christianity appears to the Christian. For this purpose it will suffice to recall how Christians regarded the pagans, considered their gods the invention of devils, their virtues splendid vices, how one of their coryphaei declared that man was merely a clod and a stone before the coming of Christ, how they declined to relate the preaching of their Gospel to man as such, how they constantly began with, 'Turn ye and be converted,' how they themselves declared that their Gospel was to the pagans foolishness and to the Jews a stumbling-block. . . . And how is it that there are actually so many who, as they say, find in their consciousness Christian impulses, yet on the other hand, neither are nor profess themselves to be Christians? It is surely because Christianity is *a radical cure* from which one shrinks; and without having precisely the same formal conceptions which led many Christians in the earliest ages to defer the decisive step until the last minute, it is surely for this reason such persons lack strength to take the desperate *leap.* In addition to this, there is the strange, stuffy atmosphere which we encounter in Christianity and which exposes every one, until he has been acclimatized, to a very dangerous climatic fever. If we look towards life here on earth, they rise up against us and declare that everything is sinful, nature as well as man; they talk about the broad way in contrast to the narrow. If we look towards the other world, it is there, as the Christians teach, we first discover how the knot is untied—the fifth act. And although the Christians have not had so grandiose an imagination as that which led the northern races to depict Loke chained to a cliff with poison dripping down upon him, while they afforded him the comfort of placing his wife by his side—the Christians, on the other hand, have known how to deprive the unfortunate of every alleviation, even of a drop of water to quench his burning tongue. Almost always where the Christian employs himself about the world to come it is desolation, punishment, destruction, eternal torture and pain which he envisages; and exuberant and extravagant as his imagination is in this regard, just so meager is it when it is a question of the blessedness of the believers or the elect, which is depicted as a blissful intentness of gaze, with fixed and vapid eyes, with great staring pupils, or with a gaze so suffused with moisture that clear sight is impeded. . . . Very much more humane, it has always seemed to me, is the notion of seeing assembled together the great, distinguished, talented men of the whole world, such as have set their hands to the wheel of human progress. My enthusiasm has always been aroused by the thought of such a veritable academy of the human race, such a republic of science and learning, in which we, ever in strife with contradictions, would be growing every moment in knowledge. . . . The Christians, however, have been loath to grant these great men entrance into their society, in order that it might not become too mixed, and that only one single chord might be struck, so that the Christians might sit like a Chinese assembly of mandarins and rejoice that they had brought to completion that high, insurmountable wall against . . . the barbarians. And why all this? Not to blame the Christians, but to show the contradictions which are recognized *de facto* in the Christian life, to warn every one whose breast is not yet tight-laced in an intellectual corset of this sort against subjecting himself imprudently to such a thing, to protect him against such narrow-breasted asthmatic conceptions. It is certainly hard to dwell in a land where the sun never shines above the horizon, but on the whole it is not particularly agreeable to dwell in a place where the sun stands so directly over your crown that it does not let you or any of your surroundings cast a shadow."

Here S.K. not only speaks of Christianity with critical aloofness but with evident petulance enumerates the worst faults he can think of, ascribing to Christianity in general the narrowness which he found in the stuffy atmosphere of his home, and plainly preferring the pagan or the humanistic ideal. There is nothing in this whole passage which the later S.K. would not have repudiated—and which he did not repent of and do penance for—except the recognition that "Christianity is a radical cure," and that it requires "a desperate leap." At a later time he insisted that a doctrine which is not "to the Jews a stumbling-block and to the Greeks foolishness" is evidently not Christian. He recognized a few years later that his state of mind meant not only revolt against his father but against God.

The immediate result of S.K.'s sudden emancipation was a febrile animation which drew him not only into new intellectual pursuits but into active participation in student life, particularly in the Student Association, before which he delivered, on November 28, 1835, a long address on the subject of "Our Journalistic Literature, a study from nature under midday illumination." On another occasion he had the responsibility of presiding over a plenary assembly of this body when a political question of immediate interest was tumultuously discussed, and when it seemed as if the decision might go against the conservative interest which he espoused he defied his brother and other advisers by proclaiming peremptorily that the meeting was adjourned. Years later on a visit to Christian VIII he was surprised to learn that the King was informed about this meeting and the part he had played in it.

Political activity was completely foreign to him in later years, but at this time, the end of the year 1835, he wrote four political articles for the *Flying Post,* organ of the great Heiberg, arbiter of literary elegance in Denmark, and this first literary venture won him enthusiastic applause. In politics he was decidedly conservative and remained so to the end of his days—even when he was attacking the Established Church. What his social philosophy was may be learned from a book published ten years later, *A Literary Review,* the second part of which has been translated by Dru and published under the title of *The Present Age.* His polemic was directed against the rule of the masses and against the right divine of mobs to govern wrong. He was not opposed to change as such but contended against the effort to impose upon Denmark the abstract theories of the French Revolution, without taking into account the character of this Nordic race, the history of the nation, and the institutions which had grown up in conformity with the genius of the people. The modern development of the Scandinavian nations, with the most liberal government in the world, but with institutions peculiar to the people and appropriate to their situation, has amply justified S.K.'s contention.

THE PATH OF PERDITION

1836

INWARDLY rent asunder as I was, without any prospect of leading a happy earthly life ('that it might go well with me and I should live long in the land'), without any hope of a happy and snug future—which most naturally issues from and consists in the historical continuity of family life in the home—what wonder that in hopeless despair I grasped solely at the intellectual side of man's nature and clung to it, so that the thought of my not inconsiderable gifts of mind was my only consolation, the idea my only joy, and that men were to me indifferent."

In the gilt-edged document this doleful entry follows the animated motto which stands at the head of the preceding chapter. It seems an incongruous conclusion to the brave spirit of independence which the motto represents; but in fact it was a natural consequence of defiance, "the shipwreck of freedom," as S.K. subsequently characterized it. In his own experience he discovered that the "aesthetical" life, that is, a life lived for enjoyment, even though it were intellectual enjoyment, leads to despair, in fact is despair, even if the individual is not aware of it. This is the lesson he sought to teach indirectly in his so-called aesthetic works, in which he exhibits himself as a deterrent example. These works, therefore, are autobiographical in a far broader sense than is implied by the apprehension that three of them contain the story of his unhappy love. To get a vivid picture of S.K. at this period of his life we have only to read the *Diapsalmata* which introduce *Either/Or,* and the colloquies (about two hundred pages in all) between Judge William and his young friend. In a sense S.K. satirized himself in these pages for the sake of representing the aesthetic life with ideal consistency; for in reality, the ethical counsels of the Judge must in some measure be included in our picture of S.K. He could not say that he was "inwardly rent asunder" unless the ethical view of life was still striving to maintain itself. But his predominant interests were "aesthetical"; they were precisely the interests which characterize the "A" who figures as author of the first part of this book, with the sole exception of the "Diary of the Seducer." Here we have proof of S.K.'s passionate interest in the theater and in the opera—especially in Mozart, and more especially in *Don Juan*. These were interests which the regenerate S.K. did not give up. He doubtless had them in mind when he said that in the ethical and religious sphere "the aesthetical is not abolished but dethroned."

The Concept of Dread, published in 1844, is a profound psychological diagnosis of his malady at this time, that is, of the dread (*Angst*) which precipitated him into despair and into sin. In his case the dread awakened in him by the Great Earthquake was what he defined as "dread qualified by reference to fate." He was doomed (as the passage at the beginning of this chapter implies) to live a short time upon earth, and he conceived that by the grim family secret he was debarred from marriage. "What wonder then" that he grasped at the intellectual side of life; and what wonder that with all his restless social activity he was "indifferent to men"? What wonder that dread as "a sympathetic antipathy" precipitated him into sin? "All sin begins with fear," he wrote in 1837 when he was slowly retracing his path; and years later, in an entry of May 17, 1843, he said, "It was dread that caused me to go astray." Dread is like the eye of the serpent which repels and yet attracts.

The intellectual and social activities remarked upon in the last chapter were by no means discontinued in 1836, although before the middle of this year the path he was treading pitched sharply down and proved to be, as he called it, "the path of perdition."

We learn from the long letter to Wilhelm Lund that in 1835 he had already begun to occupy himself with the medieval legends of Faust and Don Juan. These medieval studies first gave him an apprehension of the demoniac element in human life, "the power of the kingdom of evil here in this life." With Faust he associated the Gnostic sect of the Carpocratians whose principle it was "to pass through every vice just to acquire experience of life." The Journals show that he was strongly attracted to this principle, and was inclined to admit that as a theory there was some truth in it—if only one did not try to live up to it. He says of Faust that "he did not want to become acquainted with evil in order to rejoice that he was not so bad as that (only the Philistines do this), but on the contrary he wants to feel all the sluices of sin open in his own bosom." S.K. learned to understand the attraction of the medieval notion of selling oneself to Satan. His imagination was well able to soar to the high mountain where the devil could show him all the kingdoms of the earth and the glory of them, with the promise that "All these things shall be thine . . . if." "All these things" expresses the magnificent dream of the alchemists, of all who were seeking the philosopher's stone. In our age imagination has no such wings: men are able to think of getting possession of only a little bit of the earth —and perhaps for that they might be ready to sell their souls. Faust was typical of doubt, and Don Juan of sensuality. S.K. felt, therefore, that they were both typical of him. There is no evidence that before 1836 he began to interest himself in Ahsverus, the Wandering Jew, who typifies despair. In the first buoyant period of his revolt he did not know that he was in despair. To know that one is in despair is, of course, preliminary to the act of "choosing despair," and that, according to Judge William, is the first step towards deliverance, for it means "choosing oneself," one's own self, in all its concretion, with all its drawbacks.

But in 1836 S.K. recognized clearly that he was in despair and felt that he was the personification of Ahsverus. Among the papers of Professor Poul Møller was found a work entitled "Ahsverus"—it might well have been called, "Thus Spake Ahsverus," for it consists of apothegms such as a despairing man might utter; many of them sound like S.K.'s *Diapsalmata,* and in view of the author's intimacy with S.K. he may well have heard them from his mouth. Poul Møller doubtless knew of S.K.'s ambitious plan of writing a comprehensive work dealing philosophically and aesthetically with an aspect of the Middle Ages which is commonly ignored: "Life outside religion in its three typical aspects—doubt, sensuality and despair." Presumably Møller had this in mind when from his death bed he sent this warning to his favorite pupil: "Tell little Kierkegaard not to undertake too big a task, for that was injurious also to me." Perhaps for this reason the projected work was never carried out. At Poul Møller's suggestion he turned to the study of irony, and that is the subject of the big book he presented for his master's degree in 1841. He planned to write a book "on the use of satire by the ancients," and though such a book was never written, there can be no doubt that the preliminary studies for it contributed to make him one of the most pungent satirical writers in modern times. His interest in "the master thief" led him on through such stories as Robin Hood to an interest in fairy tales of all sorts, and although these desultory studies never resulted in a book, every reader will notice to how great a degree they served to embellish all his writings.

I mention these intellectual pursuits to show that this "student in perpetuity" did not waste all of the ten years he spent in the University, though only during the last two was he diligent in preparing for his theological examination.

But S.K. was not employed solely in studying aesthetic subjects, he was actively leading an aesthetic life. "Begging?" No!—neither from God nor man. "Youth seizes the treasure by force." S.K., defying his father, was resolved to live in the University as a rich man's son. With the tailor, the haberdasher, the bookseller, the bookbinder, the tobacconist, the coffee house and the restaurants he could run up unlimited bills—and he did. To be sure, there were occasional embarrassments. In October he was compelled to borrow from a friend the equivalent of a hundred dollars, and yet in November he was unable to pay the modest dues required by the Student Association in which he had taken so active a part. Doubtless there were other embarrassments. But for all that he could be lavish on a grand scale. A debt of five hundred and sixty dollars which the father ultimately paid to a caterer goes a long way to substantiate Brandt's theory that S.K. himself provided the lavish banquet described in the *Stages*. It is hardly a mitigating circumstance that other of his symposia may have displayed the same elegant refinement of taste. "Aestheticism is more dangerous,"

says Judge William, "in proportion as it is more refined"—
just as Burke speaks of "vice gaining more of evil by losing
half its grossness."

The motto at the head of the last chapter expresses the
spirit of defiance. S.K. knew well enough that this described
his state of mind, but he did not at once suspect that it inevitably led to despair. Years later in *The Sickness unto
Death* he described his case as the extremest form of despair: "the despair of willing desperately to be oneself—defiance," remarking that "this sort of despair is seldom seen
in the world, such figures are met with only in the works
of poets, that is to say, of real poets, who always lend their
characters this demoniacal ideality (taking this word in the
purely Greek sense)." He says there: "In order to will in
despair to be oneself there must be consciousness of the infinite self. This infinite self, however, is really only the abstractest form, the abstractest possibility of the self, and it is
this self the man despairingly wills to be, detaching the self
from every relation to the Power which posited it, or detaching it from the conception that there is such a Power
in existence. By the aid of this infinite form, the self despairingly wills to dispose of itself or to create itself, to make
itself the self it wills to be, distinguishing in the concrete
self what it will and what it will not accept. The man's
concrete self, or his concretion, has, in fact, necessity and
limitations; it is this perfectly definite thing, with these
faculties, dispositions, etc. By the aid of the infinite form
(the negative self) he wills first to refashion the whole
thing, in order to get out of it in this way a self such as he
wills to have."

S.K. believed that he was "uncommonly erotic." This
must be taken with a grain of salt; for those who knew him

well judged that he was an uncommonly pure man, and he says something of the sort himself when he speaks of a certain situation, which was certainly his own, as requiring "an extraordinary combination of purity and impurity." It is certain that he had a rare sense of shame, and possibly he was more distressed by the impure suggestions of sensuality than most men are. We must remember that it was the discovery of his father's sensuality which precipitated him into sin, and it was the puritanical training he had at home which gave to natural desires the monstrous proportion of defiant sin, of "sinning with a high hand," as the Old Testament expresses it. When, in the first part of *Either/Or,* he asserted the astonishing proposition that "Christianity brought sensuality into the world," he was not wantonly playing with paradox but was reflecting seriously upon the grievous wounds he had received in childhood from his father's stern repression of the sexual instinct. Christianity excludes sensuality, but by the fact that it is excluded sensuality is posited. "As a power, as a system in itself, sensuality was first posited by Christianity. I might perhaps adduce a further qualification which shows most emphatically what I mean: it is by Christianity that sensuality is first posited under the rubric of spirit. . . . So sensuality existed before in the world, but not as spiritually qualified. How then did it exist? It existed as soulishly qualified. So it was in paganism; and, if one would seek the most perfect expression of it, so it was in Greece. But sensuality soulishly qualified is not contradiction and exclusion but harmony and accord."

In 1845 he wrote in his Journal: "In case one had told a child that to break a leg was a sin, in what anxious dread he would be living, perhaps often breaking a leg, and the mere fact that he came near to it would seem to him a sin. Suppose that it was impossible to live down that impression of childhood; so then out of love for his parents and in order that this misconception might not become dreadful through his own ruin he would hold out as long as possible. Just as when one draws the reins too tight on a horse, pulls him back with all one's might—then he falls. And indeed one can find now and then just such misguidance with respect to what sin is—occasioned most likely by one who has the best intentions. As when a man who had been dissolute and wished to deter his son from this sort of life interpreted the sexual instinct itself as a sin—and forgot that there was a difference between himself and the child, that the child was innocent and therefore must of necessity misunderstand. Unhappy is he who already as a child is harnessed to pull and toil through life like a slave."

During this period the entries in the Journal are few and brief, but they indicate clearly enough that in April S.K. had fallen very low. They indicate frequent drunkenness and frequent thoughts of suicide. He wrote:

"When I observe that my head begins to rear up on its hind legs.—The poet must have what the Hyperboreans expected in their heaven: a pig they could always carve a piece from, and it would always grow out again."

"One blows one's brains out, bing, bang, bover, then the story is over; and snip, snap, snother, now can begin another."

"War against the Philistines! [he quotes Eichendorf] 'I believe that I am the double of all human follies.'"

"One who went out and thought of committing suicide —at the same instant a stone fell down and killed him, and he ended with the words, 'God be praised.'"

There is general agreement in placing the sexual fall in the month of May, and it is not unlikely that P. S. Møller and Jørgen Jørgensen were responsible for leading him into it. The latter was a voluptuary somewhat past his prime who attracted S.K. by his wit; the former is supposed to be the prototype of the Seducer who figures in *Either/Or* and the *Stages,* with whom, on account of his connection with the *Corsair,* S.K. came at a later time into dreadful collision.

It must be said that the "fall" rests upon an ingenious hypothetical construction which we owe to P. A. Heiberg; but the construction is so solid that no one now puts the fact of the fall in doubt, there can be a difference of opinion only about details. Heiberg reaches the conclusion that in a state of inebriation S.K. was led by a couple of boon companions to "one of those places where, strangely enough, one gives money for a woman's despicableness." These are the words S.K. uses in the story called, "A Possibility," which is inserted in Quidam's Diary on the date of April 5, midnight. It is a long story, the nearest thing to a *novella* S.K. ever wrote. Presumably it tells his story, but with so much embroidery that he was sure no one would discover in it his secret. For this, of course, was a secret he wanted to keep hid, although it was not the secret he sought to hide most deeply. It seems likely that S.K., like the hero of this story, did not remember till a long time after what had occurred. It is more doubtful if he too was tormented by the suspicion that he perhaps was responsible for the birth of a child which might then be living in misery and degradation; but his mind entertained so many possibilities that this one too might for a while have been toyed with, if it did not give him serious concern.

If we had no evidence of a sexual fall, we should have

to invent it, since it had the gravest consequences for his subsequent life and, as we shall see, he was often tormented by the question whether he ought to confess it publicly. He doubtless thought of this when in *The Concept of Dread* he wrote about "freedom lost somatic-physically." I have no doubt he reflected upon it when he wrote "The Leper's Soliloquy," which is inserted in Quidam's Diary under the date of February 5, midnight. He is reflecting upon his own case when in *The Concept of Dread* he distinguishes between "dread of the good" (which he characterizes as antipathetic sympathy) and "dread of evil" (sympathetic antipathy); and when he says of the individual, "at last it is as if the guilt of the whole world were united to make him guilty—or, what amounts to the same thing, as if by becoming guilty he became guilty in the guilt of the whole world." This book is called on the title page "A simple deliberation on psychological lines in the direction of the dogmatic problem of original sin." There has been no other man in modern times who took so seriously the problem of original sin—or inherited sin, as it is called in Danish. And no wonder, for he experienced it as continuity with his father's guilt; and when he repented he realized that he must "repent himself back into the family, into the clan, into the race, back to God." It was this sense of solidarity which gave reality to the traditional doctrine of original sin. He therefore wrestled with this problem as no one else had done and came to conclusions which no one else had reached.

In 1842 an entry in the Journal formulates his experience in these words: "People have often enough explained the nature of original sin, and yet they have lacked a principal category—namely, dread, which is the real determinant of it. For dread is an attraction to what one fears, a sympathetic antipathy. Dread is an alien power which lays hold of an individual, and yet he cannot tear himself loose from it, and also does not will to; for one is afraid, but what one fears also attracts one. Then dread renders the individual impotent, and the first sin always occurs in impotence. Apparently, therefore, he lacks accountability; but this lack is precisely what ensnares him."

It may be thought that S.K.'s sense of guilt was morbid. Everyone will think so who rejects the Christian conception of sin as sin against God. But in fact there are several entries in which S.K. appraises the sheer fact of his misdemeanors very much as any sensible man would do. For example, an entry of May 17, 1843, in which he reviews the breach of his engagement, concludes as follows: "But if I had explained myself, I must have initiated her into terrible things, my relationship to my father, his melancholy, the eternal night, my aberrations from the truth, my lusts and excesses—which yet perhaps in God's sight were not so atrocious, for indeed it was dread which caused me to go astray, and how could I seek refuge and support when I knew or surmised that the only man I had admired for his force and strength was himself tottering?"

The following definition of sin is in place here, though it was first formulated in *The Sickness unto Death,* which was published in 1849: "Sin is: before God in despair not to will to be oneself, or before God in despair to will to be oneself. But is not this definition, even though in other respects it may be conceded to have advantages (and among them this which is the weightiest of all, that it is the only Scriptural definition, for the Scripture always defines sin as disobedience), is it not after all too spiritual? To this one must first of all make answer that a definition of sin can never be too spiritual (unless it becomes so spiritual that it does away with sin); for sin is precisely a qualification of spirit. And in the next place, why should it then be too spiritual? Because it does not talk about murder, theft, unchastity, etc.? But does it not talk of them? Is it not also self-assertion against God when one is disobedient and defies His commandment?"

GROPING HIS WAY BACK

THIS period, though it covers two years, can be dealt with briefly. In my big book I called it "The Ethical Stage" —dubiously, and only out of respect for S.K.'s categories. But really S.K. never seriously conceived of an ethical stage as possible apart from a religious belief. Even Judge William, who exemplifies the ethical stage in *Either/Or,* has a vague traditional religion of immanence—and a good deal more of it than most men have. It is evident from the Journal that immediately after his fall S.K. began to think of picking himself up. He made many moral resolutions; but so many would not have been needed if he had not been continually relapsing. There was some progress evident in the long run, but it was discouragingly slow, and perhaps nothing would have come of it if he had not been aroused by a profoundly religious experience.

In *The Point of View* S.K. himself deals with this period very briefly but in a way which gives us a desolate impression of the futility of these years. "So I fared forth upon life—initiated into all possible enjoyments, yet never really enjoying, but rather (to indulge the one pleasure I had in connection with the pain of melancholy) laboring to produce the impression that I enjoyed. I fared forth into acquaintance with all sorts of men, yet it never occurred to me that I had a confidant in any of them, and it certainly never occurred to any one of them that he was my confidant. That is to say, I was constrained to be and was an observer. By such a life, as an observer and as spirit, I was extraordinarily enriched by experiences, got to see quite close at hand that aggregation of pleasures, passions, dispositions, feelings, etc., acquired practice in seeing a man through and through and also in imitating him. My imagination and my dialectic constantly had material enough to operate with, and time enough, free from all bustle, to be idle. For long periods I was employed with nothing else but the performance of dialectical exercises with an ingredient of imagination, trying out my mind as one tunes an instrument—but I was not really living. I was tossed about in life, tempted by many and the most various things, unfortunately also by errors, and, alas, also by the path of perdition. So I was when I reached my twenty-fifth year—to myself an enigmatically developed and extraordinary possibility, the significance of which and its character I did not understand, in spite of the most eminent reflection which understood, if possible, everything. I understood one thing, that my life would be most properly employed in doing penance; but in the proper sense of the word I had not lived, except in the character of spirit; a man I had never been, and a child or youth even less. Then my father died. The powerful religious impression of my childhood acquired a renewed power over me, now softened by reflection."

Observe that in the gilt-edged document S.K. provides no new motto for this chapter. In fact the period we are now dealing with is in a sense continuous with the preceding; S.K. is still on the path of perdition—only now he is trying to retrace it. He was keenly aware of his predicament. On June 12, 1836, about a month after his fall he wrote: "Reformation goes slowly. As Franz Baader justly remarked, one must retrace the same path by which one went." The reformation went so slowly that more than a year later (on October 11, 1837) he repeated the same saying and added a more disconsolate reflection, to the effect that the enchantment wrought by the fairy king can only be broken when one succeeds in playing backwards without a single mistake the same piece of music by which one was enthralled.

The outlook for release was bad—unless help came from outside. Fortunately it came, and in the moment of his greatest need. It came first from Poul Møller, his most admired teacher, whom he hailed as "the mighty trumpet of my awakening." This phrase is found in the first draft of the dedication of *The Concept of Dread,* the book in which he analysed his own situation when he was in the path of perdition, and which he dedicated to the man who first lent a hand to help him out of it. But what does this phrase mean? Again the answer is found by an ingenious piece of detective work, which this time we must credit to Professor Brandt. In my bigger book I rehearsed his argument rather fully: here I can only state the result. In the diary of the poet Hertz there is the following entry for June 4, 1836: "In the afternoon at the Heibergs' and bade them farewell before their departure for Paris. There—S. Kierkegaard and Poul Møller." Note that only these two are mentioned in such a company of wits as were likely assembled on that occasion—and that S.K. is mentioned first, as though he, a mere student, were the shining light of the party! Brandt associates this with a passage in the comic play which S.K. wrote in 1838 for the Student Association, in which he was disguised under the name of Willibald and Hertz under the name of Echo. There too an afternoon party is implied in which Willibald and Echo had been together; Willibald had departed hastily and on returning to his room was about to shoot himself when Echo came in and stopped him.

There is an undated entry in S.K.'s Journal which describes just such an occasion, and no reason can be opposed to Brandt's assumption that it describes the effect of Heiberg's farewell party on June 4.

"I have just come from a party of which I was the soul: witticism flowed from my mouth, all laughed and admired me, but I went (here indeed the dashes should be as long as the radius of the earth's orbit)——————————————————————————————————————away and wanted to shoot myself."

But what prompted S.K. to leave in haste a party in which he was so much admired? And why did he want to shoot himself? Brandt's answer is: The mighty trumpet of his awakening. He supposes that it was then, at the moment when S.K. was in his wittiest, wildest and most nihilistic mood, that Poul Møller said to him with serious concern and abhorrence, "You are so polemicalized through and through that it is perfectly terrible." It is certain that this warning was actually addressed to S.K., for he remembered it to the end of his life, as we learn from an entry of 1854. If these words were remembered so long, they must surely have been uttered in the nick of time, at the moment when such a warning was most needed, and when the effect would be greatest. And the first effect was so devastating because these words were aimed directly at "the demon of wit," which S.K. himself recognized as the most ostensible expression of his demoniac defiance of God and man. But perhaps by this trumpet call he was not thoroughly awakened at once. We have seen that it was characteristic of S.K. to be affected tardily by new experiences, after a long interval of reflection. I have no doubt that to him the trumpet sounded louder after Poul Møller's death—just as his father first acquired full authority over him when his voice came from beyond the tomb. Poul Møller died on March 13, 1838, only two months before S.K.'s religious awakening, and to prepare him for that he had heard in the mean time another trumpet call, that of Georg Hamann.

September 10, 1836, was a notable date in S.K.'s life, for it was then he first became acquainted with Georg Hamann, a German writer who died twenty-five years before S.K. was born, but whom he felt to be, as a thinker, his contemporary and his most congenial contemporary. The first entry about him is important chiefly for the passages it refers to but does not quote: "With regard to a Christian's view of paganism cf. Hamann, 1 D, pp. 406, 418*f.*, especially 419: 'No, if God Himself would speak to him, He is obliged to dispatch in advance *the authoritative word* and bring it to pass: Awake, thou that sleepest!'"

Hamann quotes from the chapter on miracles from Hume's *Inquiry concerning the Human Understanding:* "So then we may conclude that the *Christian Religion* not only was at first attended with miracles, but even to this day cannot be believed by any reasonable person without one. Mere reason is not sufficient to convince us of its veracity: and whoever is moved by *Faith* to assent to it, is conscious of a continued miracle in his own person, which subverts all the principles of his understanding, and gives him a determination to believe what is most contrary to custom and experience."

S.K. was struck by Hamann's comment: "Hume may have said this with a scornful and critical air, yet all the same, this is orthodoxy and a testimony to the truth from the mouth of an enemy and persecutor—all his doubts are proofs of his proposition."

I quote almost in full the other passage from Hamann, of which only the last sentence was quoted in the Journal: "A man who lives in God stands, therefore, in the same relation to the 'natural man' as a waking man does to one who is snoring in profound slumber—to a dreamer, a sleep-walker. . . . A dreamer may have images more vivid than a man who is awake, may see more, hear and think more than he, may be conscious of himself, dream with more orderliness than a waking man thinks, may be the creator of new objects, of great events. Everything is true for him, and yet everything is illusion. . . . The question is whether it might in any way be possible for a waking man to convince a sleeper (so long as he sleeps) of the fact that he is asleep. No—even if God Himself would speak to him, He is obliged to dispatch in advance the authoritative word and bring it to pass: Awake, thou that sleepest!"

These were precisely the words S.K. had most need of hearing at this time. They were seed thoughts, but they sprouted slowly, and not till the end of this period, that is, about eight months later, did they produce their full effect. It is a common mistake, but a very grave misunderstanding, to suppose that S.K. when he talked about the "leap" of faith meant that the will to believe could be operative, or indeed existent, in a divided mind, or in a mind which was clogged with obstacles, whether intellectual or emotional. This certainly was not his own experience; and most of his works, notwithstanding his scornful rejection of "apologetics," were designed to remove the obstacles to faith, both intellectual and emotional. Beyond that, he affirmed, no man can help another.

In the meantime things went on pretty much as before —that is, pretty badly. We have seen that in July he made a

serious resolution about his Journal, but at this time he
made no effort to carry it out. Externally his situation was
becoming more and more precarious. During the three years
covered by this chapter and the last, the breach with his
father was not healed; in a way he was living in his father's
house, he certainly had nowhere else to sleep, and presumably he often ate there. Doubtless it was hard on him "to
have to approach his father backward with averted face in
order not to behold his dishonor," and it was hard that he
had to live with the righteous elder brother; but what an
excruciating grief it must have been to the old man to see
his son daily and yet feel that they were separated by an
impassable wall, and to behold the dishonor of his Benjamin—or was it his Isaac? who was sacrificed indeed, but
not to God! Obviously, it would be better for all of them
if Søren lived elsewhere. In fact, on July 28, 1837, S.K. left
his father's house. Henceforth he was to have a room in the
town and take his meals at a boarding-house. But his father
treated him with great generosity. He promised him a
yearly allowance of 500 Rigsdaler (equivalent to $1,000),
which was about half of a professor's salary. Moreover, he
paid his debts, to the amount of 1,262 Rdl (about $2,500),
of which $400 represented debts of honor to fellow students,
$560 to a coffee house, large sums to the tailor, etc., about
$100 to the tobacconist, but the largest item, $794, was for
books and bookbinding. At a later date he wrote a receipt
for this amount in his father's account book, adding the remark: "And thus Father has helped me out of my embarrassment, for which I thank him." But the breach was
not healed.

It is a sign perhaps of greater seriousness of mind, but
perhaps also a sign of more lavish expenditure than could be

covered by his allowance, that during the next academic year S.K. taught Latin to one of the upper classes of the school he had attended as a youth.

By connecting S.K. with the poet Hertz and the group of young men who met as a clique in the back parlor of their boardinghouse, Brandt has opened a new vista into his life as a student. Hertz constructed his works of fiction realistically, and in one of them he relied upon the notes he had made of conversations in this clique. Though all the characters are referred to by nicknames it is possible to identify most of them, and several of them figure in S.K.'s works. It appears that the Banquet in the *Stages* was recruited from their number. S.K. as a member of this group does not make an agreeable impression. He was admired for his wit and his prodigious knowledge, but he was also feared, especially by those who were the butt of his terrible sarcasm. The sentimental Hans Christian Andersen was one of them, and this defenseless giant was S.K.'s favorite target. P. S. Møller (who presumably was "the Seducer") was the only one who could effectively return the blows of the Interpreter (i.e. S.K.), and P. V. Jacobsen (who was to figure as Judge William) was the only one whom he treated with respect. We get the impression here, as we do also from Judge William's description of his "young friend" and from S.K.'s account of himself in the Journals of this period, that he was a talented but insolent youth, who used his wit to wound his comrades and to triumph over them, showed no fellow feeling, but stood aloof from life and observed it superciliously. We get here the particular information that he had a harsh, grating voice. From other sources we know that it was not agreeable in public speaking and was liable to crack under strain.

On July 8 and 16 (not long before he left his father's house) he made two entries in the Journal which were certainly not meant to enlighten the reader: "O God, but how easily one forgets such a resolution! I have for some time been turned back again to the world, deposed from ruling in my inmost seat. Ah! but what doth it profit a man if he were to gain the whole world and lose his own soul! Today also (May 8) I have tried to will to forget myself, yet not with noisy bustle—that surrogate is of no avail—but by going out to the Rørdams' and talking with Bolette, and compelling (if possible) the demon of wit to remain at home, the angel with the flaming sword who, as I have well deserved, stations himself between me and every innocent maiden's heart—then Thou didst overtake me. O God, I thank Thee that Thou didst not let me become at once insane—I have never been so much in dread of it. I thank Thee that once more Thou didst incline Thine ear to me.

"Today again the same scene—I reached the Rørdams' nevertheless—merciful God, why should that inclination awaken just now—O how I feel that I am alone—a curse upon that haughty satisfaction in standing alone—all will now despise me—O but Thou my God, let not Thy hand fall upon me—let me live and reform."

About two months later he was again at the Rørdams', as we learn from a loose leaf, dated with unaccustomed precision: "Sunday, July 9, in Frederiksberg Garden, after a visit on the Rørdams: Like a solitary fir-tree egoistically separate and pointing upward I stand, casting no shadow, and only the wood-dove builds its nest in my branches."

What can be the meaning of these passionate, despairing, incoherent utterances? Not much light is thrown upon them when we learn that Bolette was the daughter of a deceased clergyman and was engaged to a theological student. S.K. professed that his interest in Bolette was merely "intellectual," yet in view of her engagement he felt a little bit guilty about this intimacy, and nevertheless, because he found in her companionship a solace which in his great loneliness he craved, he continued to visit her. This evidently does not explain such passionate despair. We get further when we discover that what he unexpectedly encountered at the Rørdams' was as terrible as an army with banners, nothing less than a pretty girl of fourteen years named Regine Olsen, with whom he fell desperately in love at first sight. The longest of the many accounts in the Journal "about my relation to Her" was written in 1849 and begins by saying: "I saw her first at the Rørdams. There it was really that I saw her during the first period, when I did not visit the family." And Regina (as she called herself in her old age because S.K. had so called her) remembered long after his death that she had seen S.K. for the first time at the house of the widow Rørdam, where she was invited to a party given for a young girl of her age. S.K. had called unexpectedly, and "the liveliness of his mind made a strong impression. His conversation welled up and was captivating in the highest degree." She believed that the passages just quoted from the Journal referred to this meeting, and she thought that he was impressed by her, as she was by him. In "The Diary of the Seducer" which concludes the first part of *Either/Or* there is a lively description of precisely this situation: the young man finds himself unexpectedly in the company of eight pretty girls and captivates them by his conversation. But though S.K. thus succeeded in hiding his emotion, he feared that he was going crazy. He was twenty-four when he fell in love with a child, and this was his first love. It was also to be his last, and in spite of all appearances to the contrary, it was to endure to the end of his earthly life—indeed like Dante he looked forward to a meeting in heaven.

Being apprised of this astonishing fact, and knowing now something of S.K.'s circumstances and disposition, we are able in a measure to piece together the incoherent exclamations which he registered on this occasion, and we find that they reflect the consequences of the Great Earthquake as they are described in the passage quoted at the beginning of the previous chapter. What "resolution" was it he was so prone to forget? Evidently a resolution to seek no intimate contacts in life, least of all with women, since he was doomed to die in a few years and by his father's secret and his own guilt was debarred from marriage. When this resolve was but for a moment forgotten, God ("the hound of heaven") overtook him, and overwhelmed him by an unlooked-for experience which brought him to the brink of madness. During this period of frequent drunkenness and constant intellectual inebriation he often felt that he was on the verge of madness, and now more than ever. And yet his terrible loneliness compelled him to go out to Frederiksberg again and again, when by the sort of espionage in which he was adept he had learned that Regina would be there. But what does he mean when he says, "all men will despise me"? Nothing less than the dread of having to reveal the sordid secret of his fall. Later entries of the Journal make it abundantly evident that, although he discussed the matter pro and con, he felt that marriage demanded absolute candor. What is far less credible, but nonetheless certain, is that he thought it necessary to make an open confession, especially if he were to enter the ministry of the church.

Such was the ominous beginning of a love which was destined to end in tragedy.

It must be said now, retrospectively and with reference to all of the eight years S.K. had already spent in the University, that there was one study which in a measure coordinated all his random interests—that was philosophy. This must be emphasized, and yet it is a matter of course when we remember the description he gives of Johannes Climacus, and when we reflect upon the philosophical profundity of all his works. Philosophy was a study he pursued, not only as a dialectical exercise, but with the passion of personal interest. He studied it, therefore, in the only way that it can be profitably studied, that is, for his own consumption, with a view to discovering a meaning in his life, when meaning had vanished with the rejection of Christianity. We have seen that in the summer of 1835 he assigned to philosophy predominant importance when he declared that Christianity cannot be reconciled with philosophy. He applied himself with the utmost enthusiasm to the study of Hegel, whose philosophy was precisely at that time welcomed in Denmark as the last word of wisdom. Little by little, before the end of the period we are now dealing with, he had become discontented with Hegelianism because it did not furnish him with *reality*. He quoted with appreciation Lichtenberg: "It is about like reading out of a cookbook to a man who is hungry." His subsequent works were either expressly or by implication a refutation of this philosophy. Under the influence of Hamann he was gradually led to suspect that religion, and particularly Christianity, was far closer to reality. Nevertheless, he continued to admire Hegel as a thinker. I have quoted in a note to the *Postscript* (p. 558) the longest expression of appreciation, but in one place he put it all in a single sentence: "If he had written his whole *Logic* and in the Preface had disclosed the fact that it was merely a thought-experiment (in which, however, at many points he had shirked something), he would have been the greatest thinker that has ever lived. Now he is comic."

It ought to be remembered that the subject of religion had a prominent place in S.K.'s philosophical inquiry, even though he had abandoned the practice of his religion. It is indeed far too real a factor in human life for any real philosopher to ignore it. It was S.K.'s constant complaint against Hegel that he had ignored not only religion but ethics. The philosopher must explain religion—perhaps by the help of psychologists explain it away. That at least. This direction of S.K.'s philosophical interests is evident in his subsequent works, which contain here and there passages which incidentally reveal the profoundest insight into the origin and nature of religion in general.

Under the influence of Hamann S.K. gradually reversed his judgment about the relative importance of philosophy and Christianity. He still used the same expression as three years earlier, "Christianity and philosophy cannot be united," but now he means that philosophy must go, or rather, to use the slogan of Johannes Climacus in the *Postscript,* Away from speculation! away from "the System" and back to reality. This is the point where the modern Existential Philosophy derives from S.K.

We find an approach to his final position in an entry of

August 1, 1838, a doggerel rhyme which I render as well as I can. S.K. is called a "poet," and yet perhaps this is the only verse he ever wrote.

> If a body meet a body
> Carrying a spade,
> And if a body has a rake,
> Need either be afraid?

This obviously means that neither Christianity nor philosophy has anything to fear from the other. In spite of the triviality of its expression, this entry had immense significance for S.K. We can measure its importance by the fact that he repeated it (without substantial change) on a loose sheet of paper without date, and that the next sixteen entries are all comments upon it. Another entry is more decisive:

Motto: [in Latin] "Cursed be he who keeps swine and teaches his son Greek wisdom." A Jewish edict of the year 60 B.C.

Christianity will have no dealing with the philosophies, even if they are willing to divide with it the spoils; it cannot endure that the King of Sodom should say, I have made Abraham rich.

But this was written *after* he had heard the authoritative word, "Awake, thou that sleepest!"

The last words in the Journal which are pertinent to this period were written on the First Sunday after Easter, April 22, 1838, only three weeks before his twenty-fifth birthday and not quite a month before the religious experience described in the next chapter: "In case Christ shall come to dwell in me, it must be as in the Gospel for today in the almanac: 'Christ enters through closed doors.'"

FATHER AND SON UNITED

TWENTY-FIVE YEARS OF AGE

> [*Lear.* No, no, no, no! Come, let us away to prison:
> We two alone will sing like birds i' the cage:
> When thou dost ask me blessing, I'll kneel down,
> And ask of thee forgiveness.] So we'll live,
> And pray, and sing, and tell old tales, and laugh
> At golden butterflies, and hear poor rogues
> Tell of court news; and we'll talk with them too,
> Who loses and who wins, who's in, who's out;
> As if we were God's spies: and we'll wear out,
> In a walled prison, packs and sects of great ones,
> Who ebb and flow by the moon.

THIS motto, which was inscribed on the third sheet of gilt-edged letter paper, finds in the reconciliation of King Lear and his daughter Cordelia in a walled prison an exact counterpart to Søren's heartfelt reconciliation with his father, which was brought about on his twenty-fifth birthday. I have, however, printed in brackets four lines which S.K. did not transcribe, for the reason that they were too poignantly appropriate.

Nothing has led us to expect such a reconciliation. It would be incredible if we had not this proof of it, and in perfect conformity with that is the adoring tribute of devotion S.K. paid to his father in his subsequent works. At this point we have to assume that something happened, something tremendously important, as prodigious as the earthquake but with precisely the opposite effect. It needs no clever detective to assure us of this, nor would his ingenuity be of any avail in this case, for here S.K. has been completely successful in obliterating all traces of his father's secret. We have to assume that the old man, now in his eighty-second year and in feeble health, took advantage of the occasion offered by the celebration of his son's legal majority, and summoning all his courage and all his remaining strength, made to him a clean breast of his sins. It is possible that Søren (as Lear's lines suggest) was moved on this occasion to ask his father's forgiveness; but it is certain that the other line describes essentially what the father did: "I'll kneel down and ask of thee forgiveness." The old man was far too sagacious not to know that it was the discovery or the suspicion of his misconduct which had driven his son away from home and away from God. Hence his heroic effort to make amends for the injury he had done.

S.K. himself has remarked that the crude fact is not nearly so dreadful as the presentiment of it. So it may have been in this case; but we must assume also that the father made clear to his son how hard he had tried to be good, and how deeply repentant he was; in short, that he was a Christian, not a hypocrite. He must have made him understand that the religious instruction he imparted to his children, however mistaken it was, was prompted by love and had the intent of saving them from the sensuality to which he had succumbed. Subsequently, this was S.K.'s interpretation of his father's "crazy" way of bringing him up. And how could he have learned it but from his father's lips? In the entry at Sæding which is quoted in the first chapter he says, "I learnt from him what father-love is, and thereby I got a conception of the divine father-love, the one unshakable thing in life, the true Archimedean point." And on July 9, two months after his birthday, he registered this prayer of thanksgiving, the first prayer which appears in the Journal, but by no means the last: "How I thank Thee, Father in heaven, that Thou hast preserved to me here on earth, for a time like the present when I stand so greatly in need of it, an earthly father, who, as I hope, will by Thy help find more joy in being for a second time my father than he did the first time." This is as though his father by his confession had begotten him again.

The entry made a few days after his father's death is as follows: "My father died on Thursday, the eighth [1838], at two o'clock in the night. I had so heartily wished that he might live a few years longer, and I regard his death as the last sacrifice his love for me occasioned; for not only has he died from me but *died for* me, in order that if possible something may be made of me still. Of all that I have inherited from him the most precious is his remembrance, the transfigured picture—not transfigured by poetic imagination (for of that there is no need), but transfigured by the many individual traits I now begin to take account of—the most precious thing to me, and I will take care to keep it most secret from the world; for I am well aware that there is only *one* person (E. Boesen) to whom I can really talk about him. He was a faithful friend."

I remark here, incidentally, that to his one friend, Emil Boesen, afterwards Dean of Aarhus, S.K. was faithful to the end, although at the end his friendship was severely tried. His letter unbosoming his grief to Boesen has been preserved; but he took such good care to keep his grief secret from the world that only when the Journal was published did those who were nearest to him have an inkling of it. His niece Henrietta Lund says that "he continued apparently in his old way of life, foregathered in cafés as usual, and promenaded the streets with his customary animation." This extraordinary ability to hide his feelings is less amazing than his desire to do so. We can perceive in this instance that to him as an introvert this was a necessity of which he tried to make a virtue by exalting the principle of "indirect communication." In the end he himself recognized that this was a form of daimonia.

But the most striking thing in the entry just quoted is the fact that he regarded his father's death as "the last sacrifice his love for me occasioned; he not only died from me [the word for deceased] but *died for* me." His heroic confession may well have hastened his death, and S.K. who was so close about his own secrets could understand what this cost his father. In 1848 he wrote: "My father was the most loving father, and my yearning for him was and is most profound—whom never a day have I failed to remember in my prayers, both morning and evening." So the reunion with his father was not only complete but lasting, capable of outliving "packs and sects of great ones who ebb and flow by the moon." The understanding between them was so deep, because in returning to his father S.K. returned to God. In his symbolism "the home" meant Christianity, as in the entry of July 10: "I hope that with respect to my contentment with the conditions of life *here at home* it may be with me as with a man I once read about, who likewise was tired of his home and would ride away from it; when he had gone a little way his horse stumbled and he fell off, and as he picked himself up he chanced to see his home, which now seemed to him so fair that at once he mounted and rode home and stayed at home. If only one gets the right view of it."

Many years later he jotted down in his Journal a plan for "a simple romance" about a father and two sons, in which the following passage occurs: " 'He came to himself'—lo, the foreign tour has now come to an end. Properly speaking, it did not end with his coming home, but with his coming to himself." It might seem natural to suppose that reconciliation with the father was a consequence of a prior reconciliation with God; but that is not borne out by the Journal, and in *The Concept of Dread* S.K. exactly reverses the sequence which seems so natural to us: "he repents himself back into the family, back into the race, until he finds himself in God." It appears that in precise correspondence with the parable, the earthly father, while the prodigal son was yet far off, "saw him and ran and fell on his neck and kissed him heartily." Yet to say that his father brought him to God would not accord with S.K.'s reiterated affirmation that no man can do for another so much as that. We must say rather that his father broke down the barriers, the "closed doors," so that Christ might enter in.

Until this moment S.K. was able to flatter himself with the notion that his defection from Christianity and from the ethical life was due to intellectual doubt and was therefore something rather superior, something Faustic. Now he learned to know that it was rebellion. Hereafter this was his constant interpretation and we may be sure that it reflected his own experience. In 1847 he wrote in the Journal: "They would have us believe that objections against Christianity come from doubt. This is always a misunderstanding. Objections against Christianity come from insubordination, unwillingness to obey, rebellion against all authority. Therefore, they have hitherto been beating the air against the objectors, because they have fought intellectually with doubt, instead of fighting ethically with rebellion. . . . So it is not properly doubt but insubordination. In vain do they try to bring the machinery into action, for the ground is bog or quicksand."

Here belongs the piece entitled "Nebuchadnezzar," which is inserted in Quidam's Diary on the date of June 5, midnight. I cannot quote it here nor comment upon it, except to say that it expresses the certain conviction of God's reality which was the paradoxical consequence of the seven years spent by Nebuchadnezzar (S.K.) "as a beast of the field eating grass." S.K. says somewhere that the man who defies God does Him the honor of acknowledging His existence.

It must have been on this occasion that S.K. had the horror of learning that he had exactly repeated the experience of his father and the guilt which three years before had aroused his abhorrence. It must have been at this time that the father told the story of his childish curse, and it may be that the sense he had as a young man of impending doom led him for a long time (remember that he married late) into excesses like those, or worse than those, into which dread had precipitated his son, so that his sin, like that of his son, was defiance of God. This must be assumed in order to account for the severity of S.K.'s judgment upon his own excesses, which yet in themselves, as he said, "were not so atrocious." From this point of view his contrition does not seem abnormal or exaggerated, and we can understand why he felt that henceforth his life must be employed in doing penance. It often occasioned surprise to his acquaintances to hear him remark casually, "I am a penitent." For this reason he felt so deeply united with his father in the walled prison that he could "repent his father's guilt." Judge William says in *Either/Or:* "And if it was a guilt of the father which descended to the son as a part of his inheritance, he will repent of that together with his own guilt. . . . The pious Jew felt his father's guilt resting upon him, and yet he did not feel it nearly so deeply as the Christian; for the pious Jew could not repent it, because he could not choose himself absolutely. The guilt of his forefathers weighed upon him, brooded over him, he sank under this weight, he sighed, but he could not lift it up. That only he can do who absolutely chooses himself."

The Saturday before the Fifth Sunday after Easter, which came fifteen days after his birthday, S.K. made this remarkable entry, which with unaccustomed precision he dated May 19, 10:30 A.M. "There is such a thing as an *indescribable joy* which glows through us as unaccountably as the Apostle's outburst is unexpected: "Rejoice, and again I say, Rejoice!"—Not a joy over this or that, but full jubilation, 'with hearts, and souls, and voices': 'I rejoice over my joy, of, in, by, at, on, through, with my joy'—a heavenly refrain, which cuts short, as it were, our ordinary song; a joy which cools and refreshes like a breeze, a gust of the tradewind which blows from the Grove of Mamre to the eternal mansions."

The reference to Gen. 18:1 has a significance we should not overlook: "The Lord appeared to him by the oaks of Mamre, as he sat in the tent door in the heat of the day." Were there no longer any "closed doors"? Was S.K. so far prepared for the Lord's visit that he had gone out to sit in the door of the tent? There are no preceding entries in the Journal which give the remotest premonition of a decisive religious change in S.K. To us this is as unaccountable as the joy was indescribable to him—unless we assume that the father's sacrificial confession had broken down the shut doors, and that Christ actually entered in.

On the face of it this seems to be a religious—I have no objection to saying a mystical—experience comparable to that of St. Paul (2 Cor. xii. 4), when he was "caught up into Paradise and heard unspeakable words which it is not lawful for a man to utter." As in the case of St. Paul this was an experience to which no reference was made again, upon which no inference was ever founded. S.K. professed that he was not a mystic, that he was too reflective, too dialectical for that. We might expect, however, that he would date the beginning of his deeper religious life from this unique emotional experience, that he would regard it as the moment of his conversion, perhaps as the authentication of an almost apostolical authority. But no, he pointed to no particular moment when he had become a Christian, for in his way of putting it he was only "becoming a Christian" up to the very end of his life; and far from assuming any authority, he described himself repeatedly as "without authority." In *The Point of View,* when he is speaking of the beginning of his religious life, he indicates rather an experience which in itself was not religious but belonged to the natural order, was, as he says, simply a "fact," namely, his engagement to Regina and the dreadful ending of it. And at that point he breaks out with an exclamation which is totally unexpected and without apparent motivation: "I beg the reader not to think of revelations or anything of the sort, for with me everything is dialectical." Evidently he himself was thinking of this strange experience; but reflectively or dialectically he knew no way to explain it, therefore he did not exploit it, did not even in his own mind appraise it as a mark which singled him out as a special object of divine favor or as a special instrument of God. To him this experience remained so equivocal that he had the audacity to travesty it in the description he gives in *Repetition* (pp. 74ff.) of a bizarre experience related by Constantine Constantius. And yet it was real to him, superreal, and it preoccupied him all his life long. It was this inexplicable experience which prompted him to apply himself so ardently to the study of "the case of Adler," that is, to the phenomenon of a Danish pastor who was deposed because he claimed to have had a revelation. It was this which riveted his attention upon the problem of the authority of an Apostle. And it was this which led him to speak of his "thorn in the flesh." We can be certain that he chose this name to express the conviction that it was like St. Paul's painful experience, which was consequent upon and "by reason of the exceeding greatness of the revelation." What S.K. meant by his thorn we cannot discover more precisely than we can in the case of St. Paul. Both of them were humiliating physical disabilities. S.K. sometimes applied this term to the "disproportion between soul and body" which he often lamented; but he must have meant something more definite, for he tells us that he consulted a physician to learn if it might be removed, and at a later period he asked himself whether he ought not to "draw it out." In this small book it would not be appropriate to delve deeper into a mystery which has not yet been solved.

The next complete entry is: "Fixed ideas are like a cramp, e.g. in the foot—the best remedy is to step on it. July 6." Were it not for the date, we should be unable to discover profound significance in this practical observation. It happens by a curious chance that thirty years later, in a letter to Barfod, Pastor Kalthoff said in a postscript: "Might it be of any interest to you that on July 6, 1838, S. Kierkegaard alone (i.e. without his father and brother) came to Confession [a public penitential preparation] and took Communion from me, I being then resident chaplain at the Frue Kirke." This is a very precious piece of information, for it shows that about seven weeks after the experience of the indescribable joy S.K. was definitely reinitiated into the Church. The contemporary entry shows that he was restrained by a scruple ("cramp") from taking more promptly this definite step which involved the reception of the Body and Blood of Christ. But perhaps he was already aware of "the sin of despairing over one's sin," which he stressed in *The Sickness unto Death,* and had learned that "the consciousness of sin is the only way of entrance into Christianity."

The father's death occurred, as we have seen, during the night following August 8. When the property was divided S.K. found himself in possession of the big house on the New Market and of a considerable fortune.

THE GREAT PARENTHESIS

WHAT I have often suffered from was that all the doubt, trouble, unrest which my real 'I' wished to forget for the sake of attaining a world-view, my reflective 'I' sought as it were to print upon my mind and preserve, partly as a necessary and partly as an interesting transitional stage, for fear I might have mendaciously appropriated a result.

"Thus, for example, when I have so ordered my life that it appears as if I were destined to read *in perpetuum* for examination, and that my life, even if it were to be longer than I expect, will not get further than the point where for good and all I broke off—just as one sometimes sees feeble-minded persons who forget all their intervening life and remember their childhood, or forget everything except one single moment of their life—that I, likewise with the thought of being a theological student, should be at the same time reminded of that happy period of possibilities (which one might call one's preëxistence) and of my arrest at that point, feeling pretty much as a child must feel when it has been given alcohol and thereby prevented from growing. Then when my active 'I' seeks to forget this in order to get to work, my reflective 'I' would so gladly hold it fast because it seems interesting, and would abstract itself from my personal consciousness while reflection potentiates itself by assuming to be a universal consciousness."

With this ends the gilt-edged document which has hitherto been our guide. It may be said that this is a very uninteresting statement. Quite true—but all the more appropriate as a description of the period S.K. was passing through when he wrote it on September 9, 1839; for to him that period was so uninteresting that he described it as "the great parenthesis." He was employed all this while in preparing for his theological examination, and he labored so diligently that in a little less than two years he was prepared to pass it *cum laude*. This he did out of deference to his father. His acquaintances expected that when he had become independent and inherited a fortune he would want to enjoy it and would be less than ever inclined to pursue the theological studies for which he had already showed his distaste. To one inquirer he said, "When my father was alive we often discussed it, and I was able to defend my contention that it was not incumbent upon me to take the examination; but after his death I had to assume also his role in the debate, and I could not any longer withstand myself." Or when it was a case of answering a fool according to his folly he said, "It's because I can no longer put the old man off with stuff and nonsense."

We can understand how irksome it must have been to a young man who already had been acclaimed as a promising author to submit again to the discipline of the school and lay aside the interesting studies which had engrossed him for so many years. This is plainly enough expressed in the motto of this chapter, and indeed not much more needs to be said about the life of the "one-time Dr. Exstaticus" during this uninteresting period. He had made a solemn resolution and he carried it out faithfully. On May 13, 1839, when he had been for nine months with his nose to the grindstone, he wrote the following: "I cannot but suppose that it is God's will I should study for the examination, and that it is more pleasing to Him that I do this than that by plunging into one inquiry or another I actually were to reach some clearer apprehension or another; for obedience is dearer to Him than the fat of rams."

This discipline was salutary. We see from the motto of this chapter that his divided mind was in the way of becoming integrated. He has already learned to regard his "active I" as his "personal consciousness," his "real" self, to which his "reflective I" is rigidly subordinated.

But though S.K. began now to integrate his own personality and ultimately attained the "purity of heart" which he defined as "willing one thing," it cannot be said too emphatically that he never succeeded in becoming integrated with what he called "the universal," i.e. with society; he remained to the end an exception, in a sense an outsider, with respect to the family, the Church and the State. He lamented bitterly his heterogeneity; and when he extolled individualism, it was not to recommend eccentric individualism, but (in Carlyle's sense) a forceful and clearly defined personality, which being integrated with the whole, would enrich society and make it something better than a mob. Therefore he was very far from regarding himself as a paradigm, a pattern or example to be followed; but, condemned to be the exception, he was able at last to comfort himself with the thought that as such he was a "corrective" and, alas, a "sacrifice." I make this observation here once for all, but it applies to his whole life. I stress it first of all as a plea for pity and as a reason for condoning S.K.'s manifest defects. For he understood that his was not a vain sacrifice but "a sacrifice for others." Who is so hard-hearted that he does not pity Nietzsche? Surely S.K. has as much claim upon our pity, and more claim upon our love, even if he was not so lovable. As a normal man, without such suffer ings as he underwent, S.K. could not have rendered to us the service he has. It was abnormal even to be so deeply engrossed in his own abnormal psychic condition that he delved deeper than other men into the secrets of personality. In advance of modern pathologists he understood that a study of the abnormal might result in a deeper and clearer knowledge of the normal, that is, of health.

During the period of the great parenthesis S.K. permitted himself only one diversion from theological study—that was the thought of Regina. Regina in the meantime had been confirmed, so she was a young lady, and without impropriety he could think of wooing her. In a later account of his love affair he said: "Before my father died I had already decided upon her. He died. I read for the examination. During this time I let her existence twine itself about mine." On October 11, 1838, he wrote: "The period of falling in love is surely the most interesting time, during which (after the total impression has been made by the first stroke of enchantment) from every encounter, from every glance of the eye (however swiftly it takes hiding, so to speak, behind the eyelashes), one fetches something home, like the bird which in its busy season fetches one piece after another to its nest and yet constantly feels overwhelmed by the great wealth at its disposal." How much he was preoccupied by thoughts of love we learn from a delightful passage in Quidam's Diary (*Stages*, pp. 193–5). He was really in love and very deeply in love; but beside the motives which ordinarily prompt a lover he had the hope that by Regina he would be reconciled with the universal. It was his only hope for a happy and normal life on earth, and it was a desperate hope. There were "moments" when he could believe in the possibility of marriage, there were other moments when he was in despair. He wrote on an undated sheet: "The only thing that comforts me is that I might lay myself down to die and in the hour of death confess the love I do not dare to reveal so long as I live, and which makes me equally happy and unhappy."

The only lyrical outburst in the Journal is the following: "Thou, my heart's sovereign, 'Regina,' treasured in the deepest privacy of my bosom, at the source of my most vital thought—where the distance is equally great to heaven and to hell—unknown godhead! Oh, may I really believe the reports of the poets that when one sees for the first time the beloved object he believes that he has seen her long before, that all love, like all knowledge, is recollection, that in the particular individual love also has its types, its myths, its Old Testament? Everywhere in the face of every maiden I see traits of thy beauty, but it seems to me as though I must have all maidens in order to extract, as it were, from all their beauty the totality of *thine;* that I must circumnavigate the whole world in order to find the region I lack and which yet is indicated by the deepest secret of my whole ego—and the next instant thou art so near to me, so present, replenishing so mightily my mind, that I am transfigured before myself and feel that it is good to be here.

"Thou blind god of love! Thou that seest in secret, wilt thou reveal to me openly? Shall I find here on earth what I seek, shall I experience the *conclusion* of all the eccentric premises of my life, shall I clasp thee in my arms—or

DOES THE ORDER READ, FURTHER?

Hast thou gone on before me, thou my *yearning?* Dost thou, transfigured, beckon me from another world? Oh, I will cast everything from me in order to become light enough to follow thee."

Here again we are struck by an ominous presage, which proved, alas, to be only too veridical.

When the examination was passed *cum laude* on July 3, 1840 and the long parenthesis was closed, S.K. found himself for the first time free to make the pilgrimage to his father's birthplace which was described in the first chapter.

But here at the end of this chapter I must refer briefly to a little event which properly belongs to the beginning of it, may in fact be regarded as S.K.'s last fling before he entered the parenthesis. On September 7, 1838 (not quite a month after his father's death), S.K. published a little book, or rather a pamphlet (a *piece,* as he called it), which bore this strange title: "*From the Posthumous Papers of one Still Living.* Published against his will by S. Kierkegaard. About Andersen as a novelist, with constant reference to his last book, *Only a Fiddler."* The phrase "one still living" expressed his genuine surprise that his father, in spite of his melancholy prognostication, had died before him. The next phrase is to be understood as a rather lame apology to the gentle Hans Christian Andersen for the harshness of his criticism, and also as a first ineffective attempt to hide behind anonymity. It must be acknowledged that Andersen, who was inimitable as a writer of children's tales, ought never to have tried his hand at a novel. But what prompted S.K. to cudgel him so severely was his pusillanimous notion that genius is a weak thing which may be snuffed out by disadvantageous circumstances. S.K. replied indignantly that "genius is like the thunderstorm which comes up against the wind, like a conflagration which the wind blows into a fiercer flame."

This little book deserves attention for the fact that it is

S.K.'s first literary production. But not only for that fact, for Professor Hirsch discovers in it abundant material for the study of his style as a thinker and a writer. Though S.K. asserts that Regina made him a poet, it is evident from this little book that he did not have to wait for her to make him a thinker and a writer. Though originally he was gifted with an extraordinary imagination, poetry was not born in him till he had been profoundly moved by love, the *primum mobile* of life in all its ranges. This at once brought him feelingly into touch with the universal; and the fact that he was unable, because of his heterogeneity, to possess concretely the "immediate" enjoyment of love left his imagination free to deal with every possibility of eros, even with its grosser aberrations, until in the end he experienced its sublimation in love for God. This thinker, therefore, when he became a poet was no ordinary thinker. No other philosopher except Plato has known how to adorn and vivify the strictest thinking with imagination and poetry.

REGINA

I WILL let S.K. tell the story of his brisk wooing as he told it in the Journal on August 24, 1849, in an entry about "My relation to Her" which occupies nine pages as it is now printed, besides several pages of marginal comment. I quote only the first part. Over it is inscribed the Virgilian line, "Infandum me jubes, Regina, renovare dolorem."

"In the summer of 1840 I took the official examination in theology. Then straightway I made a visit to my father's birthplace in Jutland, and perhaps at that time was already fishing for her a bit, e.g. by lending her books and requiring her in a particular book to read a definite passage.

"I returned in August. The period from August 9 till into September may in a stricter sense be said to be the period in which I approached her. On September 8 I started out from home with the resolute intention of deciding the whole thing. We met on the street just outside her house. She said there was no one at home. I was audacious enough to understand this as an invitation, as just the opportunity I wanted. I went up with her. There we stood alone in the sitting room. I begged her to play a little piece on the piano for me, as she did at other times. But that wasn't a success. Then suddenly I take the music book, shut it not without some violence, throw it down on the piano and say, 'Ah, what do I care about music; it is you I have been seeking for two years.' She remained silent. For the rest, I had done nothing to beguile her; I had even warned her against myself, against my melancholy. And when she spoke about a relationship with Schlegel [who had been her teacher in

135

school, had wooed her already, and afterwards became her husband] I said, 'Let this relationship then be a parenthesis, for I have the first mortgage.' (*Marginal note*. N.B. It was, however, on the tenth she talked about Schlegel, for on this occasion she uttered not a word, she was entirely silent.) [The fact is, she ran out of the room.] Finally I left, for I was fearful lest some one might come and find us two together and see her so disturbed. I went directly to the Councillor [her father]; I know that I was terribly concerned at having made so strong an impression upon her, as well as by the fear that my visit might give occasion to misunderstanding, even to the point of hurting her reputation.

"Her father said neither yes nor no; but nevertheless he was willing enough, as I could easily understand. I asked for an opportunity to talk with her. I got it for September 10 in the afternoon. I said not a single word to beguile her. She said, Yes.

"Immediately I extended the relationship to the whole family. My virtuosity was especially directed towards the father, for whom, by the way, I always had a great liking.

"But inwardly—I saw that I had made a mistake. A penitent as I was, my *vita ante acta,* my melancholy, this was enough.

"I suffered indescribably in that period."

Again the last words are ominous. The rest of this pitiful story I have no heart to tell. I told it rather fully before, and S.K. himself has told it over and over again; it can be read now in thirty-eight entries which Dru has translated from the Journals, and now also in *Repetition* and in *Fear and. Trembling,* and at prodigious length in Quidam's Diary in the *Stages*. Perhaps the story may be clearer when I tell it briefly, almost as briefly as in one of the entries made in 1849 in which S.K. distinguished five periods. The first period covered the early months of the engagement, during which he was almost too chivalrous and did his utmost to enchant her—but, as he said, "I was debating whether I could become engaged to her—and there she was, my fiancée, beside me." He described himself comically as "a lover with an artificial leg," who was unable to take a single step without reflection. He was struggling with the profoundest melancholy and suffering from pangs of conscience for the fact that he had "dragged her out with him into the current." He saw clearly that this was the point where he was guilty.

It is not easy for us to understand why he felt unable to marry the woman he loved. There may have been a psychological difficulty which escaped his sharp eye: the fact that reflection overwhelmed immediacy or the instinctive response. But here is his own explanation—in part only, for it does not mention the "divine veto."

"It does not hold good in the case of marriage, as at an auction, that everything is understood to be sold in the condition it is in when the hammer falls. Here a little honesty with regard to the earlier period is in place. Here again my chivalry is clear. Had I not honored her as my future spouse more highly than myself, had I not been prouder of her honor than of mine, I might have kept silence and fulfilled her wish and my own, let myself be married to her—there are so many marriages which conceal little stories. That I would not do, she would thus have become my concubine— I would rather have murdered her. But had I explained myself, I must have initiated her into terrible things, my relationship to my father, his melancholy, the dreadful night which broods in the inmost depths, my wildness, lusts and excesses, which yet perhaps were not so heinous in the sight of God."

The second period. "She made an attempt at boundless presumption." This needs some explanation, for S.K. writes here only for his own consumption. He tells us in another place that in a fit of petulance she said that "if she believed that I come out of habit, she would at once break off," indeed she went so far as to say that "she had accepted him out of pity." Here, as S.K. ruefully reflected later, he lost the chance of recovering his freedom and letting her enjoy "the triumph of her presumption." But for that he was too belligerent—or, as he says very plausibly, he clung to his one chance of marriage. He behaved in a masterful manner—or, as he put it euphemistically, "I took the thing up with some little reference to her."

The third period. "She surrendered and was transfigured into the most lovable being." For example, she induced him to sit in a chair—and before he knew what she was about she was on her knees before him. That was more than he could bear. His melancholy returned and was now augmented by "her womanly, almost worshipful devotion." Ah, who can blame her for her moment of petulance, when her lover read her Mynster's sermons and sometimes sat beside her silently weeping! And how lovable was her devotion!

The fourth period. He had decided that the thing must be broken off, and he sent back the engagement ring with this brief letter: "In order not to put more often to the test a thing which after all must be done, and which being done will supply the needed strength—let it then be done. Above all, forget him who writes this, forgive a man who, though he may be capable of something, is not capable of making a girl happy.

"To send a silken cord is, in the East, capital punishment for the receiver; to send a ring is here capital punishment for him who sends it."

This story, including the letter, may be read in Quidam's Diary, May 8; but I must tell it more briefly. This happened on August 11, 1841, but unfortunately, it was not the end. "In her desperation she overstepped her limit and would compel me to overstep mine. The situation became dreadful." Regina regarded this act as a symptom of his melancholy, which she had undertaken to cure. Consequently she hastened to his chambers, and not finding him at home, she left for him a note, adjuring him "in the name of Christ and by the memory of his deceased father" not to leave her. This adjuration made a prodigious impression upon S.K. And the whole family united in supplicating him. "Her father, who interpreted my behavior as eccentricity, begged and adjured me not to forsake her, 'She was willing to submit unconditionally to everything.'"

"Well, then I might have let myself get married to her (if there had not been inward difficulties on my part), at a cheap price I could have bound them all to gratitude, and for my own part have played the tyrant, having constantly at my disposal this frightful means of compulsion, that it was a charity I had done her. Truly, if I had done so, I should have been a scoundrel indeed; I should have been taking advantage meanly, with a revolting meanness, of a young girl's moan which led her to say what she never ought to have said nor could really have meant. At the same time she was not far wrong in this, inasmuch as she understood well enough that, if only I once decided to take her, I would certainly do all in my power to make her life worth living. That is to say, she trusted me.

"So let us suppose I had married her. What then? In the course of half a year, in less time than that, she would have worn herself out. About me (and this is at once the good and the bad in me) there is something rather ghostly, which accounts for the fact that no one can put up with me who has to see me in everyday intercourse and so comes into real relationship with me. Of course, in the light surtout in which I commonly appear it is different. But at home it will be observed that essentially I live in a spirit-world. I was engaged to her for a year, and still she did not really know me. So then she would have gone to smash. And she in her turn would presumably have broken me, for I should have been constantly on the point of straining myself by lifting her, her substance being in a certain sense too light. I was too heavy for her, and she was too light for me; but both cases can perfectly well cause a strain. . . .

"The case is perfectly simple. My reason told me clearly enough that what I proposed to do was the right thing, the only right thing. But had I not had a conscientious scruple to sustain me, she must have won. I could not have ventured merely at the dictates of my reason to defy her tears, her adjurations, her father's sufferings and my own wish—and I must have yielded. But I had to fight the case before a much higher tribunal, and hence my firmness, which was taken for heartlessness."

Here S.K. defends his case pretty well. It does not seem possible that Regina could have been happy as his wife, though it is clear enough that as the wife and widow of another man she continued to love and admire him.

The fifth period. A period of two months, two months of agony—for both of them. He was forced to yield—but only to the extent of prolonging the relationship until he had defended his thesis for the master's degree and published his dissertation on *The Concept of Irony.* Rightly or wrongly, he believed that the only way he could "set her afloat" or wean her from him was by pretending that he was a scoundrel who had only been playing with her affections. "She fought like a lioness." "From time to time I said to her bluntly, 'Yield now, let me go, you can't stand it.' To this she replied passionately that she would rather stand anything than let me go. I tried also to give such a turn to the thing that it was she who broke the engagement, so as to spare her all mortification. This she would not hear of. . . .

"Then it broke, after about two months. [On October 11, 1841. In the meantime the thesis had been defended on September 16, and the book was ready for the printer on the twenty-ninth.] For the first time in my life I scolded. It was the only thing to do. I went from her immediately to the theater, for I wanted to see Emil Boesen. . . . The act was over. As I went up to the second parquet, the Councillor came down from the first and said, 'May I speak with you?' I followed him to his home. 'She is desperate,' he said, 'this will be the death of her, she is perfectly desperate.' I said, 'I shall still be able to tranquilize her, but the matter is settled.' He said, 'I am a proud man; this is hard, but I beseech you not to break with her.' Truly he was proud, he touched me deeply; but I held my own. I took supper with the family that evening. I talked with her, then I left. Next morning I got a letter from him saying that he had not slept all night, that I must come and see her. I went and talked her round. She asked me, 'Will you never marry?' I replied, 'Well, in about ten years, when I have sowed my wild oats, I must have a pretty young miss to rejuvenate me.' She said, 'Forgive me for what I have done to you.' I replied, 'It is rather I that should pray for your forgiveness.' She said, 'Kiss me.' That I did, but without passion. Merciful God!

"To get out of the situation as a scoundrel, a scoundrel of the first water if possible, was the only thing there was to be done in order to work her loose and get her under way for a marriage. . . . I passed the night weeping in my bed. But in the daytime I was as usual, more flippant and witty than usual—that was necessary. . . . I journeyed to Berlin. I suffered a great deal. I remembered her in my prayer every day. To this date [eight years later] I have absolutely kept to that—to pray for her every day, at least once, often twice, besides all the times I have thought about her. [She has asked him to remember her sometimes—as he often recalled with a keen sense of irony.] When the tie was broken my feeling was this: Either you throw yourself into wild dissipations, or into religiousness absolute, of a different sort from that of the parsons."

Regina affirmed that she would die, and this made a prodigious impression upon S.K., who felt that he might have a murder on his conscience. When after not many months she proved not only to be alive but engaged to Fritz Schlegel, S.K. remarked ruefully, "She chose the cry, I chose the pain." He ought to have felt relieved by another moan of Regina's which was hardly consistent with this; for she said that she would now have to become a governess in some family. S.K. remembered it later when Schlegel was sent as governor to the Danish West Indies, and he often referred to her then as "My dear little Governess."

I conclude this chapter with a plea for pity—pity for S.K. even more than for "her," his Ophelia. Is the tribute of pity due only at the conclusion of the fifth act when the tragic hero dies? Must we not pity Hamlet when he discovers his mother's guilt? And can we not pity S.K. when he is confronted with substantially the same experience? He felt that point by point his case matched that of Hamlet. If Hamlet feigned madness, he was often on the brink of it, and many times he debated the question of suicide. He too loved a girl, and because of his secret could not marry her. He treated his girl shockingly, but so did Hamlet—and yet we can pity him. The only essential difference is that our story does not come to an end at this point with the death of both lovers. Regina had enough resilience to get engaged again, thus interjecting a comic note; and S.K., though dying daily, lived on for fourteen years and at last laid down his life in a very different cause. This, therefore, is not a simple tragedy, yet surely it presents an occasion for "purifying the passions by pity," in precisely the sense that Aristotle meant.

Iɴ Copenhagen S.K.'s conduct caused a great scandal. He faced it for a fortnight (that being a part of his plan to deceive Regina) and on October 25 he departed for Berlin with the intention of remaining a year and a half in the city which then was the intellectual capital of Europe. He was especially eager to hear Schelling demolish the Hegelian system, with the applause of the Court as well as of the University. On February 2, 1842, at the end of a long letter to Boesen he said: "This winter in Berlin will always have great importance for me. I have got a great deal accomplished. When you consider that I have heard from three to four lectures daily, have a language lesson daily, and that I have got so much written [i.e. a considerable part of *Either/Or*], and this in spite of the fact that at first I had to spend so much time writing out Schelling's lectures, which I did in a fair copy, and have got a great deal read—so that one cannot complain. On top of that, all my pains and all my monologues. I have not long to live—I never expected to—but I live for a brief term and so much the more intensely."

His enthusiasm for Schelling was short-lived. His first lectures inspired the hope that he had something real to say about "reality," but that hope was deluded, and on February 27 S.K. wrote to Boesen, "Schelling drivels inordinately . . . I am leaving Berlin and hastening to Copenhagen . . . not to bind myself by new ties . . . but to complete *Either/Or*." He got back to Copenhagen on March 6, having been away not quite four and a half months. And we learn from *Repetition* that some part of this time was profitably spent in the theater, especially in the enjoyment of a kind of farce, the *Posse,* which was then the vogue in Berlin.

The "monologues" he mentions were of course about Regina, and they were the more painful because they never resulted in a clear verdict with respect to his guilt—hence the title which he already had in mind, "Guilty?"/"Not Guilty?" He was not even clear that the possibility of a *rapprochement* was definitely excluded. He wrote to Boesen, "I regard the relationship as dissolved only in a certain sense." But it would be possible to return to her only in case she could be brought to understand him thoroughly and would accept him as he was. His introversion made it impossible to disclose himself to her directly, so he had to resort to what he called "indirect communication," which he affirmed he had learned from "her." So *Either/Or* "was written for Regina"—but not merely "to clarify her out of the situation," as he said with reference more particularly to "The Diary of the Seducer"—consciously or unconsciously he was practicing the sage counsel we find in Hudibras:

> With one hand thrust the lady from,
> And with the other pull her home.

On the short voyage to Stralsund he wrote: "You say, 'What I have lost, or rather deprived myself of!' Ah, how should you know that or understand it? When this subject is mentioned you would do well to hold your peace. And how should any one know better than I? . . . What have I lost? The only thing that I loved. What have I lost? In men's eyes my knightly word. What have I lost? That upon which I have always staked my honor, and in spite of this shock always shall:—being faithful. Yet at the moment I write this my soul is as uneasy as my body, in a cabin shaken by the double motion of the steamboat."

In Berlin he wrote: . . . "and I loved her much, she was as light as a bird, as bold as a thought; I let her rise higher and higher, I stretched out my hand and she perched upon it and called down to me, 'Here it is glorious,' and she forgot, she did not know that it was I who made her light, I who gave her boldness in thought, faith in me which brought it about that she walked on the water; and I acclaimed her, and she accepted my acclaim.—At other times she threw herself upon her knees before me, wanted only to look up to me, wanted to forget everything else."

A year later he wrote: "If I had had faith, I should have remained with Regina." In 1851, when Fritz Schlegel rejected the suggestion that he might approach Regina again on the plane of mere friendship, he made reply by dedicating anonymously to her the *Two Discourses at the Foot of the Altar:*

<blockquote>
To One Unnamed
whose name will some day be named
is dedicated
together with this little work
the whole production of the author from the very beginning.
</blockquote>

Already in 1849 he had written the following in his Journal: "My will is unaltered, that after my death the works should be dedicated to her and to my deceased father. She shall belong to history.—My existence shall absolutely accentuate her life, my work as an author may also be regarded as a monument to her honor and praise. I take her with me to history. And I who in my melancholy had only one wish, to enchant her—*there* it is not denied me, there

I walk beside her, like a master of ceremonies I lead her in triumph and say, 'Please make a little place for her, our own dear little Regina.' "

His testament was made in the form of a letter to his brother: "It is naturally my will that my former fiancée, Madame Regine Schlegel, shall inherit absolutely the little I can leave." Alas, there was very little left, and Regina declined to receive it. But this shows that the theme of the last chapter not only overlaps upon this but pervaded S.K.'s whole life, that this experience was, as he affirms in *The Point of View,* the decisive "fact" which determined the most important ethical and religious change: "I was so profoundly shaken that I understood perfectly well that I could not possibly succeed in taking the comfortable and secure *via media* in which most people pass their lives: I had either to throw myself into perdition and sensuality, or to choose the religious absolutely as the only thing—either the world in a measure which would be dreadful, or the cloister. That it was the second I must choose was already substantially determined: the eccentricity of the first movement was merely the expression of the intensity of the second; it expressed the fact that it would be impossible for me to be religious only up to a certain point."

He said in another place, "My engagement to her and the breaking of it is really my relation to God, my engagement to God, if I may dare to say so." On the other hand, he frequently affirmed, and with as much reason, that "it was she who made me a poet."

On February 20, 1843, *Either/Or* appeared and made a great sensation in Copenhagen, partly because it was such a big book, and partly because it was pseudonymous. It was the biggest book S.K. ever wrote and was published appropriately in two volumes. By resorting to the most amazing devices S.K. was able for some time to throw the public off the track. Not till 1846, in a postscript to the *Postscript,* did he acknowledge that he was the author of the six pseudonymous works which he had produced up to that date; but when once he was discovered as the author of *Either/Or,* no one was long deceived by his subsequent pseudonyms. Before this book appeared he wrote with feigned indignation to one of the daily papers, protesting against the attribution to him of several recent anonymous works which in fact no one had thought of ascribing to him. And in the Journal he tells with pride how much pains he took to fool people: "A whole book could be written if I were to relate how inventive I have been in hoaxing people about my mode of existence."

"At the time I was reading the proofs of *Either/Or* and was writing the *Edifying Discourses* I had almost no time at all to walk in the street. So I employed another expedient. Every evening when I left home completely fagged out and had dined at Mimi's restaurant I was for ten minutes at the theater—not a minute more. Being so generally known as I was, I reckoned that there would be several tale-bearers at the theater who would report, 'Every night he's at the theater, he doesn't do anything else.' O you dear gossips, how I thank you! Without you I should not have attained my purpose. In fact it was for the sake of my former fiancée I did this. It was my melancholy wish to be as much derided as possible, merely to serve her, merely in order that she might be able to put up a resistance."

We learn from S.K. that the first half of the second volume, that is, Judge William's exaltation of the beauty of marriage, was written while he was engaged to Regina but hopeless of realizing the joys he so enthusiastically described. There is profound pathos in this; and we wonder that he could find time for producing such a work when he was not only in constant attendance upon Regina but was busily employed in finishing his treatise on irony. The last half of the second volume was written in Berlin, where, as we have seen, he had many other things to do; and the whole of the first volume was written after his return to Copenhagen. He boasted that the whole book was written in eleven months.

Either/Or not only produced a sensation, being "much read and even bought," as S.K. put it; but it puzzled and amazed its readers. The reviewers, even such astute reviewers as Heiberg and Goldschmidt, were annoyed because they were unable to understand what it was all about; for no book even remotely like it had ever appeared before. The book claimed to be edited by Victor Eremita, who makes use of the papers of "A" and "B" which were accidentally discovered. "A" is a brilliant young man who depicts in glowing terms the pleasures of the aesthetic life, but reveals from the very outset—in the *Diapsalmata,* which are Byronic expressions of despair—that this is not the way which leads to happiness. The extremest aberration of the aesthetic life is exemplified in the Seducer, whose diary concludes the first volume. Knowing that he himself might reasonably be identified with "A," S.K. was careful to point out that this piece had another origin. He experienced more difficulty in writing "The Diary of the Seducer" than any other part of the work, and it gave him many pangs of conscience. It was meant to be deterrent in the highest degree, and he was disgusted to find that it was the most popular, the most attractive element in the book. With very questionable taste it was translated into English and into several other languages apart from its context and before any other complete composition by S.K. was known. "B" is an older man, happily married and occupying a responsible position, who tries to convince his young friend of the superiority of the ethical life. The reader is not told whether Judge William succeeded in convincing his young friend, or was perhaps seduced by him; and so is left free to choose for himself between the contrasted views of life which are here exemplified. Judge William is represented here as a bit prosy, as he might well be in the role of a moralist who is supported by conventional religious beliefs but has no compelling religious enthusiasm. Nevertheless, it was in the second part that Heiberg discovered a profundity of meaning which prompted him to counsel his readers to reread the first part and seek there a meaning which had likely escaped them, as it had escaped him.

Though *Either/Or* is by no means S.K.'s most admirable work even from a literary point of view, it was in his time the most popular, and perhaps it may be today. Though the brilliant papers of "A" are rather haphazard, and the Judge's letters too long drawn out, the whole is clearly a proof of genius, its defects are due to the superabundance of ideas which S.K. simply had to "expectorate" or get off his chest. S.K.'s own "verdict" upon *Either/Or* is exuberant: "There was a young man, as richly gifted as an Alcibiades. He went astray in the world. In his need he looked about for a Socrates, but among his contemporaries he found him not. Then he begged the gods to transform him into one. And, lo, he who had been so proud of being an Alcibiades became so shamefaced and humbled at the gift of the gods that when he had received just what might properly have made him proud he felt himself inferior to all."

In a certain sense the title is more important than the book. It became the name by which S.K. was commonly known to the man in the street. It represented in fact precisely what he stood for: a decisive choice between practical alternatives. S.K. understood "either/or" as the counterpart of the Hegelian "mediation," of which he says, "Give that up, and there is no speculation; admit it, and there is no either/or." He says in the Journal: "The fact that there is a plan in *Either/Or* which stretches from the first word to the last, likely never occurred to anybody, since the Preface treats the matter jestingly and utters never a word about speculation. What I am essentially concerned about with regard to the book as a whole is that the metaphysical significance at the bottom of it may become duly evident, the fact, namely, that everything brings one up squarely against the dilemma."

Again he says: "What is either/or?—if it is I who must say it who surely must know. Either/or is the word at which the folding doors fly open and the ideals appear— O blessed sight! Either/or is the pass which admits to the absolute—God be praised! Yea, either/or is the key to heaven." In another place he says, "Both-and is the way to hell."

What prompted S.K. to write a book of this character? He himself alleges so many reasons that one may be in doubt which to accept. It was "a good deed" done for Regina, "The Diary of the Seducer" in particular was meant to "clarify her out of the relationship"; it had "a religious purpose"; it exemplified a metaphysical position; it was "an evacuation of the poetical," "a necessary expectoration"; it was "a deceit" shrewdly planned to beguile men into the truth. We do not have to choose among these many reasons, for they were all operative, and there was one more which S.K. did not like to confess to himself: we have seen that while he sought to repel Regina he also desired to attract her, at least to let her see that he was not so base a scoundrel as he had pretended to be. There was an either/or addressed to her, and he addressed her more particularly in the *Two Edifying Discourses* which "accompanied" this book.

Reviewing the situation from a remote distance, he said in the year 1849: "It is true that as an author I had from the first a religious purpose; but there is another way of looking at the matter. . . . When in the Preface to the *Two Edifying Discourses* I used the expression, 'that particular individual, *"my* reader,"' I had her in mind especially, for that book contained a little hint to her, and especially at that particular time it was prodigiously true of me that I sought a single reader. Gradually this thought was assimilated"—i.e. it was generalized and became his favorite category, *hiin Enkelte,* the individual in distinction from the mass.

The religious purpose, though it is first made evident in the sermon with which the second part concludes, may also be discovered in the effort to show that the aesthetic life, ending in despair, prompts the individual to choose the ethical life, which at least is on the way to religion.

S.K. published this big book at his own expense, as he did all of his earlier works, to the number of thirteen. The booksellers received a commission of 25 percent, and he pocketed the gain—or the loss. This fact, in conjunction with S.K.'s frequent complaints that he had been obliged to "lay out money" on his works, gave some plausibility to the myth that, on the whole, he spent much more on his books than he received from the sale of them, and that a great part of his fortune vanished in this way. Only recently (in 1935), Professor Brandt and Else Rommel carried out an investigation which exploded this myth and proves that he not only made a considerable profit on the books he published at his own expense, but that, beginning with August 1847, all his subsequent works, nine of them, besides the nine numbers of the *Instant,* were undertaken by the publishers, who paid him the usual royalties. We must therefore understand his complaint to mean that, as writing was his profession, and as the laborer is worthy of his hire, his remuneration ought to have been sufficient to support him in the affluence which he required if he was to be kept in vein for an intensive production of such quality and such compass—and for this, unfortunately, it was not sufficient in a land so small as Denmark.

It is necessary to deal here, as compendiously as possible, with a question about which several books have been written to no profit—the reason why S.K. wrote anonymously, or rather pseudonymously. He himself alleges several reasons in the following passages, the first of which is from the "First and Last Declaration" which is appended to the *Postscript*. "My pseudonymity or polynymity has not an accidental reason in my person . . . but it has an essential reason in the character of the *works,*" which, as he says, required a thorough abandonment in the direction of one or another tendency such as is hardly to be found in a concrete individual. "So in the pseudonymous works there is not a single word which is mine." "My wish, my prayer, is that, if it should occur to any one to quote a particular saying from these works, he would do me the favor to cite the name of the pseudonymous author in question." The next is from *The Point of View*. "One will perceive the significance of the pseudonyms and why I must be pseudonymous with relation to all aesthetic productions, because I was leading my life in categories entirely different." But obviously there were many more reasons than these. We can dismiss briefly the superficial reason sometimes alleged, that S.K. was simply following a fashion set by the Romanticists. This does not go far to explain a pseudonymity which was also a polynymity, not only in the sense that S.K. adopted various pseudonyms for different books, for in *Repetition* there were two authors involved, in *Either/Or* five, and in the *Stages* ten. S.K. remarked with roguish delight that the thing is like a Chinese toy—boxes within boxes. In part, therefore, his exuberant use of pseudonyms may be ascribed to his love for intrigue. But it evidently goes far deeper than that and reflects the lines of cleavage which he discovered in his own personality, which perhaps were not more marked or more profound than might be discovered in many men, but which certainly were analysed by his critical introspection more sharply than has ever been the case. No one has ever followed more diligently than he the Socratic maxim, "Know thyself." Accordingly, his pseudonyms were for the most part personifications of aspects, or at least of possibilities, which he discovered in his own nature. He says in *Repetition,* "The individual has manifold shadows, all of which resemble him, and from time to time have equal claim to be the man himself." This expresses the deepest reason for his use of polynymity, and in this use of them the pseudonyms are exceedingly instructive. He hints, for example, that his choice of the name Victor Eremita for the editor of *Either/Or* signifies that he himself was victor in the conflict which resulted in the choice of the ethical life, and that when he wrote this book he was living as if in a cloister. But this is not all there is to it. His introversion for a long time inhibited him from using what he called "direct communication," and so, making a virtue of necessity, he practiced and extolled "indirect communication," using the pseudonyms as instruments to this end. After 1848, when he experienced a metamorphosis which made it possible for him to speak out clearly, he renounced essentially the use of pseudonyms. It must be said, however, that if "indirect communication" was in the first instance forced upon him by his idiosyncrasy, which he learned to regard as a demoniac trait, it was, nevertheless, an apt form for meiotic instruction, the Socratic form; and S.K., even after he had abandoned it, would not admit that he had used it inappropriately. Indeed, in so far as "indirect communication" was imparted by the use of pseudonyms, it was the only way by which S.K. could have accomplished the novel task of "making a map of the emotional cosmos" (to use Swenson's expression), of delineating the characteristic possibilities of the human soul, and thus devising a new sort of psychology in the interest of a philosophic valuation of life, or a comparative philosophy of values. To this end his characters, unlike those of the novelist, which must be quite humanly inconsistent, a mixture of good and bad, had to be inhumanly consistent, ideal exemplifications of a type, whether in the direction of good or evil, such as human life rarely, if ever, presents. But the pseudonyms also serve another use. Because S.K.'s thought was essentially dialectical, it had to be expressed in the form of dialogue, as was

the teaching of Socrates; and because he had a dramatic
instinct he took delight in this and was able to do it well.
The two lengthy letters by Judge William which fill the
second part of *Either/Or* would have been intolerably dull
if S.K. had not contrived to enliven them by quasi-colloquies
with the young friend. In *Repetition* two authors, Constantius and "the young man," were needed to exemplify contrasted attitudes. In the *Stages* Judge William's dissertation
on marriage is the answer to the frivolous speeches at the
Banquet, and Quidam is necessary to carry the movement
on in the direction of religion.

Not quite two months after the publication of *Either/Or*
there occurred on Easter (which that year fell upon April
16) an event, if we may call it such, which again gave a
new direction to S.K.'s life. It is thus described in the Journal: "On Easter Sunday at evensong in the Church of Our
Lady (during Mynster's sermon) she nodded to me—I could
not tell whether it signified entreaty or forgiveness, but in
any case it was so friendly. I had seated myself in a retired
place, but she discovered it! Would to God she had not
done so! Now the sufferings of a year and a half are wasted,
all my prodigious efforts—she still does not think that I
was a deceiver, she believes in me. What trials now await
her! The next will be the notion that I am a hypocrite. The
higher up we get the more terrible it is—to suppose that a
man with my sincerity, my religiousness could behave in
that way!"

In the preliminary draft of Quidam's Diary it is said that
he was doubtful, in view of the distance, whether he ap-
prehended aright, whether she actually did nod, or whether
perhaps she was nodding to somebody else. In any case, it
might have been "only for his eye that it had this immense

significance." Certainly this nod had immense significance for S.K. It prompted him to escape again to Berlin—not to forget "her," but to reflect upon the possibility of reunion, and to write for her two more books, which presented a different either/or. He was not able to leave at once, for not till May 6 could he get ready for the printer the *Two Edifying Discourses* which were to "accompany" *Either/Or*. Two days later he was off. Some notion of his intellectual activity is given in a letter to Boesen which was posted on May 25: "I have finished one work which I regard as important [*Repetition*—written in less than a fortnight!] and am in full swing with a new one [*Fear and Trembling*], and my library is necessary as well as the printing-press. At the beginning I was ill, now I am well, so to speak—that is, my mind is expanding and presumably killing my body. I have never worked so hard as now. During the morning I go out for a little while. Then I come home and sit in my room uninterruptedly until about three o'clock. I can scarcely see out of my eyes. Thereupon I shuffle by the aid of my cane to the restaurant, but am so weak that I believe if any one were to call out my name aloud, I should fall over dead. Thereupon I go home and begin again. During the past months [in Copenhagen] I have been pumping up a veritable shower bath, now I have pulled the cord, and the ideas stream down upon me—healthy, happy, plump, merry, blessed children, easily brought to birth, and yet all of them bearing the birth marks of my personality."

The two books which were written with such prodigious speed were from a literary point of view the most perfect he ever wrote. We may say again that no books remotely like them had ever before been produced. They were twins, for they were published on the same date, and both dealt with the same theme, his disappointed love; and yet they are as different one from the other as any two books can be. In both of them there are passages which only Regina could be expected to understand fully, or to understand the reason why they were included. Hence the name Johannes *de silentio* was adopted for the pseudonymous author of *Fear and Trembling;* hence too the choice of the motto for this book: "What Tarquinius Superbus in his garden said by means of the poppies was understood by the son but not by the messenger"; and hence Constantine Constantius, the pseudonymous author of *Repetition* says in his Letter to the Reader that "Clemens Alexandrinus did very well to write his book in such a way that the heretics could not understand it."

S.K. took no little pride in inventing the category of "repetition" to supplant the Platonic "remembrance" and the Hegelian "mediation," but it does not reappear in any of his subsequent works. It had a vivid interest for him at that moment because he treasured the hope of a repetition with "her."

S.K. returned to Copenhagen sometime in July to get his books printed. But meanwhile something had happened, something he had shrewdly designed to bring about, but which took him completely by surprise when it did occur, and at first aroused his indignation. In June Regina had become engaged to Fritz Schlegel! In 1849, reviewing this experience, he wrote in his Journal: "When she had become engaged to Schlegel she met me in the street and greeted me in as friendly a way and as ingratiatingly as possible. I didn't understand her, for at that time I knew nothing of the engagement. I merely looked at her questioningly and shook my head. Undoubtedly she supposed that I knew it and was looking for my approval."

His bitter disillusionment was promptly expressed in the Journal: "The most dreadful thing that can happen to a man is to become ridiculous in his own eyes with regard to a matter of essential importance, to discover, for example, that the sum and substance of his sentiment is bosh. A person easily incurs this danger in his relation to another person—by believing, for example, in cries and screams. Here is a case where one needs to be stoutly built."

S.K. certainly was not stoutly built, and yet he possessed a resiliency which enabled him to support this crushing experience and receive education from it. This, in fact, was the culmination of the religious crisis which was initiated by the breach of his engagement. In a remarkable passage in *The Concept of Dread* he described this experience as "education by possibility." "No one ever sank so deep in reality that he could not sink deeper, and that there might not be one or another deeper sunken than he. But he who sank in possibility has an eye too dizzy to see the measuring rod which Tom, Dick and Harry hold out as a straw to the drowning man; his ear is closed so that he cannot hear what the market price for men is in his day, cannot hear that he is just as good as the most of them. He sank absolutely, but then again he floated up from the depth of the abyss, lighter now than all that is oppressive and dreadful in life." He had already said (or at least Judge William said) in *Either/Or:* "The religious experience is essentially the expression of the confidence that man by God's assistance is lighter than the whole world, the same sort of faith which makes it possible for a man to swim." With evident reference to this experience of the swimmer, S.K. in subsequent works frequently described faith as "floating over 70,000 fathoms."

S.K., impatiently, with a heart which was angry as well as bruised, went about the task of revising *Repetition* to correspond with the altered situation. He was too impatient to rewrite this book, as he did all the others, sometimes re-writing them twice, before he sent them to the printer. He simply changed a couple of words here and there, tore out the last ten pages or so, and rewrote the ending. These aesthetic works were again accompanied by a religious book which bore his own name, the *Three Edifying Discourses,* which to maintain the transparent fiction of anonymity were issued by a different publisher but appeared on the same day, October 16, 1843. Two of the discourses dealt with the text, "Love covereth a multitude of sins," and the other with "Strengthened in the inner man." By that time S.K. was so much strengthened in the inner man that he was able to write noble sermons *ad se ipsum* which furnish an invaluable commentary to the two aesthetic books. He called them "discourses," not sermons, and he gives as his reason the fact that they are "without authority." But he may have had in his own mind another reason which we can understand better, namely, that they are unlike any sermons that ever were preached or written.

From the fact that S.K. calls these books "aesthetic" it must not be inferred that they deal solely with love and other aesthetic themes; for here, as in *Either/Or,* there are meta-physical interests which are fundamental, and here for the first time in the pseudonymous works the religious interest is prominent. In particular the Christian idea of faith is illuminated in both books, and illuminated from different sides.

But I cannot stop to describe these books. I am ever mindful of the fact that I am writing a biography—and a very short one. I have devoted to the aesthetic works a disproportionate attention because they illuminate the greatest crisis in S.K.'s life. But even if I were writing a bigger book, I should not be disposed to describe S.K.'s books so fully that the reader might think it unnecessary to read them, now that they are available in English, nor would it be appriate to repeat here the ample introductions with which I have accompanied them. It is true that S.K.'s life consisted in his thought, to a degree which has hardly been equalled; but to delineate the development of his thought more completely than I here essay to do would be incompatible with the aim of writing a short biography, and if such a work needs to be done, it had better be done in a separate volume. The public is always clamoring for results, and the results of S.K.'s thought have often been presented in big volumes. But apart from the consideration that this task is perhaps beyond my powers, I am deterred by a scruple which S.K. pointedly suggests. For in his lifetime he was indignant with people who were "eating" him and putting him into paragraphs; and he insisted that what he offered was not "results," but a *method* of reaching them, which every "subjective thinker" must follow for himself.

After the religious crisis which culminated in Regina's engagement, S.K. was for a long while occupied in writing Edifying Discourses. He soon published a little book of four, then one of two, another of three, and finally, after a collection of four had appeared on August 3, 1844, they were all published together in one volume as *Eighteen Edifying Discourses*. Each collection had been piously dedicated to his father with the stereotyped phrase:

> To the late
> Michael Pedersen Kierkegaard
> sometime hosier here in the city
> my Father
> these discourses are dedicated.

Each had also the same preface with slight variations. That of the first read: "In spite of the fact that this little book (which is called 'discourses,' not sermons, because the author has no authority to **preach**; 'edifying discourses,' not discourses for edification, because the speaker makes no claim whatever to be a **teacher**) wishes only to be what it is, a superfluity, and desires only to remain in retirement, as it was in concealment it had its origin, yet I have not taken leave of it without an almost romantic hope. Inasmuch as its publication implies that in a metaphorical sense it is about to start, as it were, upon a journey, I suffered my eye to follow it for a little while. I saw then how it made its way along solitary paths, or went solitary on the highways. After one and another misunderstanding, due to its being deceived by a casual resemblance, it encountered finally that single individual whom it sought, that individual whom I with joy and gratitude call **my** reader, that individual whom it seeks, to whom as it were it stretches out its arms, that individual who is willing enough to let himself be found, willing enough to receive it, whether at the moment of the encounter it finds him joyous and confident or weary and downcast.—In so far as its publication implies in a more literal sense that it stands stock still without budging from the spot, I let my eye rest upon it for a little while. So there it stood like an insignificant little flower in the cover of a great forest, not sought after either for its splendor, or for its sweet scent, or for its nourishing properties. But then I saw also, or fancied that I saw, how a bird which I call **my** reader suddenly cast an eye upon it, swooped down in its flight, plucked it and carried it off. And when I had seen this, I saw no more. Copenhagen, May 5, 1843."

In the meantime (not to speak of the *Philosophical Fragments,* of which I shall speak in the next chapter) S.K. published on June 17, 1844, *The Concept of Dread,* a profound "psychological" analysis of the experience he had recently gone through on the way to faith. Because it had this relation to the aesthetic period of his life S.K. reckoned it among the "aesthetic" productions, although in other respects it was furthest removed from them and, as he confessed, had a tendency to "lecture," i.e. to use direct communication. I regret that I can say no more about this book, since it is a work of immense importance, not only for an understanding of S.K.'s thought but for a comprehension of his development in the most critical period. He described it as "a simple deliberation on psychological lines in the direction of the dogmatic problem of original sin," and he attributed it to a new pseudonym, Vigilius Haufniensis (i.e. the Watchman of Copenhagen). It was this serious book he dedicated to Poul Møller.

Stages on Life's Way was published on April 30, 1845, and was accompanied by *Three Discourses on Imagined Occasions,* which was published one day earlier. This big book, the last of the aesthetic works, is in a sense a repetition of *Either/Or,* for it has the same theme, and most of the pseudonyms of the earlier works reappear as actors in this piece.

The Aesthetic Works

No other author has had the hardihood to repeat an earlier work in a totally different style. It is a marvel that the venture did not fail. In fact, S.K. produced nothing more brilliant than the speeches of the Banquet, Judge William proves to have something new to say about marriage, and Quidam's Diary, which occupies two thirds of the book, tells the story of his love candidly, that is, not symbolically as he had told it in *Repetition* and *Fear and Trembling*. So in spite of being a repetition this book is very different from the four which preceded it. I have said of them that they are totally different from one another, and totally different from any book that has been written before or since. S.K. doubtless had in mind the extraordinary diversity of his literary production when he boasted that he had written "a literature within a literature."

What prompted him to write this repetition of *Either/Or* was the consideration that the earlier book stopped with the ethical and was thus incomplete. He said of it that, like Aladdin's palace, it was left with an unfinished window, and this lack he proposed to supply by adding a story entitled "Guilty?/Not Guilty?"—the story which is told in Quidam's Diary, the story of his own love and its tragic ending. He proposed to write it immediately after he reached Berlin in 1843. An entry of May 17 of that year reads: "I have begun a new story entitled Guilty/Not Guilty; naturally it will contain things capable of astonishing the world, for during a year and a half I have been experiencing within myself more poetry than there is in all romances put together." But then he goes on to say, "But I cannot and will not—my relationship to her shall not be evaporated into poetry, it has an entirely different sort of reality, she has not become a stage princess. If possible she shall become my wife." So this story was kept for the *Stages*. It could not be written until Regina was irretrievably lost to him.

It is amazing that the entries in the Journal which were made during the two busy months in Berlin contain hardly any references to the books he was actually writing at that time, but refer to many of the themes which were developed two years later in the *Stages*—such as "The Two Lepers," "The Ladies' Tailor," "Nebuchadnezzar," and "The Mad Accountant." From this we may see how copious was S.K.'s genius, which enabled him in a little more than two years to publish fourteen books, not to speak of the two large volumes which are filled with the Journals of that period and with the Papers, which include an unfinished philosophical work ascribed to Johannes Climacus. Originally the word poet meant creator. S.K. is clearly entitled to this name—not, of course, by the sheer quantity of his production, but by the quality of it, the variety, the spontaneity, the creative exuberance. In Danish, as in German, it does not sound paradoxical to call a man a poet who writes no verse, nor do we think it strange that Plato is called a poet. But if Plato was a poet, so was Kierkegaard; he too poetized philosophy, in the aesthetic works we look for poetry as a matter of course, but perhaps it is to be found at its best where we would least expect it, in the religious discourses. The Discourses which accompany the *Stages*, though they are not the most poetic, are among the most sublime. As a commentary to this book they are invaluable. One must read them to understand how it is that Quidam's Diary leads up to and into the religious stage.

THE POSTSCRIPT

1846

THE outstanding event of the year 1846 was the publication, on February 27, of the *Concluding Unscientific Postscript to the Philosophical Fragments,* ascribed to the pseudonym Johannes Climacus, but bearing the name of S. Kierkegaard on the title page as editor. The big book (of 554 pages in the English edition) is quaintly described in the title as a "postscript" to a very small book published about two years earlier and ascribed to the same pseudonym —the same pseudonym, moreover, who was held responsible for a work entitled *De omnibus disputandum est,* which was begun in 1842 and left unfinished when, for a time, S.K. was diverted from philosophy and started upon a new train of thought by Regina's nod. Philosophy was an interest which pressed as insistently for expression as did poetry; but when poetry had had its say S.K. did not carry on the argument of the unfinished work which was directed against the followers of Descartes, since now he was intent upon opposing the followers of Hegel. In this interest he wrote the *Philosophical Fragments,* which was published on June 13, 1844.

At first I feared it might seem pedantic to say anything about the pseudonym, Johannes Climacus, to which S.K. ascribed his most stupendous philosophic works and from which he derived Johannes Anticlimacus who figures as the author of his greatest religious works. Perhaps he assumed some knowledge on the part of his contemporaries of a Greek monk, John Climacus, who died about the year 600 as abbot of the monasteries on Mount Sinai and was famous throughout the Middle Ages as the author of a treatise on ascetic mysticism entitled *Scala paradisi* (to give the name in Latin) and hence was commonly known by a surname derived from the Greek word *klimax,* a ladder. Of this S.K. deigns to give no explanation, though in his unfinished work *De omnibus dubitandum est* he alludes to this famous book when he characterizes the ardent intellectual pursuits of the youth there described as "a ladder of paradise." On the part of my contemporaries I can hardly assume any acquaintance with John Climacus or his manual of asceticism; and yet for us in the Western Hemisphere the book has a singular importance. For by chance I learned recently from a book entitled *Cuentos del México Antiguo* by Artemio de Valle-Arizpe that it was the first book translated in the New World, and the first book printed here, that it was printed by Juan Pablos on a press sent to Mexico about 1535 by Charles V, and was translated, under the title *Escala spiritual para llegar al cielo,* by the Dominican novice Juan de la Magdalena (in the world Juan de Estrada) for the benefit of his fellow novices. The translation was, of course, from Latin into Spanish. This was nearly a century before the Pilgrims landed at Plymouth Rock! For this reason Johannes Climacus can claim some importance for us who are Americans, and I insert therefore without much diffidence this little explanation.

Though I have said the same thing of so many of S.K.'s books, I can affirm without any exaggeration that the *Fragments* is absolutely *sui generis.* It pretends to be "a thought-project" which discusses abstractly the fundamental themes of Christianity without using this word or referring to the historical events in which Christianity had its origin. It held out the tentative promise of a sequel which would invest the problem with a "historical costume." The *Postscript* is the promised sequel. Of course it did much more than provide the costume, for that was given as soon as the word Christianity was mentioned. In fact, the *Postscript* deals both discursively and profoundly with the philosophic problems involved in Christianity, and it is singularly fortunate that both the *Fragments* and the *Postscript* have been translated into English by a man so competent as David F. Swenson, who not only was professor of philosophy but for more than thirty years was a devout student of S.K.

S.K. calls the *Postscript* "unscientific," the Danish word having the broad sense of the German *unwissenschaftlich,* without specific reference to "science" strictly so called—although of that he said in his Journal at this time, "All demoralization will come in the end from the natural sciences." He at first proposed to use the word "simple" instead of "unscientific," and this helps to define his meaning. He let his reader know at the outset that this book is not written in the style of the professional philosophers, that it is a revolt against the pedantry which would banish poetry and humor from the discussions of philosophy. In that sense it is "simple" and provides many attractions for a mind not versed in philosophy. For all that, S.K. was able to keep his categories clear and to satisfy the exactions of the most rigorous thinkers. For this reason it is not popular. Several years after its publication S.K. remarked that only sixty copies had been sold and it had never been reviewed. In a sense it is a very complicated work, as one may see by a glance at the table of contents, and as is suggested by the title page where the book is described as "a mimic-pathetic-dialectic composition, an existential contribution."

Another word in the title, the word "concluding," is more

important; it indicates S.K.'s purpose of making this book his last. At this time he gave thanks to God that he had been able to say what he needed to say, and, in fact, he did not again feel the need of writing anything more on the subject of philosophy. So it seemed likely enough that this would be his last book. It had not yet occurred to him that he might become a religious writer in a greater sense than he already was as the author of edifying discourses. He thought that it would be a magnanimous gesture to retire at the height of his fame as an author and accept a small parish in the country. It was a very obvious thought, for it was for this he had been preparing himself for many years, and it was his father's wish. Naturally this thought recurred again and again; in later years it became a tempting thought when his fortune was exhausted and he was in need of a "living." We shall see in the next chapter why his purpose was not carried into effect at this time, and why the *Postscript* was not his last work.

Because he expected it to be his last work he interjected a chapter entitled, "A Glance at a Contemporary Effort in Danish Literature," in which Johannes Climacus reviews the works of the earlier pseudonyms, with the intent of making clear the unity of purpose in this whole literature. S.K. had become aware that his "indirect communication" had failed to communicate the thoughts which he was eager to impress upon his generation; and not being ready to give up the principle, he adopted this indirect way of teaching people what he meant. Therefore, except for *The Point of View,* this chapter is the most authentic explanation of his works which we possess. But this elaborate fiction was not maintained, for when the *Postscript* was finished he appended to it "A First and Last Declaration," in which he acknowledged that he was the author of this and all the other pseudonymous works.

The *Postscript* was so far from being his last work that in 1848 (only two years later) he could describe it in *The Point of View,* not only as "the turning point," but as "central" to his work as a whole, remarking incidentally that it was also central in the sense that as many works had been produced after it as before. But for two years after that date he continued to write as diligently as before; his greatest religious works were written then, and therefore, at the end of his life the *Postscript* was no longer central in a superficial sense. It remained nevertheless of pivotal importance, for nowhere else have we a reasoned statement of the philosophy which underlies his religious works. It is "central," as S.K. says, for the reason that, "having appropriated the whole pseudonymous, aesthetic work as the description of *one* way to become a Christian (i.e. *away* from the aesthetical in order to become a Christian), it undertakes to describe the other way (i.e. *away* from the System, from speculation, etc., in order to become a Christian)."

The problem proposed by the *Fragments,* as Climacus expresses it, is this: *"Is a historical point of departure possible for an eternal consciousness; how can such a point of departure have any other but a purely historical interest; is it possible to base an eternal blessedness upon a historical knowledge?"* This problem is also the theme of the *Postscript,* and there "the concern of the infinitely interested individual about his own relationship to such a doctrine" is dealt with even more personally, more passionately, and consequently more "subjectively": "I, Johannes Climacus, now thirty years of age, born in Copenhagen, a plain man like the common run of them, have heard tell of a highest good in prospect, which is called an eternal blessedness, and that Christianity will bestow this upon me on condition of adhering to it—and now I ask how *I* can become a Christian."

A book which puts to philosophy this personal question must, of course, lay the utmost emphasis upon the personal appropriation of truth. It had already been said in *Either/Or,* "Only the truth which edifies is truth for you." And now the *Postscript* gives this definition: *"Objective uncertainty held fast by the personal appropriation of the most passionate inwardness is the truth, the highest truth there is for an existing individual."* But this is also a definition of faith, the faith which is figuratively described by "lying out over a depth of 70,000 fathoms of water and still preserving my faith." The believer has to be content with "a fighting certainty." "Without risk there is no faith." The above definition regards the individual as the standard of truth— not however in the sense of Protagoras, but rather in the sense in which Socrates understood the Delphic maxim, "Know thyself." "The infinitely interested subjective thinker" is contrasted by Climacus with the speculative philosopher who, as he is proud to claim, disinterestedly seeks to ascertain objective truth without any concern about his relation to it.

From another point of view this "subjective" thinking is described as "existential" thinking. In reality, therefore, S.K.'s subjectivism lays greater stress than does speculative philosophy upon an objective world in which the individual *exists.* To "exist" does not mean simply *to be* but to stand out from (*ex-stare*), and that not in the sense of being separate *from* but intimately connected with the environment from which the individual as an individual stands out. It is important to note the specific meaning of "existence" and "existential" in S.K.'s philosophy, as well as in the so-called Existential Philosophy of Jaspers and Heidegger which confessedly is derived from it. Heidegger seeks to indicate what existence implies by using the expression *Da-sein* (which we might translate by "thereness") and *in-der-Welt-sein* (the fact of being in the world). It is defined by S.K.'s emphatic use of the word "interest" (*inter-est*), which expresses the fact that we are so intimately involved in the objective world that we cannot be content to regard the truth objectively, i.e. disinterestedly. "It is impossible to exist without passion."

In the *Postscript* S.K. described "the existence spheres" more fully and more definitely than he had done in the *Stages,* even finding an appropriate place for irony and humor; and thus he completed the unique task of charting the unexplored sea of human personality.

Professor Swenson, in *Something about Kierkegaard,* begins a chapter on "Existential Dialectic" with the following paragraph: "In S.K. we have a thinker who completely reverses the Cartesian distribution of emphasis: he reflects where Descartes accepts, and accepts where Descartes reflects. He took his point of departure in something deeper than an abstract intellectual doubt, namely, in a concrete personal despair. In this despair, which was ironically witty and articulate, he questioned the meaning and truth of human life in its whole range of substantial values. The struggle to find solid ground under his feet was undertaken with a concentration of all his faculties, intellectual and passional; and, in gradually achieving this task for himself, he brought into being a revision of the basic categories of human existence. The revision is such as to have significance also for others, and it has been given expression in a literature of surpassing artistry and rare moral power."

For me to present here a summary of this great book would be manifestly absurd; I shall not even attempt to describe it; the reader must be left to find his own way as an independent subjective thinker, although I hope that the few hints I have given above may be helpful as a preliminary orientation.

But in addition to this concise positive orientation, a negative orientation may be even more necessary, i.e. a warning against what Professor Hirsch calls "the well worn paths of German misinterpretation." When Karl Barth jettisoned S.K. with the declaration that essentially he was a Catholic, he implicitly acknowledged that he had misinterpreted him in the first instance. But Barth's followers still misinterpret S.K. when they pretend to derive from him their doctrine which posits an irreconcilable opposition between the religion of transcendence ("the infinite yawning qualitative difference between God and man," to use S.K.'s phrase which defines "religiousness B" of the *Postscript*), and the religion of immediacy ("religiousness A")—as though *this* was the either/or proposed by S.K. But in fact, S.K. did not conceive that the "paradoxical religiousness" ("religiousness B") could exist apart from the religion of immediacy ("religiousness A"), which is the substratum, "the vital fluid," in which all religiousness lives. His alternative was the aesthetic life and speculation on the one hand, and the ethical *and* the religious (both A and B) on the other. Cf. the Editor's Introduction to *Kierkegaard*, pp. 10f., and the Editor's Introduction to the *Postscript*, pp. xviiif.

The essential distinction between religiousness A and B has been admirably expressed by Swenson (*op. cit.*, p. 135) in a passage which takes into account the important distinction S.K. makes between guilt and sin: "Religion A is characterized by a passive relation to the divine, with the accompanying suffering and sense of guilt. But it is distinguished from religion B, or transcendent religion, in that the tie which binds the individual to the divine is still, in spite of all tension, essentially intact. . . . The distinctive feature of transcendent religion can be briefly stated. It consists in a transformation or modification of the sense of guilt into the sense of sin, in which all continuity is broken off between the actual self and the ideal self, the temporal self and the eternal. The personality is invalidated, and thus made free from the law of God, because unable to comply with its demands. There is no fundamental point of contact left between the individual and the divine; man has become absolutely different from God."

It is very easy to misapprehend, even to caricature, S.K.'s notion of the "leap," more especially when it is a leap into the paradoxically religious sphere which S.K. characterizes as "the absurd." The leap is indeed a decisive *choice,* and as such it is an expression of the will. But this does not imply an antithesis between the intellect and the will, for the whole man, intellect, feeling and will, is involved in the choice. S.K. constantly speaks of "becoming a Christian," rarely of *being* a Christian, i.e. he never thinks of this experience in static terms. But because it is a *real* becoming, it cannot be adequately accounted for by anything that preceded it, anything like an immanent evolution. Therefore, as Swenson says, "the movement of faith seems paradoxical to the ordinary consciousness from which faith emerges"; it is "absurd" from the ordinary human standpoint, but not from the standpoint of faith. Nor is faith altogether unmotivated. S.K. would be the last to affirm such a thing, for all his works, from the first to the last, were meant as a motivation of faith. He affirmed that there can be no *proof* of faith, no compulsion to believe; but it has innumerable motivations both intellectual and passional. "The paradoxical," says Swenson, "is S.K.'s careful and precise development of a thought which the Greeks dimly shadowed forth as the divine madness (Plato's *phaedrus*)."

I might, perhaps, prefer to quote Swenson even if I were able to say the same thing better; for with respect to positions of fundamental importance which have been commonly misunderstood I would not have it seem as if I stand alone.

THE AFFAIR OF THE CORSAIR
1846

THE affair of the *Corsair*" was one of the major events in S.K.'s life, which outwardly was so uneventful but inwardly so intense. The *Corsair* was a comic paper founded by a talented young Jew, Aaron Goldschmidt, and by him so cleverly managed that it had attained the biggest circulation in Denmark. Though S.K. affirmed that it stood for no idea, Goldschmidt flattered himself that he was serving the idea of political liberalism by dragging down the great and revealing that they were not really superior to the vulgar. It paid "a glittering honorarium" to disloyal servants for betraying the secrets of the home, and its real editors hid behind blackguards who were ready to suffer the penalties of the law for libel. All reputable men declared that it was a scandal which ought to be abated—yet secretly read it with malicious enjoyment. S.K., they said, was the man to attack it, because he was so completely independent. He, with his polemical nature, was ready enough for the fray. We have seen that even in childhood he did not shrink from conflict with bigger boys.

An occasion was furnished him in 1845, when for the second time the *Corsair* praised his works to the skies and declared that his pseudonym Victor Eremita "will never die." S.K. at once wrote in the name of Victor "A Prayer to the *Corsair*," in which he lamented the cruel distinction of being made immortal...by the *Corsair*. This was not published because S.K. was then completely preoccupied with the work of finishing the *Postscript;* but no sooner was the manuscript ready for the printer than a better occasion presented itself of which he promptly took advantage. On or about December 22 appeared an "aesthetic annual" entitled *Gæa,* elegantly gotten up by P. L. Møller to serve as a New Year's gift. It contained not only a supercilious review of the *Stages* but a passage which evidently was meant as a personal affront to S.K.; and in the name of Frater Taciturnus, one of the pseudonyms of the *Stages,* S.K. replied to it promptly in a letter to the *Fatherland:* "The Activity of a Peripatetic Aesthete and how he paid for the Banquet." It was a devastating attack upon Møller personally. I can quote here only a part of the last paragraph: "Would that only I now might soon get into the *Corsair.* It is really hard on a poor author to be thus singled out in Danish literature as the only one (assuming that all the pseudonyms are one) who is not abused there. Hilarius Bookbinder has been flattered in the *Corsair* (if I remember correctly), and Victor Eremita has been obliged to suffer the wrong of becoming immortal...in the *Corsair!* And yet already I have been there, for *ubi spiritus, ibi ecclesia—ubi* P. L. Møller, *ibi* the *Corsair.*"

Goldschmidt, meeting S.K. soon afterwards, admitted that Møller had been "annihilated." It was his ambition to succeed Oehlenschläger as professor of aesthetics in the University, and that hope vanished when his association with the *Corsair* was made public. He replied in the *Fatherland* with a letter which S.K. characterized as "deferential"—"he made his bow and disappeared. I do not know whither he went, but from that moment, according to the report of my barber, there was a busy time on the dance floor of literary despicableness in the office of the *Corsair.*" At that time Goldschmidt approached S.K. with the hope that he would ask him to desist from attacking him. Unfortunately, it was not in S.K.'s nature to make such a request, and during the two months which elapsed before the *Postscript* was published he persisted in the pretense that the pseudonyms who were attacked had nothing to do with, him. So the counter attack was launched on January 2, in an article which recounted "How the Peripatetic Philosopher found the Peripatetic Virtual Editor of the *Corsair*." Though it was accompanied by a couple of caricatures, it was not very grievous. Goldschmidt was still waiting for a word which would flatter his vanity. He had a great admiration for S.K., who perhaps was the only distinguished man in Copenhagen who had not treated him condescendingly.

It was a pitiful situation, for if either man had spoken frankly to the other, the disaster which involved them both would never have occurred. Even when he had launched with full force an attack which was to last for almost a year and to be the principal feature of nearly every number of the *Corsair,* he discoursed amicably with S.K. in the street, still hoping to draw from him the word of approbation he coveted. He told him how enormously he had been influenced by encouraging words S.K. had uttered in time past; he recalled that once he had counseled him to try his hand at "comic composition," and now he asked if it did not seem to him that he had succeeded in the articles on Frater Taciturnus. S.K. extricated himself from this very dialectical situation by affirming that he "had not recognized the higher right of Frater Taciturnus." Goldschmidt relates that upon meeting him in the street a short while after the *Postscript* was published and the pseudonyms acknowledged S.K. passed him by "with a proud and furious glance, not wishing to greet or be greeted."

"The fierce glance had the effect, as it were, of drawing

aside the curtain to disclose 'the higher right' on which Kierkegaard previously had plumed himself, and which I had neither been able nor willing to see, although I had a presentiment of it. It accused me and crushed me. The *Corsair* had conquered in the fight, but I myself had drawn a false No. 1. But in this momentous instant a protest arose in my mind: I was not a man to be looked down upon, and I could prove it. Before I had walked home through the streets it was practically decided that I should give up the *Corsair*." It was not an easy resolve to carry out, for the *Corsair* brought him a fortune, and in fact it was eight months before he did give it up and retired to Germany. He returned several years later to Copenhagen, founded there a reputable monthly review, and was reinstated in the esteem of the public—but not in the eyes of S.K., who continued to regard him as "the bad boy of literature." P. L. Møller betook himself to Paris, and in France he died before long in abject misery, befriended only by two women whom he had seduced.

I have no doubt that S.K. attacked the *Corsair* deliberately (and, as he said, "prayerfully"), as "a good deed," in the defense of public decency; but likely he did not expect to suffer a persecution so painful and so prolonged. He had expected that the prominent men who had urged him on would at least support him; but they persisted in saying of the comic abuse, "It is nothing," and they did nothing; S.K. suspected that they found an invidious pleasure in seeing him mocked; but after all he too pretended that it was nothing. The *Fatherland* said not a word in his defense— but really its editors were waiting for him to tell them what he would have them do. He was well aware that he was a good subject for caricature; and he could have laughed at it with his equals, but not with the mob. In the drawings which lampooned him there was precious little wit, though they delighted the populace, especially when they drew attention to the unequal length of his trousers and prompted everybody in the street to gape at him. But the comments of Goldschmidt were calculated to wound him most deeply by seeking to make out, in the service of his political idea, that S.K., as a rich man and intellectual aristocrat, was contemptuously indifferent to the simpler classes. Nothing could have been further from the truth, for no one felt more vividly than he "the equality of all men before God," and if we cannot now believe, as was commonly believed after his death, that most of his fortune had been bestowed upon the poor, there was probably no one in his day who exercised more abundant charity in the Gospel sense; certainly there was no one who found so much pleasure in the simple acquaintances he made in the street, where he liked to converse affably with everybody. From this pleasure he was henceforth precluded; he bravely continued his walks in the street, his only exercise, but this was no longer a diversion; more than ever he found solace in long carriage drives into the country, sometimes for several days, but even in the country he could not be sure of being unmolested. When the *Corsair* had ceased to exist, the persecution it had begun went on of itself. The very name of Søren became comic throughout the whole of Scandinavia, so that fond parents no longer bestowed it upon their children; and this persecution continued as long as he lived.

I therefore cannot agree with the writers who are scornful of S.K. for taking this thing so much to heart. It is true that his lamentations would fill a large volume; but they were only confided to the Journal, and the Journal was his only confidant, which just at this time became extraordinarily voluminous. At the beginning, and for a year or so, the entries were more humorous than one might expect. S.K. made but one reply in the *Fatherland;* but he wrote many replies which are so witty that they ought to have been published. The bitterest complaint he recorded at this time is the following: "It is even possible that, in spite of my insignificance before God, personally humiliated as I was for my personal transgression, I was nevertheless 'a gift of God' to my people. They have treated me shabbily, God knows; yes, they have abused me as children abuse a costly present."

I quote here a few other entries in order that the reader may hear S.K.'s own voice: "What I lack is bodily strength. My spirit is calm, I have always considered that I must be sacrificed, now I have received my orders and stand prepared for the command. I can endure it better in its daily form. But when, for example, I have sought recreation by driving ten or twelve miles, and my body has gradually become somewhat weak, partly by the drive, and partly by the sheer occupation of my mind, when I alight from the carriage and there is sure to be some one at hand who is jolly enough to call me names—it has a very strong effect upon my bodily disposition. Or when I have made a long excursion out on the lonely roads, engrossed with my thoughts, and then I encounter suddenly three or four louts out there where I am entirely alone, and these then take to reviling me—it has a strong effect upon my bodily disposition."

"Mr. Hostrop writes a student-comedy—of course, with all possible inconsiderateness, using all possible licence. It would indeed show a poor spirit of comradeship if one were to take objection to it! Very well; but must it not then continue to be a student-comedy, i.e. for students? But what happens? The piece travels around the whole land, is performed finally in the Royal Theater—and now I see today by the paper that it has been played in Norway, and that the Norwegian paper calls the character which represents me, by my name, Søren Kierkegaard."

"Andersen can tell the fairy-tale of 'The Lucky Galoshes,' but I can tell the tale of the shoes that pinch."

"I know my exterior well, and indeed few men have so often been the object of good-natured raillery, or a little witticism, or a little banter, or a smile in passing, as I have been. And truly I have no objection to that: it expresses an instantaneous impression. The person in question cannot help it, and that is the atoning factor, and perhaps many who have thought too much of my talents have as a set-off to this got a little joy out of my legs—many a maiden who perhaps set me up too high by reason of my mental gifts has found herself reconciled to me by reason of my thin legs. All this I find in the highest degree innocent, pardonable, and indeed enjoyable. But it is another thing when an abusive person takes the liberty of egging the crowd on to observe them."

[An ale-house keeper who used to treat him with the greatest deference now shows his contempt, but the watchman in his street is sympathetic.] "My watchman's opinion about the aesthetic attack is as follows: 'If worse comes to worst, I could reconcile myself to having my trousers stolen, but that somebody should draw a picture of them—that I couldn't survive.' . . . His opinion seems strange to me; for if somebody were to steal my trousers and I had no others to put on, then perhaps I might not survive it, supposing that I was compelled to walk abroad without them and presumably would catch a cold. On the other hand, when I am allowed to keep them on I get from my trousers a profit and joy such as no one else in the realm has—I have them on (that is what I share in common with all who wear trousers), and the whole town has joy in seeing that I have them on—joy and perhaps also profit. Well, to be sure, I once thought of being able to do a little something for the individual man by my literary effort. Sheer conceit and vanity! It may be that I have merely mistaken the means and can still succeed in being of some use after all. The means of profiting people is discovered, it is constantly with me as I walk—it is my trousers. My biggest works have not made so much impression. One might think that 'what the age requires' is my trousers. Then I will wish that its every requirement might be as innocent—for the requirement is that I should wear them, and at the best that I should some day bequeath them to the city. . . . I conclude that there is some element of enchantment involved in this case. Just as Aladdin's lamp was entirely inconspicuous, so it is with my trousers, which are just as inconspicuous and as little glaring as possible. If they were red with a green stripe, or green with a red stripe! But how ungrateful it was of me to regard these trousers as a thing of no importance whatever, merely giving orders to the tailor to cut them out of the customary gray cashmere—and now it is just by the help of these trousers that I am becoming almost a person of importance. . . . Pretty nearly everybody has read the paper (in spite of the fact that they dare not confess it to one another—it is all part of the game)—a countless multitude of gentlemen and ladies have personally convinced themselves by inspection that I have on the same trousers and that they correspond to the description. In order to meet the requirement of the age I have given a frank answer to every one who has asked me whether these 'really' are the famous trousers, so that they could definitely say that they themselves had seen them . . ."

"To let oneself be trampled to death by geese is a slow way of dying. . . . Such a galling sort of abuse is about the most torturing experience. Everything else has an end, but this never ceases. To take a seat in a church and there find a couple of louts impudent enough to sit beside one, continually staring at one's trousers and scoffing at one in their conversation, which is carried on in a voice loud enough for one to hear every word. But I am accustomed to such things. . . ."

"Oh, if in eternity there is time and place for jest, I am certain that the thought of my thin legs and my scorned trousers will be a blessed amusement. And it is blessed to have boldness to say, 'God knows that what I have suffered in this respect I have suffered in a good cause and because, humanly speaking, I did a good deed with truly disinterested self-sacrifice.' This I am bold to say directly to God—and I know more certainly than I know that I exist, more certainly than anything, because I already feel it, that He will answer, 'Yes, my dear child, you are right there,' and He adds, 'On the other hand, whereinsoever you have sinned and have not been in the right, this is forgiven you for Jesus Christ's sake.' "

S.K. remarked that the affair of the *Corsair* had enriched him "with many observations of human nature." In particular this experience fixed his attention upon the influence of the press, which had the effect of reducing individuals to a mass,

"the public." The entries he made in his Journal about journalists and the press would fill a large volume. A century
before our time he urged that there should be a society to
promote temperance if not total abstinence from reading
newspapers.

But the principal effect was that "the tension of reality"
caused him to give up "the melancholy idea" of taking a
country parish and prompted him "to stay on the spot."

"The wish to be a priest out in the country has always
attracted me and has remained in the background of my
soul. It attracted me both as an idyllic wish in contrast with
a strenuous existence, and also religiously, in order to find
time and repose to sorrow rightly for the sins I personally
may have committed. I supposed then that as an author I
was about to achieve success, and hence I considered that
to end in this way was the right thing to do. However, it
seems obvious enough that *the situation here at home is
becoming more and more confused.* The question now is
—in so far as it is true (as I am confident enough to sustain before the judgment seat of God) that the literary social and political situation requires an exceptional individual—the question is whether there is any one in the realm
who is fitted for this task except me. . . . The tasks set before me as a country parson are not essentially in my line.
Therefore, my thought has constantly been merely to express the universal; and the ethical significance of this step
would lie in the fact that I preferred this to glittering success. But now, and from now on, my career as an author
is truly not glittering. It is clear enough that I am to become a sacrifice."

So he stayed and braved the storm. Not only did he put

away the thought of a country parsonage, but he would not retreat even to Berlin, except for a few days, although that would have saved him from immediate annoyance and nipped in the bud the campaign of the *Corsair,* which could excite popular interest only so long as S.K. was daily to be seen in the streets. He stayed on the spot, realizing now that as an author he had a religious work to do. In 1847 he wrote: "It is an instance of God's grace to a man when precisely in the experience of adversities he shows that he is so fortunately constituted that like a rare musical instrument the strings not only remain intact through every new adversity, but he acquires in addition a new string on his string-board." Two years later he recurred to the same figure: "It was the tension of reality which put a new string in my instrument"; and again: "As an author I have acquired a new string to my instrument, I have become capable of producing tones I otherwise never would have dreamt of."

Thus the *Corsair* brought it about that, instead of being the concluding work, the *Postscript* was "the turning point." This was not, as he remarked, a religious work in the stricter sense; but it was in the direction of the religious. He said in one place that the *Postscript* was "a deliberation" whether and in how far he was to become a Christian. But he said too of all his works that they were "my education in becoming a Christian." His education was now so far advanced that henceforth he devoted himself exclusively to the production of religious works, which became progressively more and more definitely Christian.

During the three years he was an aesthetic writer he posed as an idle man-about-town. "The costume was correct," he thought. But he reflected that with the publication

of the *Postscript* and with the inception of distinctively religious writings "the costume must be changed." That
change was accomplished for him by the persecution of the
Corsair.

On MAY 5, 1847, S.K. completed his thirty-fourth year —and was still alive! In a letter which he wrote to his brother on this date he expressed his amazement. He was inclined to suspect that his birth had been incorrectly registered and that he might still have time to die before he was thirty-four years old. This was the last vestige of the fixed idea his father's melancholy presage had implanted in him. It will be remembered that he felt the same amazement at surviving his father. Strangely enough, the fact that Peter had already invalidated his father's prophecy by living far longer than the time allowed him did not weaken S.K.'s belief in it.

Expecting to die so early, he had already used up a good part of his capital, and now, with an indefinite term of life before him, he would be obliged to dip into it more deeply, if he were to maintain his rather lavish scale of living and could find no new means of support.

S.K. has been severely blamed for squandering his fortune. But he did only what the more sober critics of capitalism advise. Being assured that he had but a short time to live, and having no dependents to whom he must leave his money, no relatives who were in need of it, he prudently (may I not say?) planned to spend it during his lifetime. Nor was it only a superstitious dependence upon his father's prophecy which caused him to believe that he would not live long. His health was so frail that this seemed only too probable. Now, however, when he had passed his thirty-fourth birthday, the thing did not seem to him so prudent.

Not knowing how long he might live, it was a serious question whether what remained of his fortune would last as long as he did. This naturally gave him a new concern, from which he was never free until his death eight years later. And it seems an amazing instance of divine providence that as he was carrying home from the bank the last money he possessed, he fell paralyzed upon the street, was carried to a hospital and died within a few weeks.

This new and very pressing concern prompted him to take various measures to secure his economic position. In August 1847 he sold to his publisher Rietzel the whole outstanding stock of his books, and from that time his works were published on a royalty basis. At the same time he tried to sell to Philipsen the right to publish a second edition of *Either/Or,* and only because he could not at once get the price he demanded the publication was delayed for over a year. But his principal asset was No. 2 Nytorv, the big house he had inherited from his father and was prompted by filial piety to keep. The house, in fact, was his only asset, for on his thirty-fourth birthday he possessed only two certificates of stock at 400 Danish dollars par, and one of them he was obliged to sell at this time. In August he thought he had a purchaser, and he moved out in September, but not till December was the house actually sold. He made a good profit on it; but one third of the price went to pay the mortgage held by his brother Peter—and, alas, much of the remainder was lost by reason of the inflation of 1848, when Denmark was engaged in a war with Germany and had at the same time a political revolution. S.K. had bought Royal Bonds, the same security which had saved his father's fortune in 1813, but which now lost half their value.

This new concern forced upon him again the thought

of a country parish, which he now viewed from a different angle when he had to look for some means of support. We must remember that S.K. had been trained for this profession, and that it would have been difficult for him to make a living in any other way. This thought was to recur many times during the next few years as his fortune dwindled; but for the sake of brevity I shall not refer again to this persistent theme, which was again and again debated in the Journal, which always ended in a negative verdict, and yet was never disposed of but only adjourned. He never got so far as to make application for a parish, although he was sure Bishop Mynster would be glad to give it to him —if only to get him out of the way. He later reflected very wisely that a position in the Pastoral Seminary would be more suitable for him, and several times he "dropped a word about it" to Mynster. The Bishop seemed to pay no heed—except once when he replied wittily enough, "Why don't you found one of your own?" On his own part there was one obstacle he could not get over: he was fearful that when he had become a parson the sin of his youth, that dreadful thing which happened to him in 1835, might somehow be revealed and bring him to shame. Having no auricular confessor, he thought of making a public confession, but could not bring himself to do so. And so the question was always cropping up and was always adjourned.

For all this, he did not resort to the most obvious means of making his fortune last—he did not plan to live more frugally. When he moved (and he moved eight times before his death), he moved into a large and costly apartment, and until his death he always kept two servants, a man and a woman. A good deal was said about his extravagant manner of life, and he felt guilty about it himself, feeling that it was not in accord with the precepts of the Gospel. His defense was that he needed luxury to keep himself in vein for such a prodigious literary production. So he had soup twice a day, his secretary Levin reports, and "very strong soup" at that! The carriage rides, which were so necessary to him, were a very considerable expense. The microscopic study of S.K.'s life has been carried so far that we now know what he ate day by day. During the month of November 1847 he had *Gänse Braten* four times, larded lamb four times, salmon twice—not to speak of more ordinary viands. The inventory of his house reveals that when he died there were thirty bottles of wine left! I do not defend him, of course, but I feel much sympathy for him. If I had to live in a hutch, I say with Bishop Bloughram, "My hutch should rustle with sufficient straw." But S.K. was not made for life in a hutch. In 1852 he tried for a year and a half an ascetic regime—"just to see how much I can stand"— but he gave it up with a feeling that it led to sophistry.

Several visits which he made to King Christian VIII at this time were doubtless a solace to S.K., although they were not recorded in the Journal till several years later. The favor of the King was a relief from the scorn of the vulgar and the "treachery" of the aristocrats, who were thus furnished with "a little difficulty to bite on." Nevertheless, he was reluctant to make these visits and did not go to the palace as often as the King wished. He held himself a little aloof because he knew that the King was inclined to offer him a sinecure in appreciation of his staunch support of the monarchy. He hinted that he could be serviceable only so long as he was independent, and characteristically he added, "I have the honor of serving a higher Power to whose service my life is devoted." (Some years later he wrote an address to the Crown, asking for a pension—but he did not send it.) Except on this delicate subject he was very frank and easy with the King, saying to him on one occasion, "I have often reflected what a king ought to be like. First of all, he had better be ugly; next, he should be deaf and blind, or at least give himself out to be, for that abridges many difficulties— a rash or untimely speech, which acquires a certain importance by the fact that it is addressed to the King, had best be disposed of by an 'Excuse me?' as an indication that His Majesty has not heard. Finally, a king must not say much; he should have some set phrase to use on every occasion, which consequently says nothing. The King laughed and said, 'Charming description of a king!' Then I said, 'Yes, there is one thing more: a king must take care to be ill now and then; it arouses sympathy.' Thereupon he burst out with an exclamation of joy and jubilation: 'Ah! That's the reason you talk so much about your ill health. You would make yourself interesting!' " S.K.'s last word on this subject is: "On the whole, Christian VIII has enriched me with many psychological observations. Perhaps psychologists ought to pay particular attention to kings, and especially to absolute monarchs; for the freer a man is, the better he can be known."

The external troubles of this time did not concern S.K. so deeply as did "the case of Adler." In the spring of 1846, on returning from a journey of only a fortnight to Berlin, he bought all the works of Adler, along with everything that had been published about his case, and with the thoughts suggested by this apparently unedifying material he was deeply engrossed for three years, writing and twice rewriting his "big book on Adler," which now is printed among his Papers. For, in spite of the pains he took in writing it, he never published it—partly because it was written chiefly to clarify his own mind, and partly because it contained a premature polemic against the Established Church.

P. A. Adler, a Danish pastor, had lately been deposed for the claim he made in the preface to his first book that it was written at the dictation of Jesus Christ, and by his awkward recantation he justified the judgment of the ecclesiastical tribunal. The polemical character of S.K.'s book appears in a passage which describes this case as "an epigram upon present-day Christianity":

"So Magister Adler was born, brought up and confirmed as a native in geographical Christendom—thus he was a Christian (just as all the others are Christians); he became a theological licentiate—and was a Christian (just as all the others are Christians); he became a Christian priest, and then for the first time the curious chance befell him that through a profound impression upon his life he came into serious touch with the decisive experience of what it means to become a Christian. Just at this juncture, when by being religiously moved he undeniably comes nearer to the experience of what it means to become a Christian than he had been all the time he was a Christian—just at this juncture he is deposed. And his deposition is quite justified because the State Church only now has the opportunity to ascertain how it stands with his Christianity. But all the same, the epigrammatical application still remains—that as a heathen he became a Christian priest, and when he had got somewhat nearer to the experience of becoming a Christian he was deposed."

His reflections upon "the *Corsair* as a phenomenon" made

it clear to him that his age was in complete confusion on the question of civil authority, and now the case of Adler showed that it was equally confused about the nature of religious authority. The title he at one time proposed for his book indicates that this was what prompted him to write it: "The Religious Confusion of the Present Time Illustrated by Mag. Adler as a Phenomenon."

He recognized in Adler a certain sort of genius—"a confused genius which can be described essentially as dizziness." Adler confounded his dizzy experience with revelation, and his contemporaries too were unable to distinguish between a genius and an Apostle. They conceived that they were exalting St. Paul when they extolled him as a genius, wondered at the profundity of his thought and his dialectical skill. Mere aesthetic categories! One might as well extol his talent as a tent-maker and affirm that there never was nor would be an upholsterer capable of doing such wonderful work. S.K. remarked significantly in his Journal, "For the Apostles I always keep a separate account." The Apostle was qualitatively distinguished by the fact that he had a direct and explicit commission from Jesus Christ. But S.K. also kept a separate account of another extraordinary ministry in the Church, namely, that of the prophet. He alone in his age had an eye open to the possibility of the recurrence of this extraordinary ministry. The authority of the prophet also was direct and "immediate," but its credentials were not so ostensible. The ordinary ministry he conceived after the analogy of the apostolate. It too was explicit and ostensible, yet it was qualitatively different for the fact that it was not direct and "immediate"; it was derived through ordination, which was its ostensible token, though not an infallible one. The only thing that S.K. salvaged from his big book on Adler was the first of the *Two Ethico-Religious Treatises* (now translated along with *The Present Age*), which was published in 1849.

But chiefly it was a personal concern which fixed his attention upon the case of Adler. The persecutions of the *Corsair* had made him feel more acutely than ever his singularity, his heterogeneity; but this experience at the same time suggested to him, who from his childhood had had an obscure sense of mission, that what was so out of the ordinary might be the extraordinary, the exception in a good sense, that he was a man "separated" in the sense in which St. Paul uses the word in Gal. 1:15. He often reflected that if he had not been so dialectical he might have become an extravagant enthusiast like Adler and others who boast of "new Light," special "guidance," or an immediate divine call. He was well protected against such temptation and stuck steadily to his category, "without authority"; but in consequence of his reflections at this time he questioned whether he might not have been singled out to bear witness to the truth as a martyr. This is the point he had reached two years later when he published the two "treatises" above mentioned, the second of which was entitled, "Has a man a right to let himself be put to death for the truth?" At that moment he answered this question in the negative; but he reversed his judgment before he launched his open attack upon the Established Church, in which he expected to be put to death.

THE EDIFYING DISCOURSES

1843 TO 1855

IF ALL OF S.K.'s Edifying Discourses must be dealt with in one chapter, though they stretch from the beginning to the end of his authorship (from 1843 to 1855), this obviously is the place for it; for it is at this point, just after the publication of the *Postscript,* and in consequence of the persecution he suffered from the *Corsair,* he became exclusively a religious author. Exclusively, he could say, except for one little piece of aesthetic criticism, an appreciation of Fru Heiberg as an actress, which he published in 1848 and which he often cited as proof that even when he was engrossed with religious themes he had not lost his taste for the aesthetic. On the other hand, he could with more reason insist upon the fact that at the beginning, when he was engaged chiefly in writing aesthetic works, he gave evidence that he was a religious writer. For not only did *Either/Or* conclude with a sermon (on "the comfort of the thought that before God we are always in the wrong"), but it was "accompanied" by *Two Edifying Discourses;* and each new pseudonymous work had a similar accompaniment of two, three, or four Discourses under his own name, until in a year and a half they had reached the number of eighteen and were republished in one volume.

The *Stages* was accompanied by *Three Discourses on Imagined Occasions; A Literary Review* by *Three Discourses in Various Spirits;* and the second edition of *Either/Or* by *The Lilies of the Field and the Birds of the Air.* With good reason S.K. could say, "With my right hand I held out the

Edifying Discourses, with my left the aesthetic works—and
all grasped with the right hand what I held in my left."
This situation which S.K. so much deplored has unfortunately remained unchanged until lately. In Germany,
where his works have been most industriously studied, the
Discourses were tardily translated, for the most part per-
functorily, merely for the sake of completing the edition;
and because these were not available to students, the pseudonymous works were not rightly understood. Since the
pseudonymous works are in the form of "indirect communication," they stand in need of interpretation, and the
Discourses, which always were in the form of "direct communication," afford in some instances (especially in the case
of *Repetition, Fear and Trembling,* and the *Stages*) a very
precious and specific illumination of S.K.'s meaning, not
merely a proof of his religious intent in general.

Besides the Discourses alluded to above, there was published in 1847 a big volume entitled *The Works of Love;*
in 1848 *Christian Discourses,* and in 1849 *"The High Priest"*
—*"The Publican"*—*"The Woman that was a Sinner."* The
greater works of this period—which were not greater in
bulk but more tremendous—will be dealt with in a subsequent chapter. But even after *Training in Christianity* was
published there appeared three groups of Edifying Discourses. One of them, *Two Discourses at the Communion,*
he dedicated in 1851 to "One Unnamed." It was his reply
to Schlegel's refusal to encourage a renewal of his acquaintance with Regina. The last, *God's Unchangeableness,* appeared only three months before he died, in the very midst
of his attack on the Established Church, and was meant as
a gesture of farewell to his father, to whom it was dedicated
in exactly the terms he had used in the first Discourses. In

all there were eighty-six Discourses, which now are published in English in seven volumes.

As a translator I began with the religious discourses, and I went on with the aesthetic works only because no one else was prompted to do them. Professor Swenson very properly began with the philosophic works (*Fragments* and *Postscript*), but simultaneously he worked on the Discourses, and Mrs. Swenson has finished what he began. Five others have been active in translating the Discourses—eight writers in all, contrasted with the four who have dealt with the pseudonymous works. In England and America four publishers have been interested in publishing the Discourses, whereas only two have published pseudonymous works. This is a striking and spontaneous testimony to the pertinence of S.K.'s religious works to our situation at this time, and it shows that we at last are putting out the right hand to grasp what S.K. offered us with his right. The Discourses are not like other sermons, and S.K. had good reason for not calling them by this name. Free thinking Jew as he was, Georg Brandes said of them: "Judge William remarked in *Either/Or,* 'I have an idiosyncrasy against edifying works and printed sermons.' But even if in general one shares this feeling, one reads Kierkegaard's Edifying Discourses with respect. A noble spirit of moderation prevails in them. It makes a profound impression to hear this same man who is able to make himself the interpreter of the wildest passions speaking here to his fellow men so simply, so composedly, so solicitously, and offering them the best comfort he knows how to give for their pilgrimage through life."

One of S.K.'s important contributions to the philosophy of religion is the distinction he made in the *Postscript* between two types of religiousness, "A" and "B," i.e. the re-

ligion of immanence, and a religion of transcendence characterized by the specifically Christian sense of sin. At first
one may be amazed at hearing him say of his Edifying
Discourses that they correspond to religion "A"; for one
will recognize that they are more genuinely Christian than
most sermons one hears; and the further S.K. went with
them the more distinctively Christian they were. Yet such
is the fact. Whereas all the pseudonyms, except Anti-
Climacus, represent positions which S.K. had already transcended, yet when he wrote under his own name, as in the
Discourses, he was careful to register precisely the position
he had reached on the way to becoming a Christian, for
he was fearful of attributing to himself a result he had
not really acquired or had not personally appropriated by
"double reflection." This is an example of honesty which
might be recommended to preachers, who are always exposed to the temptation of saying more than they mean.

When at the end of his life, in the midst of his fierce contention with the "parsons," he affirmed, "All I demand is
honesty," his own position was impregnable, for he had always been honest even with himself. When he said of his
works in general, "They were my own education in Christianity," he doubtless had in mind the Discourses in particular. Of them Swenson says justly, "The development of the
Christian thesis is gradual, careful, methodical, advancing
step by step." Some of the steps are indicated by the titles.
S.K. called the first collection *"Edifying* Discourses," being
inhibited by a strange scruple from affirming that they were
issued authoritatively "for edification"; yet in 1848 he ventured to apply this "higher category" to the third section
of the *Christian Discourses;* in 1847 he had already characterized *The Works of Love* as "Christian reflections"; and

in 1849 the Discourses on the Lilies and the Birds were called "Godly Discourses." These are subtle distinctions, but they clearly indicate a sense of progress. For all that, he regarded even the last Discourses as examples of religiousness "A": they were distinctively Christian, yet not exponents of the paradoxical religiousness which is peculiar to Christianity. This in itself is enough to prove that in discriminating between the religion of immanence and the religion of transcendence S.K. did not radically disparage the former, far less discard it; for not only did he affirm that it is the permanent substratum of all religion, but it was the religiousness which he expounded in eighty-six Edifying Discourses, and the religiousness which he personally exemplified. Therefore, when it came to publishing *Training in Christianity* and *For Self-Examination,* his most stupendous religious works, he felt the need of using a pseudonym, Anti-Climacus, who instead of ranking lower than he in the religious scale stood far higher. As for himself, he recognized humbly that even when in his perception of what Christianity is he had attained the highest point, he was not yet adequately expressing it in his life, had not yet *become* a Christian—until he died for his faith.

METAMORPHOSIS

1848

In 1848 S.K. was an old man—an old man at thirty-five—and yet not too old to experience a profound transformation which made this year the most productive of his whole life. This year, which was so momentous in European history for the external effects produced by a belated concretion of the ideas of the French Revolution, was for S.K. the period of his most intense spiritual activity, which resulted in the production of his most admirable works. Professor Hirsch says that "the year 1848 represents the climax of Kierkegaard's intellectual productiveness. . . . *The Sickness unto Death* and *Training in Christianity* (his two masterpieces as a Christian author) and *The Point of View* (a religious autobiography so unique that it has no parallel in the literature of the world) have more prospect than any other Christian theological productions of the nineteenth century of finding a place among the imperishable writings of the Christian Church."

About this year S.K. himself says in an entry made a year later: "In one sense 1848 potentiated me, in another sense it broke me, that is to say, it broke me religiously, or, as I put it in my language, God had run me to a standstill. He allowed me to undertake a task which even in reliance upon Him I was unable to lift in a higher form; I had to take it up in a lower form. And hence this thing has become my own religious or more inwardly religious education in an inverse fashion. In a certain sense I would be so glad to venture [i.e. to make an open attack upon the Established Church], my imagination lures and incites me; but I must just be good enough to venture in a lower form [i.e. pseudonymously]. It [i.e. *Training in Christianity*] is certainly the truest and most perfect thing I have written; but my relation to it must not be such as to make it seem as if it is I who come down upon all the others with an almost damning judgment—no, I myself first of all must be educated by it; no one perhaps has a right to be so deeply humbled under it as I, before I have a right to publish it. . . . Economic anxiety came suddenly upon me and all too close. Two such heterogeneous weights as the opposition of the world and anxiety about my subsistence I am unable to lift at the same time. . . . Then suddenly the confusion [war and revolution] broke loose. For a few months the situation was such that tomorrow I might possess nothing at all but would be literally without a penny. That went hard with me. All the more powerfully did my mind react. I produced more powerfully than ever, but more than ever like a dying man. In the direction of Christianity it is the highest yet accorded me, that is certain. But in another sense it is, in turn, too high for me to assume responsibility and step forth openly in character. That is the deeper significance of the new pseudonym [Anti-Climacus], who is higher than I."

Even to this day it is commonly believed that S.K. was so absorbed by his religious thoughts—or, as some think, by petty egoistic interests, like the loss of his competent servant Anders, who was drafted into the army just at the time when his master had to change his dwelling-place and was most in need of him—so absorbed in this that he was indifferent to the great issues involved in the brief war of his country with Germany and the bloodless revolution which put an end to the absolute monarchy. But the fact is that

S.K. had already discounted the events of that year and transcended the political ideologies which were dominant in his day. Two years earlier (in the second part of *A Literary Review* which Dru has translated under the title *The Present Age*) he had discerned, almost prophetically, the consequences which have become to us a century later only too apparent and for us discredit the ideologies of 1848 as thoroughly as they were discredited for S.K.

Fortunately, in this chapter I can tell much of the story in S.K.'s own words, supplying merely the connective tissue which may be necessary to hold his scattered utterances together.

S.K. had the psychic disposition characteristic of twice-born men, as we have seen already in his experience twelve years earlier of the "inexpressible joy." But twice-born men are apt to be thrice-born, and S.K.'s subsequent experience was no less vivid and no less momentous in its results. In both cases the Journal makes it possible to observe a period of incubation. However sudden the event was, it was not without motivation. In this case it was anticipated by an entry dated eight months earlier, on August 16, 1847. Referring to his resolution not to go off for a brief visit to Berlin, he says: "The fact that I remain at home has a far deeper reason, and I feel impelled to it. Sometime I must begin to accustom myself to do without such strong diversions. . . . I feel now impelled to come to myself in a deeper sense, by coming closer to God in the understanding of myself. I must remain on the spot *and be renewed inwardly*. . . . I must try to get a better hold upon my melancholy. Hitherto it has reposed in the deepest recesses, and my prodigious mental exertion has helped to hold it down. That I have profited others by my work, and that God has approved it and has helped me in every way, is perfectly certain. I thank Him again and again that He has done for me infinitely more than I had expected. Sure as it is that no man has any merit before God, it is my comfort, nevertheless, that He has been well pleased to behold my endeavor and to see that in my frightful sufferings I have held out to the last by His assistance. I know of myself before God that my work as an author, my readiness to obey His signal, to sacrifice every earthly and worldly consideration, will mitigate the impression of the evil I personally have committed. Just because I began my work as an author with a troubled conscience I have striven with the utmost diligence to make it so pure that it might be a little abatement of my debt. This purity, disinterestedness, diligence, is what appears in the eyes of the world to be madness—without implying that in His eyes it might be so pure that before Him I can dare to boast of it.—But now God would have it otherwise. There is something stirring in me which indicates a metamorphosis. Precisely for this reason I did not dare to take the trip to Berlin—for that would be to produce an abortion. I shall therefore keep quiet, not work too hard, yea, hardly at all, not begin a new book, but try to come to myself, *to think thoroughly the thought of my melancholy together with God on the spot*. In that way my melancholy may be relieved and *Christianity come closer to me*. Hitherto I have defended myself against my melancholy by intellectual labor which keeps it at a distance—now, by faith that in forgiveness God has forgotten what guilt there is in it, I must myself try to forget it, but not by any diversion, not by any remoteness from it, but in God, so that when I think of God I may think that He has forgotten it, and thus learn for my part to dare to forget it in forgiveness."

The novelty of the thought that God "forgets" may for a moment obscure to us the pathos of this experience. It was a crucial experience for S.K., who did not find it as easy as most men do to believe in the reality of God's forgiveness. In the entry below not a word is said about God "forgetting," for it dwells exclusively upon the effect of this experience, upon the sudden sense of liberation; and yet the subsequent entries show conclusively that what underlay and accounted for this sudden liberation was the conviction that God had not only forgiven but forgotten. The entry follows:

NB NB

"Wednesday, April 19 [Wednesday in Holy Week, 1848].

"My whole nature is changed. My close reserve, my introversion, is broken—I must speak. Great God, give me grace!

"After all, that is a true word my father said of me, 'Nothing will come of you so long as you have money.' He spoke prophetically, believing that I would drink and revel. But not exactly that. No, but with my mental acumen and with my melancholy and then with money—oh, what a favorable condition for developing the torments of self-torture in my heart! (Such a strange coincidence: just when I had resolved to speak, my physician comes in. However, I didn't speak to him, for me that is too sudden. But my resolution stands fast, to speak.)"

[The following was appended, presumably on Friday.] "Maundy Thursday and Good Friday have for me become true Holy Days. Alas, she was unable to break the silence of my melancholy. That I loved her—nothing is more certain—and thus my melancholy got plenty to feed upon, and it got, in addition, a dreadful perquisite. The fact that I became an author is due essentially to her, my melancholy and my money. Now by God's help I shall become myself, I believe now that Christ will help me to triumph over my melancholy, and then I will become a priest.

"In this melancholy I nevertheless loved the world, for I loved my melancholy. Everything has helped to heighten the tension of my position: her sufferings, all my exertions, finally the fact that I have been an object of derision, has now at the end, when I am brought to the pass of needing to be anxious about my subsistence, conduced by God's help to prompt me to break through."

[Alas, he soon had to register a relapse:]

NB NB

"Monday after Easter.

"No, no, my close reserve cannot be broken, at least not now. The thought of wanting to abolish it by force of will has the effect of preoccupying me so much, and therefore every instant, so that it merely gets more and more firmly imbedded. . . . I cannot achieve such confidence of faith as to believe this painful recollection away. But by believing I defend myself against despair, bear the pain and punishment of introversion—and am so indescribably happy or blessed in the activity of spirit which God has so richly and so graciously granted me."

Immediately following this we have: "It was a miracle when Christ said to the paralytic, 'Thy sins are forgiven thee' or, 'Arise and walk.' But if this miracle does not now happen to me—what a marvelous boldness of faith is involved in believing that the sin is entirely forgotten, so that the memory of it has nothing alarming about it, thus truly believing oneself into being a new man, so that one can scarcely recognize oneself again."

On a loose leaf we find this: "When a man has thus verily experienced and experiences what it is to believe in the forgiveness of his sins, he has certainly become another man, everything is forgotten—but in his case it is not as it is with a child, which when it is forgiven becomes the same child again. No, he has become an eternity older, for he has now become spirit, the whole of immediacy with its selfish clinging to the world and to itself is lost. Humanly speaking, he is now old, prodigiously old, but eternally he is young."

At this point I must begin, alas, to abbreviate exceedingly, if I am to keep within the limits prescribed by the definition of a "small book." It is hard to tell briefly the story of S.K.'s last years; for this period, in spite of the fact that no external events occurred except the agitation which he precipitated, is the most interesting phase of his life, and to me the most edifying. During the six penultimate years (1849 to 1854), when S.K. was writing little or nothing for publication, the Journal grew enormously, not only in mass but in quality. In the recent Danish edition the entries of that period occupy 2,845 big pages, and among them are some of the most finished products of his pen. Fortunately, about one-tenth of them (270 pages) are available to English readers in Mr. Dru's translation, and I take comfort in the thought that the interested reader can turn, if he will, to the last chapters of my bigger book, where the story of these years is told in as many words as are comprised in the whole of this book.

However, I am not sorry that I have to bring this chapter

to an abrupt conclusion. For it is painful to dwell upon S.K.'s frequent relapses—and neither is it necessary, seeing that the outcome of the Easter experience was a radical cure, as is clearly proved by the fact that from this time on he never again resorted to "indirect communication," nor to the use of pseudonyms in the sense in which he had hitherto used them. There was no more "ventriloquism," as he put it. In the Edifying Discourses he had always used direct communication; but in the *Christian Discourses* one can easily recognize by the more polemical note that the last section ("Thoughts which Wound from Behind") was written after the Easter experience. The five books which were written during the year 1848 and published subsequently I shall describe briefly in the next chapter, merely remarking here that from one to another there is a very observable advance in plain speaking. When S.K. said in the entry of Wednesday in Holy Week, "I must speak," he implies, "I can": what one must do one can do. He learned to believe in the forgiveness of sins when he realized that this was a *must:* "Thou *shalt* believe in the forgiveness of sins." *Training in Christianity,* the last work written in 1848, could hardly be exceeded for plainness of speech, and yet it *was* exceeded two years later by *For Self-Examination,* and that in turn was exceeded by *Judge for Yourself*—and yet to S.K.'s thinking this was not downright enough to be used in the last polemic for which he was all this time sharpening his weapons.

Having been so indiscreet as to admit that I am a lover of Kierkegaard, I would have it known that *this* is the Kierkegaard I love—not the dissolute and despairing youth, nor the returning prodigal, nor the unhappy lover, not the genius who created the pseudonyms, but the frail man, utterly unfitted to cope with the world, who nevertheless was able to confront the real danger of penury as well as the vain terrors his imagination conjured up, and in fear and trembling, fighting with fabulous monsters, ventured as a lone swimmer far out upon the deep, where no human hand could be stretched out to save him, and there, with 70,000 fathoms of water under him, for three years held out, waiting for his orders, and then said distinctly that definite thing he was bidden to say, and died with a hallelujah on his lips. I could not love him as I do unless I could venerate him, and I learned to venerate him only when I saw that he had the courage to die as a witness for the truth.

VENTURING FAR OUT

1849–1851

At the beginning of 1849—the year when gold was discovered in California—S.K. held in his hands a more precious treasure...and did not know what to do with it. Since the Easter experience of the preceding year he had written his three greatest books: *The Point of View, The Sickness unto Death,* and *Training in Christianity.* These were the captain jewels in the coronet, but there were others: "A Cycle" of essays (the final recast of the book on Adler), of which a part was ultimately published in the *Two Little Ethico-Religious Treatises; Armed Neutrality* (not quite finished and never published); and *The Lilies of the Field and the Birds of the Air*—altogether eight works. He experienced no difficulty about publishing the last I have mentioned, for it was in the style of the previous Discourses; and in fact he wrote during this year another series of Discourses entitled *"The High Priest"—"The Publican"—"The Woman that was a Sinner,"* and published it on November 13. During this whole year hardly anything else was written for publication, because the question of publishing the works already in existence was a problem which absorbed him completely.

He was embarrassed by the fact that a second edition of *Either/Or* was called for, and because he needed the money he had to consent to it, though it seemed to him inappropriate that his first aesthetic work should reappear at a time when he was engaged in the most decisively religious production. It was published on May 14 and accompanied by "the godly discourses on the lilies and the birds," which he conceived of as poetry to end poetry. The idea of these Discourses came to him immediately after the experience of Wednesday in Holy Week, probably on Easter Even, when he said: "The purpose of these discourses will be to make evident the conflict between poetry and Christianity, how Christianity, in a certain sense, when compared with poetry (which is wishful, infatuating, benumbing, tending to transform the reality of life into an oriental dream, as when a young girl could wish to lie all day upon a sofa and let herself be enchanted)—how Christianity in comparison with this is prose . . . and yet is precisely the poetry of eternity. Consequently the lilies and the birds (i.e. the description of nature) will on this occasion receive a more poetical coloring and splendor of hue, just to show that the poetical shall be given up. For when poetry really must fall (not before the rant of a glum and sullen parson) it must wear its festal dress."

The experience that he could and therefore must speak, and speak out clearly, prompted S.K. not only to use direct communication for the future but to do what he could to make clear the religious purpose of his previous pseudonymous works. To this end he promptly wrote *The Point of View for My Work as an Author*. He experienced no difficulty in writing it, notwithstanding the fact that it was a most personal revelation of himself, and he was able to finish it in about a month, because, carefully as it was expressed, almost every phrase had been formulated in many entries of the Journal which he called "Report" or "Accounting." But when it came to publishing, the difficulties proved to be insurmountable. He had expected to die soon after it was finished, and so to leave it for posthumous publication. After many debates this is what he ultimately concluded to do: he called it on the title page "A Report to History," and it was given to the press four years after his death by his brother Peter. But something had to be done at once. He said in the Journal: "It is as if one possessed a great treasure and kept it securely hid by throwing away the key. The thought that troubles me is whether I have a right to do this, whether it is permissible with respect to a productivity which is so infinitely indebted to Him for its meaning, to let it remain an enigma and for many a mere curiosity." Accordingly he wrote a dry and less personal account, entitled *About My Work as an Author,* which was published in 1851, accompanied by *Two Discourses at the Communion on Fridays.*

With the same aim of insuring that after his death his works should not be totally misunderstood, he decided "to draw to me," as he said, Rasmus Nielsen, professor of philosophy in the University—that is, he accorded him the privilege of accompanying him on his promenades and discussing philosophy as they walked. Nielsen had shown that he was eager to be "drawn," and though this experience confirmed S.K. in his opinion that "a disciple is the greatest of all calamities," it was, nevertheless, an advantage to his cause that when he died in the midst of his violent attack upon the Church there was someone at hand who could explain to a bewildered nation what it all meant.

It must be clearly understood that S.K.'s difficulty about the publication of *The Point of View* was not the old reluctance to use direct communication; no, it was a scruple which would not occur to many men: "whether a man has a right to let people know how good he is." And in part it was this same scruple which for a long time delayed the publication of *Training in Christianity*. This book was not personal in the same sense, but it is evident enough that none but a good man—or a hypocrite—could write such a book as this, which insists upon the imitation of Christ, upon "following" and discipleship, and in our language finds its closest counterpart in Law's *Serious Call*. But in this case there was an additional difficulty, which was very grave and yet did not prove to be absolutely deterrent. For beside being a call to a devout and holy life, this book contained a sharp polemic against the easy-going Christianity which was represented by the Established Church. In an entry of this year (which was quoted at the beginning of the previous chapter) S.K. says: "Two such heterogeneous weights as the opposition of the world and anxiety about my subsistence I am unable to lift at the same time." He means that when by attacking the Church he had aroused the opposition of the world, the authorities might not be willing to appoint him to a living when the last remnants of his fortune had disappeared. It must be confessed that he was confronted by an appalling situation. If a man physically stronger than S.K., capable of earning a livelihood in various ways, and better able to put up with hardships, were to feel appalled by the prospect of total penury, one would not blame him very harshly. So the difficulty about publishing was complex. It had three elements: the fear of letting it be known how good he was; the fear of utter destitution; and the fear of "the opposition of the world," which to his vivid imagination meant physical maltreatment and perhaps martyrdom. It occurred to him that he might avoid this painful dilemma by first getting a parish or a chair in the Pastoral Seminary—and *then* publishing his polemical works. This was a shrewd plan. S.K. boasted that his mind was fertile in shrewd plans—and that habitually he scorned to follow them.

Eventually this plan was rejected with the strongest expressions of disgust and self-reproach. "Fie, fie! So I have been willing (or at least had the thought) to act shrewdly in order to assure myself first of a position, and then publish the works pseudonymously. A capital interpretation of 'Seek first God's kingdom!' "

Yet this plan was not quite so crass as it seems. He reflected that this was the humble thing for him to do, so that as a parson he would evidently fall under the reprobation he pronounced. Moreover, this was the purpose he had always had, and no man was more faithful in cherishing an original purpose. It should be remembered that when the Easter experience gave him confidence that he could speak, he exclaimed, "Then I will become a priest," joyful at the thought that in this respect he at last would be able to "realize the universal."

The difficulties he felt about publishing the polemical works were further complicated by the thought of Regina. We find to our surprise that he was then thinking of the possibility of a *rapprochement* with Fru Schlegel. Yet we might have guessed it. There was a hint of it in a significant entry celebrating his new-found power to speak, which reminded him that, if earlier he had been able to speak out, he would not have lost her. Besides this, he had hoped that his renown as an author would be to her glory—but the direction his writings had now taken was likely to involve him—and "her"—in a notoriety the very opposite of renown. The obstacle to a *rapprochement* with her now was the inveterate enmity of her father. But just then Councillor Olsen

died, in the night of June 25/6. It happened that just then
S.K. had definitely resolved to publish *The Sickness unto
Death*. On the afternoon of June 25, after a vain attempt to
see Bishop Mynster and the Cultus Minister, Madvig, from
whom he meant to inquire about the possibility of an
appointment to a living, he rather petulantly resolved to ask
the printer if he was free to begin to print this book at once,
meaning to bring it out under his own name. Learning
that the way was clear, he sent the manuscript at once.

Not till the 27th did he learn of Councillor Olsen's death,
and that at once raised "a multitude of difficulties." That is,
it opened up the possibility of approaching Regina and
prompted him to withdraw a book which might hinder the
realization of this hope. He relates that the following night
he slept uneasily and heard, as it were, a word about plunging to destruction. The contemporary entry which records
this experience is so laconic that we can make little of it.
But from entries made several years later we learn that he
then experienced an auditory hallucination which might
well have frightened him into making a final decision. He
remembered distinctly almost every word of a conversation
he seemed to be carrying on with himself: "So then this
is what is required of me?"—"What does he imagine?"—"I
might well wait a week."—"Look, now he is willing his own
destruction." According to his final interpretation, it was not
his better nature but his "common sense" which tried to
hold him back with the query whether so much was required of him, and whether he might not at least be allowed
a brief delay. This experience decided him not to withdraw
the book, but still he hedged a little by ascribing it to a new
pseudonym, Anti-Climacus, his name remaining on the
title page as editor.

On November 19 he made a move to establish with Regina a "sisterly relationship," believing that he had "data" which indicated that she desired it. After he had rejected many forms of a long letter to Schlegel, which of course were all of them admirably expressed, he sent a short one, enclosing a sealed note to Regina which her husband might give her if he thought fit. Two days later the note was returned to him unopened, with an indignant reply from the husband. This was a cruel blow, but I cannot think that the triangular relationship he proposed would have added to the happiness of any of the three.

The Sickness unto Death was quickly printed, and was published on July 30, 1849. The following entry gives a notion of S.K.'s state of mind at that time: "Till now I am a poet, absolutely nothing more, and it is a struggle of desperation to will to go out beyond my limits.

"The work on *Training in Christianity* has great importance for me—does it follow from this that I must at once make it public? Perhaps I am one of the few who need such strong remedies. And instead of profiting by it and beginning myself quite seriously to become a Christian, I would first make it public. Fantastical!

"This work and others are actually in being; the time may perhaps come when it is appropriate and I have strength to do it and it is right for me to do it. . . .

"So *now* then *Sickness unto Death* is coming out pseudonymously with me as editor. It is called 'for edification'— that is more than my category, the poetical category, 'edifying.'

"As the river Guadalquivir plunges underground at one place, so there is a stretch (the edifying) which bears my name. There is something lower (the aesthetical) which is

pseudonymous, and something higher, which is also pseudonymous, because my personality does not correspond with
it.

"The pseudonym is called Johannes Anti-Climacus, in
contrast to Johannes Climacus who said he was not a
Christian. Anti-Climacus is the opposite extreme, that of being a Christian in an extraordinary degree—whereas I manage only to be a very simple Christian."

It needs to be understood that S.K. wrote all of these later
works in his own person and intended to publish them in his
own name. Anti-Climacus was an afterthought. In fact,
when *Training in Christianity* had finally been sent to the
press in 1850, S.K. ran to the office in the hope that it had
not gone too far for him to remove the name of Anti-
Climacus. Alas, it was too late. But at least it did not appear
on the title page of *For Self-Examination,* which was published the following year. It cannot be said too emphatically
that in this case the use of a pseudonym did not mean, as it
had meant in the past, that the subject of the book was removed to a distance by "double reflection"; on the contrary,
it meant that the subject was pressed upon the reader objectively, without regard to the authority or the personal
character of the author, and (as the title of the last book puts
it) that the reader was left to judge for himself in the light
of the New Testament. Anti-Climacus meant simply that
S.K. wanted to "draw attention," to "compel people to take
notice" of Christianity as it really is.

Although *Training in Christianity* was not published till
September 27, 1850, the idea of it first occurred to him in
connection with the Easter experience two and a half years
earlier. At least the text of the first part, "Come unto me,"
was almost forced upon him while he worshiped in the Frue

Kirke on the last days of Holy Week; for it faced him in the conspicuous letters carved on the base of Thorvaldsen's statue of Christ.

About the four great books which are the principal subject of this chapter I say almost nothing here, except to implore my reader to read them. They bear witness so directly that they need no introduction. I have hardly any other purpose in writing this book but to induce people to read these great works.

But I will say something with a view to avoiding a misunderstanding to which S.K. himself gave occasion when the second edition of *Training* appeared in the midst of his open attack and to sharpen his polemic he declared that if the book were published then for the first time he would withdraw the Preface which was three times repeated and the Moral which concludes the first part. They then seemed to him to soften too much the severity of the book and might even be regarded as a retraction. I quote here the first paragraph of the Moral: "And what does all this mean? It means that everyone for himself, in quiet inwardness before God, shall humble himself before what it is to be in the strictest sense a Christian, admit candidly before God how it stands with him, so that he might accept the grace which is offered to everyone who is imperfect, that is, to everyone. And then no further; then for the rest let him attend to his work, be glad in it, love his wife, be glad in her, bring up his children in joyfulness, love his fellow men, rejoice in life. If anything further is required of him, God will surely let him understand, and in such case will also help him further; for the terrible language of the Law is so terrifying because it seems as if it were left to man to hold fast to Christ by his own power, whereas in the language of love it is Christ that holds him fast. So if anything further is required of him, God will surely let him understand; but this is required of everyone, that before God he shall candidly humble himself in view of the requirements of ideality. And therefore these should be heard again and again in their infinite significance. To become a Christian has become a thing of naught, mere tomfoolery, something which everyone is as a matter of course, something one slips into more easily than into the most insignificant trick of dexterity."

I cling to this moral—not merely because I personally need the comfort of grace, but because I believe that it is an integral factor in the thought of S.K., who was not only severity but also leniency. Compassion and leniency were expressed, as he himself affirmed, in the Discourses published under his own name, whereas until the open attack severity was expressed only by the pseudonyms.

This is an appropriate place to affirm that S.K. was in the broadest sense of the word a Catholic Christian, because in the best sense of the word he was a humanist. He revolted against the one-sidedness of the Protestant Reformation, and more violently against every sectarian division in the Lutheran Church. Strangely enough, he ignored the Calvinistic branch of Protestantism as completely as if it did not exist. He expected that in view of the fierce polemic in which his life ended, future generations would regard him as an exponent of surly and narrow-minded religiosity, though even then he was contending for no sectarian interest but for the Christianity of the New Testament, and he counted that the copious aesthetic production of his early period ought to be enough to refute such a false judgment. The aesthetic, he affirmed, is not abolished in the religious stage but merely dethroned, and he plumed himself upon the fact that when he was engrossed with the most decisive religious writings he had published an aesthetic appreciation of a favorite actress.

One of the difficulties we encounter in the effort to understand his works is due to the fact that his interests were so many, and his culture so broadly humane. Not many theologians of any age have been more familiar with, or so enamored of, the culture of Greece and Rome, or with the early Christian authors, or with the secular interests of the Middle Ages, not to speak of contemporary literature, of music, of the modern drama, even of the farce. It was this broad humanism which in his early days made him critical of "the stuffy atmosphere" he found in the churches, and inclined him later to regard with sympathy the Church of Rome. Brandes may not have been quite right in the opinion that, if S.K. had lived longer, he would have had no alternative but "to make a leap into the black abyss of Catholicism, or over to the headland of freedom"—meaning the land of free-thought which he represented. Perhaps this was a misunderstanding; yet it is a fact that in his own day and during the century following it he has prompted many to enter the Church of Rome.

The "Moral" which prompted me to make this comment expresses a position which is very characteristic of Catholicism, whether S.K. was aware of it or not. I cannot pursue here the remoter implications; but essentially it means reintroducing the notion of the *consilia,* the distinction between "counsels of perfection" and the duties which are imperative for every Christian. This distinction Protestantism rejected with disdain; but the consequence, instead of being a leveling up has been a leveling down of the sterner maxims of the Gospel, which literally required a following of Christ through suffering to martyrdom. As S.K. put it, "place No. 1 has fallen out, and place No. 2 has become the first place"—in other words, the place of the "disciple," "the witness," the saint, the martyr, even the monk, has fallen out, and the highest thing left, even as an ideal, is the average Christian practice in Christendom. This was the gist of S.K.'s complaint against the Established Church, "especially in Protestantism, and more especially in Denmark"; and all he demanded was that the Church, through the mouth of its chief bishop, should admit that the Christianity commonly inculcated was only a mild accommodation to human weakness. With that admission, he thought, a little honesty would be introduced into the situation, and by holding high the ideal men would be taught in their weakness to take refuge in grace. Then he would be ready to say of the Established Church, "Seest thou these great buildings? . . . not one stone shall be torn down." He believed that he was proposing to Bishop Mynster the one way of vindicating the Church.

The title of this chapter recalls the expression S.K. used to describe his perilous position in 1849: he was "venturing far out." That made this uneventful year one of the most agitated, if not the most crucial year of his whole life. The point to be noted is, that in spite of all his fear and trembling, in spite of his titubation on the brink of the abyss, and in spite of the fact that hitherto he had in no single instance succeeded in overcoming his scruples and accomplishing boldly what he had undertaken to do—whether it was to marry, or to follow the profession for which he was prepared—he now took the plunge and ventured indeed far out. We shall see in the next chapter that this plunge was decisive.

HOLDING OUT

1852–1854

INCREDIBLE as it may seem, the Kierkegaard we are dealing with now is a resolute man. His Journals, which during these three years are more voluminous than ever, no longer contain excruciating debates as to whether he should seek an appointment in the Church, whether it would be given to him, how long his money will last, how clearly he ought to speak his mind, etc., etc. His resolution was definitely made, and never again was it shaken. From a very early period he had an exceedingly complicated knot to unravel. We have seen with sympathy, or perhaps with impatience, how long and desperately he struggled with it; and it seemed as if, in spite of the most eminent dialectic skill and the most tireless reflection, he would be unable to solve the problem. But now we behold with amazement that all this labor was not in vain, that he has reached a simple, clear and definite solution, which illuminates for him only too searchingly the defects of his behavior hitherto, and indicates precisely the path assigned him for the few remaining years of his life, which terminated, in fact, four years later in the midst of the resolute act which he understood as the definite task appointed him to do in the service of God and man, so that his death, as he regarded it, was the appropriate conclusion of his task.

I quote a few paragraphs from two very significant entries which were written near the beginning of this period, in June 1852: "The fact that I do not make my life more comfortable, do not seek to assure myself of a livelihood, one might ascribe to pride, to arrogance. Is it that? Well, who knows himself so perfectly? But should it be that, or at least something like that, my thought is that just by holding out in this way this fault must eventually be manifested, and I must suffer my punishment. Moreover, my thought is as follows: It seems to me that I am morally bound by what I have understood, that the higher interest can require me to hold out as long as there is even the least possibility. As soon as I make my life finitely secure (while it still would be possible for me to hold out a little longer) I am finitized, and the whole power of worldliness will at once understand that there is no more any danger. I have constantly the feeling that there is something higher stirring within me, I believe that I am not justified in any other course but in holding out as long as possible in order to be at its service. If I should have made a mistake—in God's name!—this sin can be forgiven, and its punishment will come in this life; but if I should break off wilfully, true as it may be that I need to do something for my living—if I thus break off...and there was something higher stirring which would come to evidence in and through me—ah, this I shall first discover in eternity, when it will be too late."

" . . . And now I have reached the point where I was in '48, but with a higher understanding. I understand myself in my heterogeneousness, my unlikeness to others. On the other hand, I stand in a direct relationship to Christianity, so that what I now shall have to suffer does not come under the rubric of intellectual enthusiasm for the question what Christianity is, but under that of suffering for the doctrine, so that in bearing it I have the direct support of Christianity.

"What must be emphasized is the following of Christ— and I must remain as I am in my unlikeness to others. O my God, it was Thou indeed that didst hold Thy hand over me, so that in the long period of my anxiety I did not set out and take a step in the direction of likeness, and thereby become guilty of procuring an abortion (to use the strong expression employed in one of the Journals of that time to describe what I then feared), becoming entangled moreover in something in which I should discover nothing but worry, because I am not at home in it, and finally might incur a protest when I arrive in eternity. 'Imitation' must be insisted upon. But 'without authority'—this is and remains my category.

"O my God, how clearly now it all stands out before me. How infinitely much has already been done for me. It is not heterogeneity I must now pray myself out of, that is not the task, but, alas, I shall never know the security which consists in being like others. No, I remain in unlikeness. There I remain with Thee—and verily I recognize the blessedness of it. The only thing which made me fearful was the thought that possibly the task was a different one, that I ought to get out of my unlikeness—a thought which may very well have been prompted by the wish to make my life secure.

"So I am courageous and joyful—not indeed with an ebullient joy as in '48, for then anxiety about my livelihood was more remote—if at this moment I were free from it, I should exult again, for all things are good. However, during the past year I have suffered so much and have been compelled to view my task so seriously that doubtless I am a good deal changed. But even with such economic anxiety as I have, conjoined with the picture my knowledge of the world enables me to paint of the uproar which will ensue, I am calm and joyful, perhaps more definitely so, with a more tranquil confidence, than in '48."

From this time on there was no relapse, no symptom of

the hesitation which is so painful a feature of the earlier Journals. His duty became more and more definite. In 1853 he wrote: "I have something on my conscience as a writer. Let me indicate precisely how I feel about it. There is something quite definite I have to say, and I have it so much upon my conscience that (as I feel) I dare not die without having uttered it. For the instant I die and thus leave this world (so I understand it) I shall in the very same second (so frightfully fast it goes!), in the very same second I shall be infinitely far away, in a different place where still within the same second (frightful speed!) the question will be put to me: 'Hast thou uttered the definite message *quite definitely?*' And if I have not done so, what then? . . ."

This is not in the Journal, it is an article written as if for publication, and therefore as if in a public confession he reviews with the utmost candor the reluctance he had felt at every step in his career as an author against uttering clearly this definite message. At every step conscience had upbraided him. At first he had said it enigmatically—and then done everything to insure that no one would give heed to it. When he had said it more distinctly he tried all the harder to obscure the impression. And in this he succeeded, even in the case of so plain a book as *Training in Christianity*. This, I suppose, is the most humiliating confession he was ever obliged to make, for it amounts to a retraction of the pseudonyms and the whole elaborate apparatus of "indirect communication." But for this reason it shows better than any other passage the degree of lucidity he had attained in self-knowledge. For all that, he did not of course know definitely what he was to do, and in October 1854 he said to God: "Thou knowest that it has not been made quite clear to me what I must do. Only so much have I understood, that I must hold out." In fact, during these three years there was nothing for him to do but to hold out. At the end of his life he expressed his situation in these figurative terms:

"Imagine a big, well-trained hunting dog. He accompanies his master on a visit to a family where, as all too often in our time, there is a whole assembly of ill-behaved youths. Their eyes hardly light upon the hound before they begin to maltreat it in every kind of way. The hound, which was well trained, as these youths were not, fixes his eye at once upon his master to ascertain from his expression what he is expected to do. And he understands the glance to mean that he is to put up with all the ill-treatment, to accept it indeed as though it was sheer kindness they conferred upon him. Thereupon the youths of course became still more rough, and finally they were agreed that it must be a prodigiously stupid dog which puts up with everything.

"The dog meanwhile is concerned only about one thing: what the master's glance commands him to do. And, lo, that glance is suddenly altered; it signifies—and the hound understands it at once—use your strength. That instant with a single leap he has seized the biggest lout and thrown him to the ground—and now no one stops him, only the master's glance—and the same instant he is as he was a moment before.—Just so with me."

And he follows this with another picture:

"Hast thou ever seen a hound—all bloody, exhausted by the effort and by the loss of blood incurred by the struggle within the hole of the fox? Yet he does not let go; he has fastened his fangs in the fox and then dies. I too am exhausted, but I have not let go of my thought, I have not made my life more comfortable, which only would have made less evident what I required. As I have often said,

'The end must be made fast' [that is, the end of the thread must be knotted if one would sew effectively—as he said once with reference to his father's death, and now with a thought of his own]. . . . The lecturing habit cannot be stopped by a new doctrine, but only by a personality."

During this long pause S.K. was of course not idle. He was "loading the gun"; or rather he was setting down in the Journal or on loose sheets observations which might be serviceable when the attack was launched, and which at all events afforded practice in plain speaking and sharp speaking. In a sense he was never more a poet than at this time, for he knew how to use significant images to express his devastating polemic against the establishment.

I must refer to my bigger book for an account of S.K.'s relation to Professor Martensen and Bishop Mynster, who were necessarily the first objects of his attack because they were the most prominent exponents of the Established Church; but here I must say emphatically that the attack upon these two men was not animated by personal hostility. It is true, he had never liked Martensen, yet he had publicly defended him against his detractors by affirming that he was not only the most eminent theologian in Denmark but one who would shine in any university in Germany. But Mynster he admired above every man of his time, and loved him with a singular devotion—which, alas, was destined to be an unhappy love, like his love for Regina. In the public attack these men had to be named, but in the Journal they commonly figure as "the Professor" and "the Prelate." I quote here (omitting quotation marks) three entries which imply Martensen, and one which only in the title names Bishop Mynster.

Holding Out

Let us take mathematics. It is perfectly possible that a celebrated mathematician, for example, had become a martyr for his science—there is nothing therefore to hinder me from becoming professor of what he brought to light; for in this case the essential thing is the teaching, the scientific acquisition, the personal life of the teacher being accidental to that.

But ethico-religiously, and Christianly in particular, there is no teaching in the sense that it is the essential thing and the person is the accidental; in this case imitation is the essential. What nonsense it is therefore that instead of following Christ or the Apostles and suffering as they suffered, one should become professor—of what? Why, of the fact that Christ was crucified and the Apostles scourged. If only at Golgotha there had been a professor at hand who had installed himself at once as professor...of theology? Well yes, you see, at that time theology had not yet emerged, and hence at that time it would have been as clear as could be that, if one were to become professor of anything, it must be of the fact that Christ was crucified. So then to become professor of the fact that another person was put to death. It might be very curious to let such a professor take part in the whole campaign. So then he first became professor of the fact that Christ was crucified. At this point the Apostles began. Then Peter and James [*sic*] were arraigned before the Council and then scourged—that at once becomes a new paragraph, and the professor becomes the very same day professor of the fact that Peter and James were scourged. Thereupon the Council forbids the Apostles to preach Christ.

But what do the Apostles do? They don't let themselves be put out, they continue their preaching, for one must fear God more than men—and neither does the professor let himself be put out; he becomes professor of the fact that Peter and James, in spite of their scourging, didn't let themselves be restrained from preaching the truth. For the professor ought to love the new paragraph more than God and the truth.

The professor constantly follows along. Indeed it is also the cue for the professor to follow—to follow the times, not, however, to follow after or imitate Christ. Assuming that there was a contemporary theological professor at that time when theology had not yet emerged, one would be able to go through the Acts of the Apostles and be oriented by observing what he was now professor of. So it ended with the Apostle being crucified—and the professor became professor of the fact that the Apostle was crucified. Thereafter the professor departed this life with a calm and peaceful death.

Behold, this is the way to put an end to all this scientific method when it becomes too self-important and pretentious: one seizes "the professor" and puts him outside until the admissions are made [i.e. the admission that the whole thing was not genuine Christianity]—and then the whole existing establishment may as well continue to exist.

In any case, "the theological professor" is a *point de vue* in Christendom: in the same degree that "the professor" is regarded as the highest thing, in that same degree one is most disoriented in Christianity; by the way "the professor" is judged one can see the status in Christendom and the doom of Christianity.

Passages are to be found in the New Testament from which one can justify bishops, presbyters and deacons (however little the present examples resemble the original picture), but one will search in vain in the New Testament for a passage where professors of theology are mentioned. Hence one would be tempted to laugh involuntarily if in that passage where it is said that God appointed some to be prophets, others to be apostles, others to be pastors—one would be prompted to laugh involuntarily if it were added, some to be professors of theology. It might just as well read, God appointed some to be privy councillors. "The professor" is a later Christian invention. A later Christian invention indeed, for it was about the time when Christianity began to go backward, and the culminating point of "the professor's" ascent coincides exactly with our age when Christianity is entirely abolished.

JUDAS ISCARIOT

The dreadful word pronounced upon him by Christ Himself was: "It were better for this man if he never had lived." But when in Christendom everything has been set in motion to make Judas out the blackest that was possible, I may nevertheless remark that I could imagine him a whole quality worse. So, as I imagine it, Judas Iscariot was not, as indeed in reality he was, a man in despair who in an instant of fury sells his master for the paltry thirty pieces of silver—where in the smallness of the sum there is a kind of extenuation, as also after a sort in his frightful end. No, Judas is a much more highly cultured man, calm, and in possession of a shrewder understanding of life, of profit. So he goes to the high priests and says to them: "I am willing to betray him. But now hear my conditions. I don't care much about getting a large sum once for all which I might squander in a few years. No, I wish something certain yearly. I am a young man, well and strong, having in all human probability the prospect of a long life before me—and I could wish to lead (married and with a family) an agreeable life with rich opportunity for enjoyment. That is the price." This, according to my notion, is a whole quality more odious—nor do I believe that anything so odious could have occurred in the earlier times, it is reserved for our intelligent times. It is easily seen that I have represented Judas a little *à la* professor. . . .

HOW I FELT WHEN I WAS CONTEMPORARY WITH BISHOP MYNSTER

Imagine a very great ship, greater, if you will, than the biggest ships we have at present, suppose it has room for 1,000 passengers, and of course it is equipped on the greatest possible scale with conveniences, comforts, luxuries, etc. It is towards night. In the cabin they are having a merry time, everything illuminated in the most resplendent way, everything glitters; in short, all is merriment and good cheer, and the joy and tumult of their joyous abandonment to mirth carries out into the night.

Above on the bridge stands the captain, and beside him the next in command. The latter takes the glass from his eye and hands it to the captain, who replies, "There is no need of it, I see well enough the white speck on the horizon—it will be a dreadful night." Thereupon he gives his orders with the noble and intrepid composure which befits an experienced seaman: "The crew will stay on deck all night; I myself will assume command." Then he goes to his berth. It is no great library he has with him, yet he has a Bible. He opens it, and strangely enough he opens it precisely at the text, "This night thy soul shall be required of thee." Strange! After a moment of devotion he dresses for night duty, and now he is the practiced seaman through and through. But in the cabin the merriment goes on; song resounds, and music and noise, the clatter of dishes and flagons, champagne sparkles, and the captain's health is drunk, etc., etc.—"It will be a dreadful night," and perhaps this night thy soul shall be required of thee.

Is not this dreadful? And yet I know of a still more dreadful thing. All is the same, except that the captain is another. In the cabin all goes merrily, and the merriest of all is the captain.

The white speck is there on the horizon; it will be a dreadful night. But no one sees the white speck or divines what it means. But no—this would not be the most dreadful thing—there is one that sees it and knows also what it means—but he is a passenger. He has no command on the ship and is unable to do anything decisive. However, to do the only thing in his power, he sends a message to the captain to come on deck for an instant. There is considerable delay; finally he comes out but will listen to nothing, and with a jest he hastens down to the noise and reckless joy of the society in the cabin, where the captain's health is drunk and he responds complacently. In his anguish the poor passenger ventures once more to disturb the captain; but now the captain has even become discourteous to him. Nevertheless the speck on the horizon remains unchanged —"it will be a dreadful night."

Is not this still more dreadful? It was dreadful for those

thoughtless, noisy passengers, dreadful that the captain is the only one who knows what impends—ah, but the important thing is that the captain knows it. So it is more dreadful when the only one who sees and knows is...a passenger.

That (in a Christian sense) there is to be seen a white speck on the horizon which means that a dreadful tempest is impending—that I knew; but, alas, I was and am only a passenger.

Imagine a young officer—we can imagine him a competent young officer. There is a battle. Our young officer commands half a battery. He sees (and we can imagine that he sees aright), he sees: "my three cannon trained upon that spot—and the victory is ours." But just at that spot (or if not exactly at that spot, yet in such a position that it is impossible to train the cannon upon that spot), just there stands his own general, the old Fieldmarshal Friedland, with his staff. Imagine what that young man must suffer! "I am young," says he to himself, "my future would be made if I could succeed in using my cannon. Oh, but this is the instant to do it!" The instant passes. "A fig for myself," says the young officer, "but the battle could be decided if only I could use my cannon. Oh, this is indeed dreadful that it is my own general who stands there so that I cannot succeed in using my cannon."

S.K.'s aim was the deplorable state of Christianity in Christendom, his "one thesis" was that "Christianity no longer exists," but he could not shoot without wounding his old bishop and the professor who succeeded him as Primate of Denmark. I conclude this chapter with four entries which in one way or another depict the deplorable state of the Church. It will be seen that these passages, though they were not written expressly for publication, are as perfect in form as anything that can be found in his books, and it would be a shame if some of them were not made available in English. Thirty of the polemical entries made during this period (that is perhaps one-tenth of them) can be read in Dru's translation of the *Journal,* but only one of those which I quote here is included.

CHRISTIANITY A FORTRESS

Imagine a fortress, absolutely impregnable, provisioned for an eternity.

There comes a new commandant. He conceives that it might be a good idea to build bridges over the moats—so as to be able to attack the besiegers. *Charmant!* He transforms the fortress into a country-seat—and naturally the enemy takes it.

So it is with Christianity. They changed the method—and naturally the world conquered.

CHRISTIANITY—THE STATE

Take a symbol. When a cabman, for example, sees a perfectly admirable horse five years old and without a blemish, the very ideal of what a horse should be, a fiery, snorting steed such as never before was seen—then says the cabman, "No, that's a horse I can't bid on, nor can I afford to pay for it, and even if I could, it wouldn't be suitable for my use." But when some half score years have gone by, when that splendid horse is now spavined and lame, etc., then the cabman says, "Now I can bid on it, now I can pay for it, and I can get so much use out of it, or what is left of it, that I can really take pleasure in spending a little to feed it."

So it is with the State and Christianity. With the proud air Christianity had when it first entered the world—"No," every state might say, "that religion I can't buy, and not only that, but I can say, Good Lord deliver me from buying that religion, it would be certain ruin to me." But then as Christianity in the course of some centuries had become spavined, chest-foundered, and generally made a mess of, then said the State, "Yes, now I can bid for it; and with my cunning I perceive very well that I can have so much use and profit out of it that I can really take pleasure in spending something to polish it up a bit."

If only Christianity in gratitude for its polishing doesn't become itself again and polish off the State!—"Ouch! Good Lord deliver us! Every state can see that this religion is my ruin." The cabman is well secured, he has bought shrewdly, he runs no risk that the twenty-year-old hackney jade can become again the five-year-old, which, according to the cabman's judgment, no cabman can be served by, just as little, precisely as little as the State can be served by... Christianity eternally young.

THE DOMESTIC GOOSE

A Revivalistic Meditation

Suppose it was a fact that geese could talk. They then would have so arranged it that they could have their religious worship, their divine service. Every Sunday they came together, and a gander preached. The essential content of the sermon was: what a lofty destiny the goose had, what a high goal the Creator (and every time his name was mentioned the geese curtsied and the ganders bowed their heads) had set before the goose; by the aid of wings it could fly away to distant regions, blessed climes, where properly it was at home, for it was only a stranger here. So it was every Sunday. And as soon as the assembly broke up each waddled home to his own affairs. And again the next Sunday to divine worship, and then again home—and that was the end of it, they throve and were well-liking, became plump and delicate—and then were eaten on Martinmas Eve—and that was the end of it.

That was the end of it. For though the address sounded so lofty on Sunday, the geese on Monday were ready to recount to one another what befell a goose that had wished to make serious use of the wings the Creator had given him, designed for the high goal that was proposed to him—what befell him, what a terrible death he encountered. This the geese could talk about knowingly among themselves. But of course to speak about it on Sundays would be unseemly; for, said they, it would then become evident that our divine worship is really only fooling God and ourselves.

Among the geese, however, there were some individuals which seemed to be suffering and grew thin. About them it was currently said among the geese, "There you see what it leads to when flying is taken seriously. For because their hearts are occupied with the thought of wanting to fly, therefore they become thin, do not thrive, do not have the grace of God as we have who therefore become plump and delicate."

And so the next Sunday they went again to divine worship, and the old gander preached about the lofty goal the Creator (here again the geese curtsied and the ganders bowed their heads) had set before the goose, whereto the wings were designed.

So with the divine worship of Christendom. Man too has wings, he has imagination . . .

And then when someone reads this he says, "That's pretty" —and there it ends, he then waddles home to his affairs and becomes (or at all events endeavors with all his might to become) plump, delicate, fat—but on Sunday the parson preachifies thus, and he harkens to it—exactly like the geese.

THE SPIRIT

It is not as scoffers and freethinkers boldly affirm, or as the half-experienced in despair or in revolt say with a sigh, or noisily, that there exists no such Spirit which when one summons it will entirely recreate a man, renew him, give him strength for self-denial, all possible self-denial. No, it is not thus. Such a Spirit really exists. But the fact is that for one who is aware of this it is so terrible a thing to call this Spirit that he dare not do it, especially one who from childhood is coddled by grace, coddled by being told that everything is leniency. For in that way he must get an entirely different conception of God, and, ah, his prayer must become entirely different from that to which he was accustomed from childhood and which was his blessed delight.

Take a symbol. There is a winged horse, more than winged, it has an infinite speed, once you mount it you are at more than a world's distance away from this world and its way of thinking and its life and its conceptions and the understanding of your contemporaries. The freethinkers, the scoffers, the half-experienced, are all on the alert to deny that such a horse exists—all with the hypocritical pretence that, if such a horse did exist, they would be ready enough to mount it.

And, ah, here lies the difficulty for all of us in Christendom who yet have some Christianity. We cannot deny that such a horse exists, that it is only waiting for us to give ourselves up to it entirely—then it will surely take care of the rest.

GODLY SATIRE

WHEN the time came for him to speak S.K. did indeed say the definite thing he had to say, he said it again and again, and he said it very definitely. Essentially he had only one thesis, that "Christianity no longer exists." "O Luther," he exclaimed, "you had ninety-five theses—terrible! And yet, in a deeper sense, the more theses there are, the less terrible it is. The situation now is far more terrible—I have only one thesis." But this one thesis was accompanied and illustrated by a torrent of satire. His attack upon the Established Church of Denmark, and implicitly upon Christianity as a whole wherever it has settled contentedly upon the lees, ought to be widely known. In fact, it was the first thing to be translated into German and into Italian —in the interest of anti-clericalism or anti-Christianity. That was a misunderstanding, and in a very different interest I am eager to see it translated into English—now that S.K.'s other works are known and this will not be misunderstood. At this moment it is the only important part of his production which has not yet found a translator, and if no one else will undertake it, I will, though I am not eager to do it, for I have done my share and would willingly be relieved. It must be made known, for it is a godly satire, and it is important that the clergy at least should hear it. A godly satire—for on his death-bed S.K. said to his old friend Pastor Boesen, "You must note that I have seen from the very inside of Christianity." It is the only notable satire upon the Church which was not written by an outsider and an opponent. And yet it was satire. Hence it was one-sided and

239

exaggerated. When Pastor Boesen tried to get him to retract some of his statements, affirming that they "did not correspond to reality and were more severe" than need be, S.K. patiently replied, "So it must be, otherwise it is of no avail; that I am sure of—when the bomb bursts it must be thus." Not only was the attack one-sided, but I have the impression that S.K., who with good reason could boast that "the other side always finds in me its warmest advocate," had in the heat of controversy ceased to be dialectical in this sense, did not see or would not permit himself to see "the other side."

The controversy was so sharp that not much of the material he had amassed in three years of waiting was appropriate when the bomb burst and the attack had to be sharply directed to the need of the instant. But his resourcefulness was limitless. What he published in these nine months fills 369 pages in the latest edition of his *Works*. But that is not nearly so much as he wrote in his Journal during the last five months of waiting. S.K. was a copious man; he wrote big books, and often wrote diffusely. Everything he wrote now was pungent, brief, addressed to the man in the street, so written that he who runs could read. It had an immense effect, an effect which was the more profound for the fact that it drew attention to his later works, and the publication of a new edition of *Training in Christianity*, which came out in the midst of the fray, added weight to it. Though it did not avail to destroy the Established Church, it upset the colossal figure of Bishop Mynster and the less imposing figure of Martensen.

But after this preliminary orientation I must start at the beginning.

Reluctant as S.K. was to begin the attack while the old

Bishop still lived, he was many times on the point of doing
it. For how could he be sure that he would outlive the
Bishop, or that his money, the little that was left of his
fortune, would hold out? Bishop Mynster died on June
30, 1854, he was buried on July 7, and on July 5, the Sunday preceding the funeral, Professor Martensen pronounced
the official eulogy upon the deceased prelate, in which he
affirmed that the "irreplaccable" Bishop (whom he expected to replace) was "a genuine witness for the truth,
not only in word and profession but in deed and in truth,"
that he formed part of "the holy chain of witnesses which
stretches from the days of the Apostles." S.K. had no doubt
that the use of this term, "witness for the truth," which he
used so emphatically and had so highly exalted, was intended to pique him, and he took it as the signal for as-
sault. He wrote at once a scathing denunciation of Martensen, in which he exposed the serious shortcomings of the
late Bishop, and asked insistently whether the Professor
was telling the *truth*. This was written for publication in
a daily paper and was dated February 1854. But a very
delicate point of honor held him back. He felt that he could
not publish such an attack upon Martensen before he was
appointed to the vacant see, as he was sure to be, if there
were no such interference. Martensen was appointed to the
bishopric on April 30 and consecrated on June 5—and still
S.K. did not feel free to begin until there had been brought
to completion a popular subscription which had been started
for a memorial to the late Bishop. Were it not for this delay his period of waiting would have been shortened by
almost a year.

Not till December 18, 1854, did he publish in the *Fatherland* the attack he had written in February, but he pub-

lished it with the original date, to show how long he had waited. It produced the utmost consternation—and also incredulous surprise. For S.K. had always been known as a conservative, a loyal supporter of Church and State; and his contemporaries could only suppose that he had gone mad. So people often think today. For how could so religious a man attack the Church unless he had lost his senses? The fact that he died in the midst of this attack lends color to the suspicion that all this was a symptom of his illness. But the extraordinary ability of the attack, and the concentrated power with which he sustained it for nine months, is sufficient proof of his mental soundness; and we who have followed the course of his life up to this point are in a position to perceive that he was never more sane, and that the attack upon the Established Church was the logical and necessary outcome of all his thinking.

Beginning with the thin edge of the wedge, i.e. with a polemic narrowed down to two persons, which was no part of his original plan for the campaign, he continued with twenty articles in the *Fatherland*—averaging one a week—which gradually widened the field of discussion. Just before the last of them appeared at the end of May he issued as a separate tract what he called "The Cry," referring to Matt. 25. 6. The gist of it was expressed in few words:

THIS MUST BE SAID; SO BE IT SAID

"Whoever thou art, whatever thy life may be, my friend —by ceasing to take part (if in fact thou dost) in the public performance of divine worship as it now is, thou hast one guilt the less, and a great one, that thou dost not take part in holding God to be a fool, and in calling that the Christianity of the New Testament which is not the Christianity of the New Testament."

This was dated December 24, 1854, to show that it was with this he had meant to begin. S.K. expected that this would "bring about a catastrophe"—by which he meant that he would be arrested, probably imprisoned, and perhaps put to death by the mob. In this instance his vivid imagination led him far astray. The Cultus Minister happened to be a wise man, and it is said that the Prime Minister let it be known that if an author who had shed so much luster upon Denmark were arrested, he would at once release him; and among the people, especially the youth of the land, he found his most enthusiastic supporters. The clergy were for the most part exasperated; but since they were generally ignorant of S.K.'s works, they were neither able to understand what the conflict was all about, nor to make any adequate reply. Most of the replies were anonymous. Bishop Martensen, after a lame attempt to answer the charge brought against him, thought it more dignified to keep silent. "The establishment," said S.K., "is so demoralized that one can spit in its face, and it takes care to sneak away." Doubtless he was disappointed that no violence was done him—for that would have helped his cause. He wondered that people who were accustomed to go to church still continued to do so. This shows that with regard to the "Midnight Cry" he had a blind spot. To me it seems the least effective feature of his campaign, if it was not a tactical blunder. He was himself a regular church-goer up to the time when he wrote this "cry." He had not missed hearing a single sermon of Mynster's except the last. And certainly he did not expect the Establishment to fall like the walls of Jericho, for he knew that it was "a machine which would go buzzing on."

"Let us try a thought-experiment," he said. "If one could establish the fact that Christ never existed, nor the Apostles either, that the whole thing was a poetical invention—in case nothing was done on the part of the State or the congregations, no indication that they would suppress the livings, I should like to see how many parsons would resign their posts." He expected a reformation, because it was obviously needed; but he could not tell when it would come —and it has not come yet. In an entry entitled, "How I understand the future," he said: "Certainly things must be reformed, and it will be a frightful reformation, compared with which the Lutheran Reformation will be hardly more than a jest; a frightful reformation which will have for its watch-word, 'Will faith be found upon earth?' and it will be characterized by the fact that men will fall away from Christianity by the millions, a frightful reformation; for the fact is, Christianity really does not exist, and it is horrible when a generation coddled by a childish Christianity, deluded into the vain notion that they are Christians, have to receive again the death-blow of learning what it is to become a Christian, to be a Christian."

After the "Midnight Cry" he published his last article in the *Fatherland* and then began the publication of a little pamphlet which he called the *Instant,* to which he asked the public to subscribe. It had such success that the circulation was larger than that of the daily paper which he had been using, and he could be sure that it was bought only by persons who were interested in his "plea." It was issued at intervals of about a fortnight; each number was about twenty-four pages long and contained some seven or eight brief articles—of course all by S.K. The ninth number was published on September 24, and the tenth was ready to be printed when he died.

In Denmark the effect of these tracts was enormous, and they were promptly translated in the Swedish papers. S.K. had become again a popular figure. "It was time for him to die," said Goldschmidt in an appreciative notice, "for popularity was the last thing he could endure." It was a matter of course that freethinkers and sectaries should welcome S.K.'s attack upon the Established Church, but the sequel proved that it was welcomed by many within the Church, even among the pastors. The effect of S.K.'s works at that time was, as it has been ever since, to persuade some that they did not properly belong to the Church, to stimulate others to become better Protestants, and to induce a few to become Catholics.

During this period of strife S.K. received no visitors, replied to no letters, and commonly conversed with no one in the street. But Hans Brøchner relates that he encountered him several times and was amazed at the confidence and peace expressed in his countenance and by his speech.

No adequate notion of the character of this polemic can be had by reading a few samples; but here are six which I have selected. The first three are from the *Fatherland,* the others from the *Instant,* the last of them being from that number which was not published

WHAT I WANT

Quite simply—I want honesty. I am not, as one man with the best intentions has desired to represent me, I am not Christian severity contrasted with Christian leniency.

Not at all. I am neither severity nor leniency—I am...
mere human honesty.

I want honesty. If that is what this race and this generation want, if it will uprightly, honestly, frankly, openly,
directly rebel against Christianity and say to God, "We can,
but we will not subject ourselves to this authority"—but observe that it must be done uprightly, honestly, frankly,
openly, directly—well then, strange as it may seem, I am for
it; for honesty is what I want. And wherever there is honesty I can take part. An honest rebellion against Christianity
can only be made when one honestly admits what Christianity is and how one is related to it.

And what have the clergy done for their part? They have
(and I am sorry to be compelled to be so courteous, but it
is true), they have preserved a significant silence. It is curious: if they had replied, something fatuous was sure to come
out, perhaps the whole of it would have been fatuous; now
on the contrary how significant the whole thing has become by reason of this significant silence.

What then does this silence signify? It signifies that what
concerns the clergy is their livings. In any case it signifies
that the clergy are not witnesses for the truth, for in that
case it would be inconceivable that the clergy as a whole—
especially after the Right Reverend Bishop Martensen had
made such a luckless attempt at speaking—could want to
preserve silence when it was openly made evident that official Christianity is both aesthetically and intellectually
ludicrous and indecent, a scandal in the Christian sense.

Assuming on the other hand that a living is what concerns the clergy, this silence is perfectly understandable. For
it was not the livings in a finite sense I was aiming at in my
attack; and well known as I am to the clergy they must

know that such a thing could never occur to me, that not only am I not a politician but I hate politics, that I might indeed be disposed to fight for the clergy were anyone to attack the livings in a finite sense.

Hence this complete silence—my attack did not really concern the clergy, i.e. it has nothing to do with what does concern them. Take an example from—I had almost by a slip of the tongue said "another world"—take an example from the same world, the shopkeeper's world. If it were possible to make an attack upon a merchant in such a way as to show that his wares were bad but without this having the least effect upon the customary turnover of his wares—then he will say, "Such an attack is entirely indifferent to me; whether my wares are good or bad does not concern me at all in and for itself; remember that I am a merchant, what concerns me is the turnover. In fact I am to such a degree a merchant that if one could show not only that the coffee I sell is damaged and spoiled, but that what I sell under the name of coffee is not coffee at all—if only I am assured that such an attack will have no effect whatever upon the turnover, such an attack is entirely indifferent to me. What does it matter to me what sort of thing people guzzle under the name of coffee? All that concerns me is the turnover."

WITNESSES FOR THE TRUTH

This is the point—and it can be shown that the new Bishop by thus canonizing Bishop Mynster makes the whole church establishment an impudent indecency.

For if Bishop Mynster was a witness for the truth, so likewise—as even the blindest can see—every parson in the land is a witness for the truth. For what was aesthetically distinguished and extraordinary in Bishop Mynster has nothing whatever to do with the question whether he was or was not a witness for the truth, a question which has to do with life, character, existence, and in this respect Bishop Mynster was completely homogeneous with every other priest in the land who does not offend against the requirements of civil righteousness. Hence, every priest in the land is also a witness for the truth.

It is quite true that I am acquainted with several men who are in the highest degree respectable, capable, remarkably capable clergymen, but I venture to assert that in the whole realm there is not one who as "a witness for the truth" would not be comical.

THE RELIGIOUS SITUATION

We have, if you will, a complete garrison of bishops, deans, and parsons—learned men, eminently learned, talented, or gifted. With well intentioned zeal they all declaim —do it well, very well, exceedingly well, or fairly well, indifferently well, badly. But not one of them is in the character of the Christianity of the New Testament, and [alluding to a recent article] not even in the character of endeavoring in the direction of the Christianity of the New Testament. But such being the case, the existence of the Christian garrison is so far from being advantageous to Christianity that it is actually a peril, because it so very easily gives rise to the misunderstanding and the erroneous inference that when we have such a complete garrison we naturally have Christianity too. A geographer, for example, having assured himself of the existence of this garrison, would consider that he was completely justified in introducing the statement in his geography that the Christian religion prevails in the land.

We have what one might call a complete inventory of churches, bells, organs, foot-warmers, alms-boxes, hearses, etc. But when Christianity does not exist, the existence of this inventory, Christianly considered, is so far from being advantageous to Christianity that it is actually a peril, because it so very easily gives rise to the misunderstanding and the erroneous inference that, having such a complete Christian inventory, we naturally have Christianity too. A statistician, for example, having assured himself of the existence of this Christian inventory, would consider that he was completely justified in introducing into his statistics the statement that the Christian religion is the prevailing one in the land.

Annoyed by well intentioned efforts to restrain him and quench the fire he had kindled, S.K. wrote

WHAT SAYS THE FIRE CHIEF?

So also in the case of a fire. Hardly is the cry of Fire! heard before a crowd of people rush to the spot, nice, cordial, sympathetic, helpful people; one has a pitcher, another a basin, another a syringe, etc., all of them nice, cordial, sympathetic, helpful people, eager to help put out the fire. But what says the Fire Chief? The Fire Chief he says—to be sure, on other occasions the Fire Chief is a very agreeable and cultured man; but at a fire he is what one might call coarse-mouthed—he says, or rather he bawls out, "Go to hell with your pitchers and squirts." And then when these well intentioned people are perhaps offended, regard it as highly improper that they should be treated in this way, and require at least that they should be addressed with respect—what says the Fire Chief then? Well, on other occasions the Fire Chief is a very agreeable and cultured man who knows how to show to every man the respect which is his due, but at a fire he is rather different, he says, "Where the deuce is the police force?" And when several policemen arrive he says to them, "Rid me of these damn people with their pitchers and squirts; and if they won't yield to fair words, smear them a few on their backs so that we may be rid of them and get to work."

FREDERICK AND JULIANA

A living—and then Juliana—that Frederick and Juliana can come together. Oh these proofs which are produced for the truth of Christianity, these devilish learned and profound and perfectly convincing proofs—what do they all amount to in comparison with Juliana and the fact that in this way Frederick and Juliana can come together? If at any moment the thought should struggle in Frederick, "I myself do not really believe this doctrine, and then to have to preach it to others—" if such thoughts should struggle in Frederick, go to Juliana, she can drive such thoughts away. "Sweet Frederick," she says, "only let us manage to come together. Why do you go and torment yourself with such thoughts? There are surely 1,000 parsons like you; in short, you are a parson like the others."

Juliana, indeed, plays a great role in procuring clergy for the State. And hence they should have been wary about introducing Juliana, and also about introducing livings. For it is possible, as Don Juan says to Zerline, that only in the soft arms of a blameless wife does true felicity reside, and possibly it is true, as both poets and prose writers have testified, that in these soft arms one forgets the world's alarms; but the question is whether there is not also something else one can only too easily forget in these soft arms —namely, what Christianity is. And the older I grow, the clearer it becomes to me that the prattle into which Christianity has sunk, especially in Protestantism, and more especially in Denmark, is due in great part to the fact that these soft arms have come to interfere a little too much, so that for Christianity's sake one might require the respective proprietors of these soft arms to retire a little further into the background.

It is pathetic to reflect that this next passage, which was the last word S.K. wrote in this controversy, and which is so ironical, was not made public because of his sudden illness.

THOU PLAIN MAN!

The Christianity of the New Testament is something infinitely high; but note that it is not "high" in such a sense that this has to do with the difference between man and man with respect to intellectual capacity, etc. No, it is for all. Every one, absolutely every one, if he absolutely wills it, if he will absolutely hate himself, will absolutely put up with everything, suffer everything (and this every man can if he will)—then this infinite height is attainable to him.

Thou plain man! I have not separated my life from thine; thou knowest it, I have lived in the street, am known to all; moreover, I have not attained any importance, I do not belong to any class-egoism, so if I belong anywhere, I must belong to thee, thou plain man, thou who once (when one profiting by thy money pretended to wish thee well), thou who once wast too willing to find me and my existence ludicrous, thou who least of all hast reason to be impatient at or ungrateful for the fact that I am of your company, for which rather the superior people have reason, seeing that I have never decisively united myself to them but merely maintained a loose relationship.

Thou plain man! I do not conceal from thee the fact that, according to my notion, the thing of being a Christian is infinitely high, that in no age are there more than a few who attain it—as Christ's own life attests when one considers the age in which he lived, which His preaching also indicates if one takes it literally. Yet nevertheless it is possible to all. But one thing I adjure thee for the sake of God in heaven and by all that is holy, shun the parsons. . . .

DEATH AND BURIAL

WHILE he was working on the last number of the *Instant* S.K. fell to the floor unconscious. Subsequently he had difficulty in walking, but he recovered sufficiently to take his customary promenades. On October 2 he fell unconscious in the street. His legs were paralyzed. He was carried to Frederik's Hospital, and as he entered it he said, "I have come here to die." His trouble was vaguely attributed to disease of the spine. He affirmed that his ailment was psychic, and that their physical remedies were tried in vain. Forty days later he died.

In the hospital he was tenderly cared for, and he thought it appropriate that he who had lived as the exception to the common rule should die in the common way. His brother Peter was not permitted to enter his room, nor was Giødwad, the editor of the *Fatherland*, with whom he must have had a falling-out of which we know nothing. But Christian and Ferdinand Lund, his two brothers-in-law, were admitted to the sick room, and the most welcome guests were their children, his nephews and nieces. Peter, who had rarely a good word to say for his brother, once remarked that he had "an especial aptitude for being an uncle." His nieces and nephews adored him, and Henriette Lund, in a book called "Memories of Home," has left a charming picture of her beloved Uncle Søren, depicting him in happier times, and finally on his death bed. As she entered the sick room she was overwhelmed by the gleam of light which seemed to radiate from his face: "Never in such a way have I seen the spirit break through the earthly husk and impart to it a

glory as of the transfigured body on the resurrection morning." Her half-brother, Trols Lund, a distinguished his-
torian in later years, was a boy of five, but he remembered
vividly, as one of the most significant experiences of his life,
the visit to Uncle Søren: "He took my hand in both of his
—how small they were and thin and palely transparent—
and said only, "Thanks for coming, Trols; and now farewell'; but these simple words were accompanied by a look
the match of which I have never seen. It shone out from a
sublime and blessed splendor which seemed to me to make
the whole room light. Everything was concentrated in these
eyes as the source of light: heartfelt love, blissful dissolution
of sadness, penetrating clearness of mind, and a jesting
smile." Henrik Lund, a son of Christian, was then a young
physician, living as interne in the same hospital and deeply
attached to his uncle. He tended him devotedly but has left
no report.

The most invaluable information about these last days we
get from Pastor Boesen, the friend of his youth, who visited
him daily, until near the end, when he was called away from
Copenhagen. As a faithful pastor he subjected S.K. to a
catechetical inquisition which must have been very trying to
a dying man, but was borne patiently. The important thing
is that he daily recorded his conversations with S.K. I have
already referred to one of them, and I report here a few
more, distinguishing S.K.'s replies by quotation marks.
When asked if he did not desire to receive the Holy Communion he said, "Yes, but not from a parson." Then it would
be difficult to do it. "Then I die without it." That is not
right. "I will not dispute about it. I have made my choice.
The parsons are royal functionaries, and royal functionaries
are not related to Christianity." That is not true, it does not

accord with reality. "To be sure God is the Sovereign; but then came all these men and wanted to arrange things in Christianity for their convenience—and the 1,000 parsons— so no one can die blessedly without belonging to them, and so they become the sovereign, and it's all over with God's sovereignty. But He must be obeyed in everything." On being asked whether he was able to pray to God in peace, he replied, "Yes, that I can. So first I pray for the forgiveness of sinners, that it may be forgiven them all. Then I pray that I may be free from despair at the moment of death. And then I pray for what I so much desire, that I may know some time beforehand when death will come." And this then is all because you believe, and take refuge in God's grace in Christ? "Why, of course. What else?" When Boesen remarked that he looked so well, as though he could get up and go out, he replied, "Yes, the only trouble is, I can't walk. But indeed there are other means of transportation, I can be lifted up; I have had a feeling of becoming an angel and acquiring wings; and that indeed is what is to come to pass: to sit astride the cloud and sing, Hallelujah!"

S.K. died on November 11. His brother Peter hastened to Copenhagen. The question of his burial was a ticklish one, and it was very ineptly resolved by the decision to hold the funeral service in the Frue Kirke, the most important church in Copenhagen (which was also the Bishop's cathedral), and on November 18, which was a Sunday, when the greatest crowd would be free to come. Peter was to preach the sermon. The church was crowded long before the hour, and a multitude of shabby-looking people had pressed forward near the coffin. There were no priests in the church except Peter Kierkegaard and Dean Tryde, who was to conduct the service at the grave. It looked as though there might be a popular protest against the high-handed way in which the Established Church had taken possession of the body of this man who had so publicly defied it. But at the last moment a large body of students resolutely forced their way to the front and stood guard around the coffin. Peter's sermon was very tactfully calculated to allay the animosity of the crowd, and all went quietly.

At the cemetery things did not go so smoothly. Henrik Lund claimed the right to speak, not merely as a nephew, but as one who was closely related to the deceased by sympathy with his thought. He hotly contested the right of the Church to appropriate his uncle, he read from the Revelation of St. John the letter to the Laodiceans who were neither hot or cold, proving that S.K. was supported by the New Testament, and he commented upon the article in the second number of the *Instant,* "We are all Christians." The Dean reminded him that the law allowed only ordained ministers to speak at a funeral. Whereupon Professor Rasmus Nielsen, who had intended to speak, shrugged his shoulders and went away. It was cold, and the crowd gradually dispersed.

S.K. was buried in the family lot, but no one knows precisely where. Peter did nothing to mark the spot, and only long after was Søren's name inscribed upon a marble slab along with the verse he had chosen from a Danish hymn, and this slab still leans against the pedestal of his father's monument.

EVERY "intellectual tragic hero" must have a last word to say which illuminates the significance of his life and makes clear the pertinence of his sacrifice. So said S.K. (or Johannes de silentio) in *Fear and Trembling*. Hence he sought for the last word of Abraham, and the last word of Socrates. Of course he did not mean the last, half-articulate groan of a dying man; and I do not seek for S.K.'s last word in the account of his death at the hospital. He had been provident enough to utter his last word betimes, and to register it in his Journal as a "report to history." I should not be in doubt as to what he regarded as his "last word," were it not that there are two passages which seem to have equal claim to this distinction. Both were expressed with consummate art, although long ago he had abjured poetry. I cannot choose between them, and therefore must quote them both. The first illuminates figuratively the significance of his life; the second is more pertinent to his death. The first was written in 1854, not long before he died, and it is a strange coincidence that when Andersen was relating the story of his own life in the tale of "The Ugly Duckling," S.K. was giving an account of his in "The Wild Goose," which only in the notion that he might have become a tame goose fails to accord with his history. The last of these "last words" was written prophetically two years earlier.

THE WILD GOOSE

A Symbol

Everyone who knows even a little bit about life in the bird world is aware that between the wild goose and the tame geese, different as they are, there is a sort of understanding. When the flight of the wild geese is heard in the air and there are tame geese on the ground below, the latter are aware of it at once; up to a certain point they have an understanding of what it means; so they too get under way, flapping their wings and cackling as they follow along the ground for a short distance—then it is over.

Once upon a time there was a wild goose. In the autumnal season when the time for migration was near he took notice of some tame geese. He conceived an affection for them, it seemed to him a shame to fly away from them, he hoped to win them to his side so that they might resolve to follow when the flock took flight.

To this end he sought in every way to get in touch with them, trying to allure them to rise a little higher, and then a little higher, with the hope that possibly they might be able to follow the flock, liberated from this pitiable life of mediocrity, waddling on the ground as respectable tame geese.

In the beginning the tame geese thought this very entertaining; they liked the wild goose. But soon they grew tired of him, so they gave him sharp words and derided him as a fantastical fool, without experience and without wisdom. Alas, the wild goose had so deeply committed himself to the tame geese that they had power over him, their words counted with him—the end of the story was that the wild goose became a tame goose.

It can be said in a certain sense that what the wild goose wanted to do was very pretty, yet for all that it was an error; for—this is the rule—a tame goose never becomes a wild goose, but a wild goose can very well become a tame goose.

If what the wild goose did could in any way be accounted

praiseworthy, he should have attended above all to one thing: self-preservation. As soon as he observed that the tame geese were in any way acquiring power over him—then away, away with the flock!

This applies to a genius—the rule is that a tame goose never becomes a wild goose, but on the other hand a wild goose can very well become a tame goose—therefore, be on the alert.

This rule does not apply to Christianity. Doubtless the true Christian over whom the Spirit broods is as different from other men as the wild goose is from the tame geese. But the thing Christianity teaches is what a man can *become* in life. Here then there is hope that a tame goose may become a wild goose. Therefore stay with them, occupied only with one, to win the individual to a transformation—but for the love of God in heaven, take care of this: so soon as thou dost observe that the tame geese are beginning to acquire power over thee, then off, off and away with the flock! lest it end with thy becoming a tame goose blissfully content with a pitiable condition.

"THE SACRIFICED ONES," THE CORRECTIVES

As a skillful cook says with regard to a dish in which already a great many ingredients are mingled, "It needs just a little pinch of cinnamon" (and we perhaps could hardly tell by the taste that this little pinch of spice had entered into it, but the cook knew precisely why and precisely how it affected the taste of the whole mixture); as an artist says with a view to the color effect of a whole painting which is composed of many, many colors, "There and there, at that little point, must be applied a little touch of red" (and we perhaps could hardly even discover that the red is there, so carefully has the artist suppressed it, although he knows exactly why it should be introduced), so it is with divine governance.

Oh, the governance of the world is a prodigious house-keeping and a grandiose painting. Yet He, the Master, God in heaven, behaves like the cook and the artist. He says, "Now there must be introduced a little pinch of spice, a little touch of red." We do not comprehend why, we are hardly aware of it, since that little bit is so thoroughly absorbed in the whole. But God knows why.

A little pinch of spice! That is to say: Here a man must be sacrificed, he is needed to impart a particular taste to the rest.

These are the correctives. It is a woeful error if he who is used for applying the corrective becomes impatient and would make the corrective normative for others. This is the temptation to bring everything to confusion.

A little pinch of spice! Humanly speaking, what a painful thing to be thus sacrificed, to be the little pinch of spice! But on the other hand God knows well the man whom He elects to employ in this way, and so He also knows how, in the inward understanding of it, to make it so blessed a thing for him to be sacrificed, that among the thousands of divers voices which express, each in its own way, the same thing, his also will be heard, and perhaps especially his, which is truly *de profundis,* proclaiming: God is love. The birds on the branches, the lilies in the field, the deer in the forest, the fishes in the sea, countless hosts of happy men, exultantly proclaim: God is love. But underneath all these sopranos, supporting them as it were, as the bass part does, is audible the *de profundis* which issues from the sacrificed one: God is love.

1. *Either/Or*, Feb. 29, 1843, 792 pp., Princeton University Press 1944 in 2 volumes, the first by Mrs. Swenson, based on her husband's translations, the second by Walter Lowrie.

2. *Either/Or*, Doubleday 1959, Anchor paperback A 181 a-b, translated by David F. and Lillian Marvin Swenson and Walter Lowrie. Translations and notes revised together with a foreword by Howard A. Johnson.

3. *Fear and Trembling*, 1843, Princeton University Press 1941, translated by Walter Lowrie.

4. *The Sickness unto Death*, 1849, Princeton University Press 1941, translated by Walter Lowrie.

5. *Fear and Trembling & The Sickness unto Death*, Doubleday 1954, Anchor paperback A 30, translated by Walter Lowrie. Translation revised by Howard A. Johnson.

6. *Repetition*, 1843, Princeton University Press 1941. Harper Torchbook TB 117, 1964. Translated by Walter Lowrie.

7. *Edifying Discourses*, 1843-1844, Augsburg Publishing House 1948, Vols. I-IV, translated by David F. and Lillian Marvin Swenson.

8. *Edifying Discourses*, Harper & Row 1958, Torchbook paperback TB 32, edited with an introduction by Paul L. Holmer. Translated by David F. and Lillian Marvin Swenson.

9. *Philosophical Fragments Or A Fragment of Philosophy*, 1844, Princeton University Press 1941. Translated by David F. Swenson. Published for the American Scandinavian Foundation.

10. *Philosophical Fragments*, Princeton University Press 1963. Originally translated and introduced by David F. Swenson; new introduction and commentary by Niels Thulstrup; translation revised and commentary translated by Howard V. Hong.

11. *The Concept of Dread*, 1844, Princeton University Press 1944. Translated by Walter Lowrie; 2nd edition, translation revised by Howard A. Johnson, 1957.

12. *Stages On Life's Way*, 1845, Princeton University Press 1940. Translated by Walter Lowrie.

13. *Thoughts on Crucial Situations in Human Life*, 1845, Augsburg Publishing House 1941. Translated by David F. Swenson, edited by Lillian Marvin Swenson.

14. *Concluding Unscientific Postscript to the Philosophical Fragments*, 1846, Princeton University Press 1941. Translated by David F. Swenson and Walter Lowrie. Published for the American Scandinavian Foundation.

15. *The Present Age & Two Ethico-Religious Treatises*, 1846 & 1859, Oxford University Press 1940. Translated by Alexander Dru and Walter Lowrie.

16. *Works of Love*, 1847, Princeton University Press 1946. Translated by David F. and Lillian Marvin Swenson.

17. *Works of Love*, Harper & Row 1962. Translated with an introduction and notes by Edna and Howard Hong.

18. *Purity of Heart*, 1847, Harper & Row 1938; revised edition 1948; Torchbook paperback TB 4, 1956. Translated by Douglas V. Steere.

19. *Purify Your Hearts!*, C. W. Daniel Co. 1937. Translated by A. S. Aldworth and W. S. Ferrie.

20. *Consider the Lilies*, C. W. Daniel Co. 1940. Translated by A. S. Aldworth and W. S. Ferrie.

21. *The Gospel of Suffering & The Lilies of the Field*, Augsburg Publishing House 1948. Translated by David F. and Lillian Marvin Swenson.

22. *Gospel of Sufferings*, J. Clarke 1955. Translated by A. S. Aldworth and W. S. Ferrie.

23. *Christian Discourses*, 1848, Oxford University Press (New York) 1938; Galaxy paperback 49. Translated by Walter Lowrie. This volume also contains: *The Lilies of the Field and the Birds of the Air*, 1849, and *The High Priest—The Publican—The Woman that was a Sinner*, 1849.

24. *Training in Christianity*, 1850, Oxford University Press

(New York) 1941. Translated by Walter Lowrie. This volume also contains *An Edifying Discourse*, 1850.

25. *For Self-Examination & Judge for Yourselves!*, Oxford University Press (New York) 1941. Translated by Walter Lowrie. This volume also contains *Two Discourses at the Communion on Fridays*, 1851, and *The Unchangeableness of God*, 1855.

26. *Attack upon "Christendon,"* 1854-1855, Princeton University Press 1944; Beacon Press paperback 1956.

27. *The Point of View for My Work as an Author*, 1859, Oxford University Press (New York) 1939; newly edited with a Preface by Benjamin Nelson, Harper & Row 1962, Torchbook paperback TB 88.

28. *On Authority and Revelation*, Princeton University Press 1955. Translated with an introduction and notes by Walter Lowrie.

29. *Johannes Climacus*, Stanford University Press 1958. Translated with an assessment by T. H. Croxall.

30. *The Concept of Irony*, 1841, Harper & Row, *forthcoming*. Translation and introduction and notes by Lee M. Capel.

Selections and Anthologies

31. *The Journals of Kierkegaard*, Oxford University Press (New York) 1938; Harper Torchbook edition *forthcoming*. Edited and translated by Alexander Dru.

32. *The Journals of Kierkegaard*, Harper & Row 1959; Torchbook paperback TB 52. Edited and translated by Alexander Dru (an abridgment of No. 31).

33. *Kierkegaard's Diary*, Philosophical Library 1960. Edited by Peter P. Rohde, translated by Gerda M. Andersen.

34. *A Kierkegaard Anthology*, Princeton University Press 1946; Random House (Modern Library) 1959.

35. *Kierkegaard*, Cassell 1955. Selected and introduced by W. H. Auden.

36. *The Living Thoughts of Kierkegaard*, David McKay 1952. Edited by W. H. Auden.

37. *Selections from the Writings of Kierkegaard*, The University of Texas Bulletin, No. 2326, 1923; revised edition, Doubleday 1960, Anchor paperback A 210. Edited and translated by Lee M. Hollander.

38. *The Prayers of Kierkegaard*, University of Chicago Press 1956; Phoenix paperback 1964.

39. *The Witness of Kierkegaard*, Association Press 1960. Edited and translated by Carl Michalson.

40. *Meditations from Kierkegaard*, Westminster Press 1955. Edited and translated by T. H. Croxall.

HOW KIERKEGAARD GOT INTO ENGLISH

MR. CHARLES WILLIAMS of the Oxford University Press, who from the first affectionately fostered the enterprise of publishing S.K.'s works in English, proposed to me several years ago that I ought to write a little book about this story. Although the story contains episodes of some interest, a whole book about it would be pretentious, I thought, and for the very fact that I was *gars magna* in the undertaking I was shy at the thought of telling the tale. But after all who else could tell it? Now, too, when the edition is almost complete the reason for telling it is more obvious, and, as I remarked in the Preface, an occasion here presents itself for telling the story without claiming for it undue importance. Regarded as "padding" it may be said that the purchaser of the book is not paying for it, and no one is required to read it. I might appropriately have introduced it by the caption: To whom it may concern.

Before telling a story which may concern only "that single individual" to whom S.K. addressed himself, I would give a succinct account of the present status of Kierkegaard publications in English, which at this juncture may be of interest to more than one individual, even if it does not interest many. It will be seen from the two lists which follow that six publishers have had a part in the publications of translations of S.K. and that five more have published things about him. I take no account here of articles in reviews, and I include only books which deal exclusively with S.K. It will be seen that Oxford is responsible for ten volumes, large and small, including Dru's big volume of selections from the *Journal* and my big biography, also three big volumes of mine which contain six works which originally were published separately— in all, sixteen translations besides the *Journal*. It is not so evident, but it is true nevertheless that Princeton will be responsible eventually for as great a mass of translation, though it is all comprised in seven volumes, three of which are S.K.'s biggest works. The Augsburg Publishing House at

Minneapolis is a close third with seven volumes to its credit, four of them being translations. Harpers has published one translation, Daniel one, and the short-lived Dragon Press published in its day another. The second list shows that five additional publishers have issued books *about* S.K. For the sake of making these lists more concise I indicate the Oxford University Press by "Oxon.," Princeton University Press by "Prin.," and the Augsburg Publishing House by "Augs." The number of pages (which sometimes I have merely estimated) gives only an approximate indication of the size of the book, inasmuch as the pages vary greatly in dimension and in the character of the type.. Although the translations were made without any regard to the order in which the works were originally published, they now can be listed in the order in which they were produced by S.K.

KIERKEGAARD'S WORKS IN ENGLISH

1 *The Journals, 1834–1855*, selections from 20 vols. translated by Alexander Dru, 665 pp., Oxon. 1938.
2 *The Concept of Irony*, 1841, his Dissertation for the Master's Degree. Mr. Lund, Librarian of Duke University, has undertaken to translate it. 288 pp. A pity that it cannot be ready this year to celebrate the centennial of its production.
3 *Either /or*, Feb. 20, 1843, 792 pp. Mrs. Swenson and I are translating it, being stimulated to this task by the fact that Professor Swenson left translations of nearly half of it. All that has been published of this first and most brilliant work of S.K. is *The Diary of a Seducer* (which ought not to be published separately), translated by Knud Fick, The Dragon Press, 1935.
4 *Eighteen Edifying Discourses*, published from time to time in twos and threes etc. to "accompany" the pseudonymous works, and ultimately collected in one volume. Swenson has translated a few of them, and Mrs. Swenson is translating the rest for publication in 1942. They come to 360 pp.
5 *Repetition*, Oct. 16, 1843, 200 pp., by W.L., Prin. 1941.

6 *Fear and Trembling*, Oct. 16, 1843, 200 pp. by Payne, Oxon. 1939; by W.L. (a duplication), Prin. 1941.

7 *Philosophical Fragments*, June 13, 1844, by Swenson, 135 pp., Prin. for American Scandinavian Foundation 1936.

8 *The Concept of Dread*, June 17, 1844, 280 pp., by Dru, who promises to publish it soon. Oxon.

9 *Prefaces*, June 17, 1844, an amusing book only for those who are familiar with Copenhagen in that age. It will never be translated.

10 *Three Discourses on Imagined Occasions*, April 29, 1845, 160 pp., by Swenson, Augs. 1941.

11 *Stages on Life's Way*, April 30, 1845, by W.L. 479 pp., Prin. 1940.

12 *Concluding Unscientific Postscript to the Philosophical Fragments*, Feb. 27, 1846, by Swenson (finished and edited by W.L.), 584 pp., Prin. for American-Scandinavian Foundation. 1941.

13 *Edifying Discourses in Various Spirits*, March 13, 1847, 416 pp. The first discourse, by Professor Steere, *Purity of Heart*, 207 pp., Harper's, 1938; and (a duplication) by Mrs. Aldworth and her brother the Rev. Mr. Ferrie, *Purify Your Hearts!* Daniel (London) 1938. In 1941 they issued the whole work through the same publisher.

14 *A Literary Review*, March 30, 1846. The latter part (all that need be translated) by Dru, *The Present Age*, 70 pp., Oxon. 1940.

15 *The Works of Love*, Sept. 29, 1847, 400 pp., by Mr. and Mrs. Hong, presumably to be published by Augs.

16 *Christian Discourses*, April 26, 1848, by W.L., 309 pp., Oxon. 1939.

17 *The Crisis and a Crisis in the Life of an Actress*, July 1848. It need not be translated.

18 *Two Minor Ethico-Religious Treatises*, May 19, 1849, 93 pp., No. 1 by Dru, No. 2 by W.L. (in *The Present Age*), Oxon. 1940.

19 *Discourses about the Lilies and the Birds*, May 14, 1849 (to accompany the 2nd ed. of *Either/Or*), by W.L. (in *Christian Discourses*), Oxon. 1940.

20 *The Sickness unto Death*, July 30, 1849, by W.L., 125 pp., Prin. 1941.

21 "The Big Book on Adler," though twice revised, was never published in Danish.

22 "*The High Priest*," "*the Publican*," and "*the Woman that was a Sinner*," Nov. 13, 1849, by W.L., 30 pp. (in *Christian Discourses*), Oxon. 1940.

23 *The Point of View for My Work as an Author*, 1849 (published posthumously), by W.L., 103 pp., Oxon. 1939.

24 "*The Individual*," 1849 (published posthumously), by W.L., 36 pp. (in *The Point of View*), Oxon. 1939.

25 *About My Work as an Author*, about Aug. 7, 1851, by W.L., 24 pp. (in *The Point of View*), Oxon. 1939.

26 *Training in Christianity*, Sept. 27, 1850, by W.L., 254 pp., Oxon. 1941.

27 *An Edifying Discourse*, Dec. 20, 1850, by W.L. (included in the above), Oxon. 1941.

28 *Two Discourses at the Communion*, 1851, by W.L., 25 pp. (included in the next volume), Oxon. 1941.

29 *For Self-Examination*, Sept. 10, 1851, by W.L., 81 pp., Oxon. 1941; and (a duplication) by Mr. and Mrs. Hong, Augs. 1940.

30 *Judge for Yourself!* written in 1851/2, first published in 1876. By W.L., 115 pp. (bound with the foregoing) Oxon. 1941.

31 *God's Unchangeableness*, Aug. 1, 1855 (preached May 18, 1851), by W.L., 18 pp. (bound with the foregoing) Oxon. 1941.

32 The pamphleteering attack upon established Christianity, 381 pages, must eventually be published. It is well that it has not been published in English before all the other works are known. In an anticlerical interest it was the first thing published in German and in Italian—and the only thing in Italian.

BOOKS ABOUT KIERKEGAARD

At this moment a list of all the books published about S.K. in English can be handled easily and briefly. It is a good sign that till now more has been published of S.K. than about him, although of course within a few years the situation will be inverted, and quite rightly.

The Rev. Francis M. Fulford, *Sören Aabye Kierkegaard*, a brochure of 75 pp. privately printed in Cambridge. It has, as the writer confesses, little worth, but it deserves honorable mention as the first attempt to make S.K. known in England.

Professor L. M. Hollander, *Selections from the Writings of Kierkegaard*, 239 pp. University of Texas Bulletin, 1923. This book is out of print, but it too deserves honorable mention as a pioneering venture, the first attempt to translate S.K. into English.

E. L. Allen, *Kierkegaard, his Life and Thought*, 210 pp. Nott, 1935.

The Rev. John M. Bain, D.D., *Sören Kierkegaard, his Life and Religious Teaching*, 160 pp. Student Christian Movement, 1935. (These two books are unsympathetic toward S.K.)

Alexander Dru, translation of Haecker's *Sören Kierkegaard*, 67 pp., Oxon. 1937.

Professor Eduard Geismar, *Lectures on the Religious Thought of Sören Kierkegaard* (with a long and valuable introduction by Professor Swenson), 147 pp., Augs. 1937.

Walter Lowrie, *Kierkegaard*, 656 pp., Oxon. 1938.

M. Channing-Pearce, *The Terrible Chrystal*, 250 pp., Kegan Paul, 1940.

The Rev. William F. Riviere, D.D., *A Pastor Looks at Kierkegaard*, 231 pp., Zondervan (Grand Rapids), 1941.

Professor David F. Swenson, *Something about Kierkegaard*, 300 pp. Augs. 1941.

Coming back home eleven years ago as a superannuated clergyman, after having lived, off and on, for twenty-seven years on the Continent of Europe, I could not but regard myself as a missionary called (though not sent) to mediate the mature culture of Continental Europe to the insular Britons and the still more insular mind of the North American

Continent. The latter more especially, for it is notorious that of late we have been steadily receding from intellectual contact not only with the ancient culture of Greece and Rome but with the traditional culture of Europe, so that in the religious field we have got so far away that Medieval Christianity is almost totally incomprehensible to us, and in the plane of a far distant perspective the Protestant Christianity of the Reformation seems to merge indistinguishably with Catholicism. For this reason our spokesmen are uncomfortably aware that in every ecumenical conference in which they take part they are speaking a language utterly strange to their colleagues. This is certainly not a proud view of my mission, even if it seem supercilious, for I never have claimed to have anything of my own to offer.

After the last war I was impressed by the importance the name of Kierkegaard had acquired throughout the Continent, especially in Germany. I could hardly pick up a serious book without finding his name in it. Every writer who claimed to be abreast of modern thought had to say something about him, and every reputable publisher had to bring out something. S.K. had already taken the place of Nietzsche as the literary vogue in higher circles. I sought to orient myself in this new field, but it was not easy. S.K. was accessible to me only in German translations, most of which were not faithful interpretations. I read many commentators, but I confess that I got precious little out of them, except from Geismar and Hirsch. It is not creditable to German scholarship that few of those who lately have been writing about S.K. had taken the pains to learn Danish. At that time I wondered greatly at Unamuno, who in his *Del sentimiento tragico de la vida* traced all his quotations from S.K. to the Danish text. I learn lately from Dr. John Mackay that Unamuno said somewhere, "I learned the language for the sake of reading Ibsen, and I was rewarded by reading Kierkegaard." At that time the excellent French translations of S.K. were not yet in existence. Now that the French display so fervent an interest in him I remember with amusement the remark made by

S.K.'s one-time fiancée in her mature years: "The French will never be able to understand Kierkegard."

But at the time of which I am speaking Karl Barth began to make S.K. widely known in religious circles, and his works were being rapidly translated into English. Seeing that Barth expressly claimed S.K. as his spiritual progenitor, it seemed only courteous to take him at his word. This proved to be a misunderstanding, for in 1934 he excommunicated S.K. and Brunner in the same breath . . . on the ground that they were essentially Catholic. However, two years before he uttered his famous NEIN ! I naively set about interpreting Barth in terms of S.K. in a series of lectures I delivered on the Bohlen Foundation (to an audience of one). In publishing these lectures (*Our Concern with the Theology of Crisis*) I stuck into it a short list of books of and about S.K. in German (there being no others available) and half apologized for this "accusing bibliography as an intrusion," but I added, perhaps impertinently, "But for what reason have we so many universities? Is it to insure that studious youth shall be shielded from all contacts with contemporary thought?" This was printed in such small type and in so insignificant a place that I could reasonably hope it might be overlooked. However, as it has been quoted by two reviewers of the translations of S.K. it may be regarded perhaps as the first shot, a mere pistol shot, in the campaign to introduce S.K. to the English speaking world.

I did not know then that David F. Swenson, Professor of Philosophy in the University of Minnesota, had for many years been trying in a more mannerly way, and therefore with less obvious success, to put S.K. over. He was by far the most competent translator and expounder of S.K. in the English-speaking world, and now after his death the rich fruit of his study has been made available to the public.

My campaign in favor of S.K. was at first exceedingly desultory—in the literal sense which S.K. attached to that word, that is to say, I was hopping about from place to place. "Superannuated" as I was, I declined no invitation to talk in any theological seminary or before any group of ministers. I sometimes used Karl Barth as an entering wedge. I think still that my misunderstanding of Barth was excusable; for when I became acquainted with S.K.'s works I saw that Barth owed much more to him than he could acknowledge without pedantry, for he owed to him very many of his most telling phrases. At that time I chided Professor Wilhelm Pauck for not expressing wholehearted admiration for Barth, and he replied not ineptly that he might have written as enthusiastically as I if he had felt as free to select only those parts of his doctrine which he liked.

In my desultory campaign I made a tremendous hop to China, where I was invited to lecture to the professors of Yenching University. I grasped eagerly at that invitation, not because I cherished any illusions about furthering there the cause of S.K., but because from my childhood I had a passionate interest in China, and as a serious man I could not without loss of face make so long a journey unless I could allege a serious pretext. The winter in Peking was a memorable experience, but of course I made no converts to S.K. Modern China looks so exclusively to America for its modern culture that since S.K. was not known there the inference was inevitable that he could not be worth knowing. But, as I said, the winter in Peking was a memorable one. We discarded the palace of Marquis Li Hung Chang in favor of the more glorious residence of the Prime Minister of Chien Lung, who impoverished the Empire and provoked rebellion in the provinces by the exactions he made to provide for his private extravagances, and was sentenced to death by the next emperor. Yenching University is established in the beautiful park of the Prime Minister's summer residence, and in one of the American mission compounds I looked with wonder at the monument he was politely allowed to erect in commemoration of his virtues. All this for the glorification of S.K. But to tell the truth we took this big house because we were unable to find the little one we wanted. With scant justification I adopted as my style: Dr. Lowrie of Rome and Peking. But S.K. got precious little out of it.

In Japan the situation was very different, for Japan looks quite as much to the Continent of Europe for the enrichment of its culture. There I found myself compelled by a mere chance to make an address before the whole University of Doshisha. I protested that I could not speak about S.K. before so general an audience, but I was assured that no subject could be more acceptable, since several articles had lately been written about him in the *University Review*.

But my interest is in home-missions, and here at home I was soon in touch by correspondence with all the men in England and America who were then known to be interested in S.K., and enough interested to want to do something about it. How few there were! In Great Britain I knew of only three besides Alexander Dru. Two of them, Dr. Bain and Mr. Allen, when in an incredibly short time they had finished their little books, washed their hands of Kierkegaard—Mr. Allen the more vigorously because like Schrempf he had been led by him to renounce the Christian faith . . . and he could not forgive him for the embarrassment in which that had placed him. In America besides Swenson I can enumerate only six, and in the end only one of these did something. The voluminous correspondence I carried on with Professor Swenson for seven years has been collected by Mrs. Swenson and presented to the University of Minnesota. It was exceedingly encouraging and helpful to me.

For some years my correspondence with Mr. Dru was quite as active, and on his side it was highly entertaining. My correspondence with him and Mr. Williams, supplementing the letters which passed between me and Swenson, provides abundant documentation for the whole story. Charles Williams is the only man I have ever taken to my heart "unsight unseen." It was a wrench to both of us when eventually I had to withdraw from my association with the Oxford Press. But Dru was twice in the States, and therefore I had the pleasure of knowing him face to face. He was perhaps more inclined to accept me as a partner because I am not a don like Professor Swenson and because I do not live in the Middle West. One summer when I was in Italy we almost got together. He had promised to bring Haecker to meet me there in a remote Alpine valley, and I agreed to bring Ferlov, who was cooperating in the French translations, and Professor Lombardi, who had just written the first Italian book on S.K. . . . and then washed his hands of the subject. But the best laid plans . . . Dru's very liberal education includes even Danish. He is a young Catholic layman, and (if I may say so without offense) a man of fashion. He seemed to me ideally fitted to be a translator and expounder of S.K., who only too rightly feared that he would fall a prey to the pedantry of the professors and might with even more reason have feared the narrowness of the parsons. In fact Dru has done notable service to the cause of S.K. and had proposed to do so much more when his plans were nipped by the war. And yet perhaps his big plans might not have materialized in any case, and that precisely for the reason that he was not a professor or a parson and therefore lacked the indefatigable industry the professor and the parson sometimes have.

Lately I was struck by the justice of an expression which Dr. John McConnachie applied to me: "the indefatigable Dr. Walter Lowrie." At least so I read it at first. It is hardly a flattering expression. And yet how true! I am exceedingly industrious—and I know that the definition of genius as "an infinite capacity for taking pains" is as far as possible from the mark. I must be indefatigable if, besides having other things to do, I managed to publish four volumes of Kierkegaard translations last year and six this. But in fact Dr. McConnachie described me as "irrepressible." I don't like that word. And yet Dr. McConnachie has commonly been generous in his reviews of my books. But this particular book was not about S.K., it was about *SS. Peter and Paul in Rome,* and because I was spending that winter in Rome I did not go far out of my way when I drew a comparison between the Empire of Augustus and the Fascist regime. But in the meantime came the war. And I have some acquaintance with the *perfervidum ingenium scotorum.* And yet perhaps there may be some justification for the word "irrepressible." Mrs. Swenson said of her husband that he did not succeed in making S.K. widely known because he was not so "aggressive" as Dr. Lowrie. That is a hateful word, and yet I know that it is commonly used in America without any notion of implying belligerency. Not travelling salesmen only but simple Christians are told that they must be aggressive. Perhaps I am aggressive in the proper sense of the word. I have had an experience which suggests that this may be so. At the annual garden party of the Graduate College at Princeton I was told that Henry Goddard Leach is looking for me. Mr. Leach is editor of the *Forum* and also president of the American-Scandinavian Foundation. I found him surrounded by several admiring youths whom he was about to send with scholarships to Sweden. When I approached he drew their attention to me and apostrophized me in these words: "The man who has done more than any other to bring Scandinavia and America together . . . and done it by making everybody mad." These words were a revelation to me—but thereby hangs a tale which I must tell at some length because this is where Providence comes in, the Providence which rules and overrules, the Divinity which shapes our ends, rough hew them as we will, the Providence for which Danish has a distinctive name, *Styrelsen,* which I have ventured to translate by Governance, and which I am too aggressive to give up, although it has met with no commendation and with some criticism. For it seems to me a pity that in English we have no name to distinguish the Providence which rules from the Providence which provides.

It seemed to me obvious that a fund must be secured for the publication of S.K.'s works, inasmuch as the public could not be expected to support the venture in its initial stage. It was natural to appeal to the American-Scandinavian Foundation, and Mr. Leach was well known to me. He entered ardently into the plan and made no doubt that ten thousand dollars could be raised by appealing to the friends of the Foundation. It happened at that moment that Mr. Cumberlege of the Oxford University Press was in New York. Mr. Leach charged me to draw up a contract with him. The contract proposed was agreeable to everyone. Mr. Leach was ready to sign it as soon as he had the money in hand, and he drew up at once the preliminary draft of a letter which was to be sent to prospective donors, sending it to me first with a request for my criticism of its form. I was naïve enough to take him at his word, and perhaps I criticized that letter too drastically. At all events I was told by return post that unexpected obstacles had arisen and the whole thing was off. Even then it did not occur to me that I had made "everybody mad." I learned that some years later at a garden party.

But this is where Providence comes in. Mr. Cumberlege returned to England impressed by the importance of S.K. Mr. Dru wrote to me at once that at last the doors of the Press at which he had knocked in vain were open to him. He had already gained the adhesion of Mr. Charles Williams, who has continued to be the foster father of our undertaking. While Dru held the door open I walked in—metaphorically. This was in 1936. By that time I had ready my big book on *Kierkegaard. I* could be sure that Oxford would publish it, Dru could go ahead confidently with his big work of translating the *journal,* and Swenson, having translated the *Philosophical Fragments,* got ahead of us all and had it published by the Princeton Press for the American-Scandinavian Foundation, which again later displayed its magnanimity by contributing a part of the cost of publishing Professor Swenson's translation of the *Postscript.*

But of course the Oxford Press had not yet committed itself to the plan of publishing all of S.K.'s works, it was prepared only to take one step at a time, tentatively, and therefore to encourage it in this enterprise I undertook to defray the cost of publishing whatever I might produce, with the tacit understanding that it would assume responsibility for all other translations it would publish. I had no notion then how much I was letting myself in for, since at that time I did not think of translating anything more than *The Point of View,* which was published in 1939, and the two volumes entitled *Training in Christianity* and *For Self-Examination,* which for various reasons were not published till the middle of this current year. On the other hand, the English collaborators seemed to be going ahead with all sails set. A letter from Mr. Williams of January 21, 1938, said, "*Fear and Trembling* and *Repetition* are done . . . the translations of *The Concept of Dread* and *The Sickness unto Death* are well on the way." Nothing came of all this except the publication the following year of *Fear and Trembling*—and that I have had to do over again. The consequence is that, while Oxford has received all the praise it merited for launching out upon so bold an adventure, I have borne most of the expense. And now that because of the war, and for other reasons, I have had to transfer to the Princeton Press the responsibility of completing the English edition, the cost of it still rests upon me, except so far as it is shared by Mrs. Swenson. I may remark by the way that the total costs involved in the publication of S.K.'s works in English far exceed the sum Mr. Leach and I originally reckoned, and that in spite of the fact that translators have been paid nothing at all. That had to be a labor of love. And yet that sum as a revolving fund might have been sufficient if the production had been less rapid and more time had been left for the turnover.

It was not until May of 1938 that the Oxford Press resolved to commit itself to the plan of publishing all of S.K.'s works, and as that too came about in a providential way I must express my gratitude by telling the story in some detail. I can say of the success of this edition, as S.K. said of his works, that if I must ascribe it to anyone, I must ascribe it to Governance.

From the moment my *Kierkegaard* biography was published I have been engaged in a constant struggle to keep prices down. I was concerned chiefly about the American price, for, strange as it may seem, we have never been willing in America to pay extra for quality; and in this case the American prices were necessarily enhanced by the duty exacted on books printed abroad, an exaction which, when the author happens to be an American, is so considerably increased that it may be regarded as a penalty upon disloyalty. But surely it was going too far when the New York branch advertised at ten dollars my *Kierkegaard* when it was sold for half that price in Great Britain, i.e. for 25s. I was so indignant at this that I wrote at once (perhaps "aggressively") to the Oxford Press, demanding the return of the manuscripts they then held in order that I might have them published in America. By return post on the date of May 26, 1938, Mr. Williams wrote what he himself characterized as "a passionate appeal" to me to reconsider my decision. He promised, "officially and unofficially," to remedy the grievances I complained of, which besides the question of price included vexatious delay in printing and negligence on the part of the New York branch in failing to keep on hand a stock of books sufficient to supply the demand. To this letter was appended the following postscript:

> Sir Humphrey has been at Oxford while I was writing this letter. He has just returned and has seen the correspondence. He endorses everything I have said above, and has asked me to tell you that the Vice-Chancellor (Dr. Lindsay, Master of Balliol) was so excited by the copy of your book which he had, that he found it difficult to turn to the business of the meeting before him. He insisted on being given all possible information about it, and about any further possibilities.

This was decisive. Not only did it decide me to continue with the Oxford Press on the assurance that prices would be kept at a tolerable level (my *Kierkegaard* being at once reduced to seven dollars), but it decided Sir Humphrey Milford to proceed resolutely with the publication of S.K. Dru wrote to me at once:

> Now that the OUP are really excited (as much as they can be) about SK, all should go smoothly. Williams is always good about it, and now, as you know, Sir Humphrey is convinced that he is backing the right horse.

The question of the price of these books continues to be a serious problem. It cannot be greatly reduced by the Princeton Press, for most of the volumes are not only bulky but difficult to print, and at this stage the editions are necessarily small. I rejoice that the Augsburg Publishing House is able to issue books at a cheaper price, for I desire above all to see them made available to the clergy. But it must be admitted that these are cheaper books, and I have often thought that preachers, if only they knew how many headaches they would be saved in a frantic search for a theme, might count that they could well afford to spend fifty dollars for a whole shelfful of S.K.'s works. Or a parish might well make this gift to their preacher, with better effect and at far less cost than if, as sometimes is done, he were to be sent on a trip to the Holy Land with the vain hope that this experience might make his sermons more glamorous.

But here I exaggerate. For I am well aware of the fact that a great many parsons, especially in America, if they were to become acquainted with S.K., would indignantly reject him. He is a "corrective," and they want no correction. Today as in his own age he presents an either/or—either New Testament Christianity/or none at all—and perhaps there are not many willing to face that dilemma. Moreover, it is true now as then that not all-not even all the reverend parsons—are competent to understand him. For them, if they are men of good will, his thought must be popularized (preferably in cheap books), otherwise he must remain inaccessible to them. For, eager as he was to be heard by the "simple man," his works, even the Discourses, were addressed to the cultured classes. It is appropriate therefore that in English they are published by a university press. In spite of war and everything else, it has proved to be a great advantage that the first works were launched by the Oxford Press. But for that the reviewers would hardly have been so friendly. And again it was providential that, when I resolved to have my translations printed in my own town, Princeton University Press was under the able direction of Mr. Joseph A. Brandt, who has taken a lively interest in this edition. It should be understood that this change did not involve an absolute breach of continuity, inasmuch as Princeton is careful to maintain the uniformity of the edition, and Oxford is not merely the agent for sales in

Europe but in certain cases has adopted the policy of purchasing in sheets a considerable number of copies of translations published here.

But I have got too far ahead with the story. I must return to a point near the beginning.

At the beginning it was obvious that before S.K.'s works were sprung upon a public totally unprepared to understand him, an entering wedge was needed, in the form of a pretty big book about him. I wonder now that I had the temerity to undertake such a thing, that is, to write a life of S.K. on a large scale. I hardly realized then that, although an immense amount of biographical material had been collected by Danish scholars, nothing that could properly be called a biography had yet been written. I was not so much dismayed as I ought to have been at the necessity of learning Danish; for, though I have no aptitude for learning languages, I have from time to time been obliged to learn so many that the thought of adding a new one to the list was not an appalling obstacle. When I had barely acquired the rudiments my wife and I made a visit to Denmark, which was made profitable by the extraordinary kindness of Dr. Johannes Prip-Møller and his wife, friends we had made in China, who were our constant guides and instructors during our whole stay in their land. Upon returning home I took the precaution to engage a Danish butler, to help me if necessary over hard places. He was more capable of rendering such aid than one might suppose, for it chanced that he had a passion for philology. Though I rarely had to appeal to him, it gave me peace of mind to have him in the house. Although one-third of my book was translation from S.K., I was in this case free to sidestep or leap over passages which were too hard for me. I did not then foresee that I must subsequently undertake the more exacting task of translating the works as a whole, which did not permit me to avoid difficulties—as the German translators commonly have done. In one way or another I gathered only too much material for my book, and in the end I had to eliminate one-third of what I had written in order to reduce the volume to a possible size.

Mr. Brandt now asks me to write for the Princeton Press a briefer sketch, and to me this invitation is very alluring. What should be written about him after all his works are published in English is of course very different from what had to be written before a single work of his had been published. There is now no necessity for such abundant quotation, and it is possible now to offer some analysis of his thought and to trace in a measure the lines of its development. I mean no disparagement of my first book when I say that now after I have translated the greater part of S.K.'s works I possess a more intimate acquaintance with his thought.

At first I regarded myself merely as a promoter. It was as a promoter I wrote a book about S.K. I did not conceive that I was competent to be a translator. But gradually I learned to translate S.K. by translating him, and little by little I was compelled to go further. I began with the distinctively religious works of the last period, but because few translators volunteered I was forced to go backward, reversing the direction S.K. had taken, so that I ended with the "aesthetic" works. I wonder now at my simplicity in supposing that if only an ample fund could be raised, the translation would take care of itself. Dr. Swenson experimented with several translators who came to naught. Several Danes sent to me their translations in manuscript, but they were not written in "English as she should be spoke." I soon realized that not everyone who knows Danish is therefore capable of understanding S.K.'s thought, and that it is necessary first of all for a translator to know how to write English. For S.K. was a great stylist, and it is a crime to render him dull or ineffective. It is to my mind as great a crime to replace his style by another. Our idiom is enough like his to make a literal translation possible. Both Dru and Swenson adhered to this principle, but neither was bold enough to carry it out as I did. This boast will likely be taken as a condemnation of my work. For the academical tradition of translating Greek and Latin by elegant paraphrases has corrupted many translators. To be sure, the concise phrases of Roman rhetoricians like Cicero cannot be translated briefly in English, but this is not true to the same extent of any modern language, though there is a Latin quality in S.K.'s style. A curious story was told after his death by one of his schoolmates, to the effect that young Søren's Danish style was so involved as a result of his study of Latin that his comrades had to rewrite his school exercises. This story was heard incredulously at a time when S.K.'s works were quoted in schoolbooks as models of Danish diction; but I can believe it when I note that, though he overcame his awkwardness, he retained to the end a certain abruptness (due for example to a sparing use of the conjunction "and") which tempts most translators to pad him. One may remember that he was not only proficient in Latin ("both in its written and in its spoken form," as his teacher said of him) but was for a while a Latin teacher.

Another providential dispensation was Dr. Eduard Geismar's visit to the United States for a series of lectures on S.K., which he was invited to give in the spring of 1936 on the Stone Foundation at Princeton Theological Seminary, and which he repeated many times on a journey which took him across the continent and back. Dr. Geismar, Professor of Theology in the University of Copenhagen, was the most distinguished European authority on S.K.'s life and works. His tour of the United States was at that precise moment the most effective propaganda we could have devised. His lectures, with an admirable introduction by Professor Swenson, were published the following year by the Augsburg Publishing House in Minneapolis, and the edition was soon exhausted. To this initial success was doubtless due the interest this house has since taken in the publication of translations from S.K. The journey to America proved to be Dr. Geismar's last service in a life-long devotion to the cause of Kierkegaard, for he died not long after his return to Denmark.

His visit to America came about on this wise. Professor Adolf Keller of the University of Geneva had not long before delivered the Stone Lectures at Princeton, and at that time he had suggested that Professor Geismar would be an apt choice for this lectureship—so he told me when I met him somewhere in Europe. This information emboldened me to press the matter upon the attention of Dr. J. Ross Stevenson, at that time President of Princeton Theological Seminary. I was dismayed to find that Dr. Keller's proposal had been forgotten. However, my suggestion was considered with favor, and owing chiefly to the zealous intervention of Dr. John Mackay, who was one of S.K.'s most enthusiastic champions, and soon succeeded Dr. Stevenson as President of the Seminary, the committee in charge accepted my proposal and invited Dr. Geismar to come to America. It was left to Professor Swenson and me to organize the lecture tour throughout the country. Professor Swenson's amazing efficiency in arranging the railway schedule led me to suspect that he could not be a real philosopher. So far from resenting this imputation, he humbly explained that he was "only a professor." But I think it is true of professors in general that they cannot be expected to handle time-tables with such extraordinary dexterity. I loved Dr. Geismar, and his visit was the happiest episode in this story.

In spite of the fact that this edition has come about without an editor there is more uniformity than one might expect. At the very outset I took tremendous pains to provide against divergence in the translation of S.K.'s most distinctive terms and more especially of the titles he used for his books. I corresponded in this interest with everybody who might be interested. This effort did succeed in some degree. But a little controversy I had with Professor Swenson about the title of the book which I called *Scraps* and which he tardily decided to call *Fragments* shows how hopeless my effort was. I told this story in the first note to the *Stages*. Other divergences, though they are of no great importance, may be worth mentioning lest the reader who reads more than one book might be puzzled by them. For *Øjebliket* which Dru and I translate by "the instant" Swenson uses "the moment"; for *Moment* he also uses "moment" whereas I commonly use "factor"; for *Praest* he commonly uses "clergyman" where I use "parson"; and Dru is singular in using "scandal" for the New Testament notion of "offense" or "stumbling-block." If the American-Scandinavian Foundation had sponsored the undertaking, there would of course have been an editor, and undoubtedly it must have been Swenson, however reluctant he was to assume such a responsibility. Then the books would have been issued in a more reasonable order. As things turned out the edition grew all by itself, and now that it is finished there is not much reason to repine. Not long ago Professor Reinhold Niebuhr complained to me that there ought to be an editor. He was vexed that the books he most wanted had not yet been published. I was able to content him by the reply that all these books would be published within a year, and as for the lack of an editor I called his attention to the fact that undesignedly I had become something more than that, having translated most of the works myself and collaborated in editing others.

Apart from the substance of S.K.'s teaching there are two factors which will be repellent to most modern readers: One is his Biblicism, the other his Classicism. On the part of the reader he expects a knowledge of the Bible which is rare in our day, and he exacts at the same time a thorough acquaintance with the literature of Greece and Rome, the Classical heritage. That, too, has become rare in our day, even among the cultured classes. This puts to a severe test the translator. Besides the Danish dictionary he must have at hand a Danish Bible and a concordance—preferably the old text which S.K. used. Still more striking perhaps, and even more remote from the interest of the generality of readers is his constant reference to the literatures of Europe from the Middle Ages down to his own day. But this is an expression of the fact that S.K. was a Humanist in the most eminent sense. If ever I get to the point of writing a second and last book on S.K., I shall stress this fact emphatically. For it is commonly overlooked. On account of the severity of his Christian teaching (which he protests is many degrees more lenient than the Gospel) he is often regarded as intolerant, narrow and morose-and this in spite of the fact that his major works were "aesthetic." True, his tendency was "away from the aesthetical" toward the ethical and the religious; but he said emphatically that by the religious "the aesthetical is not abolished but dethroned." He would have said the same about Humanism, Classical culture in the broadest sense. He was not disposed like St. Augustine to discard all this that he had once loved, to suppose that he must offer it as a sacrifice to a serious view of Christianity. In his own experience of "becoming a Christian" the Humanistic spirit was indeed dethroned from the chief place it is wont to claim, but he boasted that it was not abolished. He remained a Humanist when he became a serious Christian, and for this reason he was essentially a Catholic, as Father Przywara recognizes. And for this very reason Barth rejected him. It was owing to his Humanism that he disdained every sectarian movement however zealous. Yet for all that he is often regarded as a narrow and bigoted Christian. Nothing could be further from the truth. In his last and most trenchant religious works he often protests, "I am not severity, I am leniency"; and when he proposed to the leaders of the Church that they should formally admit that the religion they taught and practised was not in the strictest sense Christianity, the Christianity of the New Testament, he was recommending in a way the Catholic doctrine of the *consilia*. His Humanism will endear him to some men of today, and to some it will damn him. But if this is to be my last word about Kierkegaard, I would assert emphatically that he was a Humanist as well as a Biblicist. The proof of this affirmation is now clearly furnished by the complete edition of his works. And yet it may not be credited, for in a modern man, especially in a Protestant, this combination is all but unique.

It was lately suggested to me that Paul Elmer More was such an exception. He justly called himself a Humanist, and he became a Christian . . . without renouncing his Humanism. At my exhortation he read one work of S.K.'s not long before he was taken ill, and of course at the first reading he understood very little of it. To me it was exasperating that he could not go further, for I was exceedingly eager to witness his reaction. It was like Brandes' disappointment when he sought to introduce Kierkegaard to Nietzsche and found that his mind was already too clouded to read him.

Among my personal friends Professor Ernesto Buonaiuti of Rome combines most perfectly the ideal of the Humanist and the Christian. In his first stage he was a Humanist and a Liberal—but that is hardly a combination, it is not a synthesis but rather a relation of identity. But at the same time he was a Catholic, and became a profound Christian through the fact that he was excommunicated. He became even, I would say, a more profound Catholic when he found refuge in the lofty spiritualism of Giocchino da Fiore and the later followers of St. Francis . . . yet still remains a Humanist, capable of expounding the Greek tragedies as profoundly as he does the Gospel.

S.K., too, is a profound expositor of the Greek religion. Nothing that is religious is foreign to him. While as a corrective, in view of current aberrations, he insists upon the transcendency of God, he insists less frequently but no less emphatically upon God's immanence. His constant "practice of the presence of God" almost justifies the common notion that he was a mystic. While he insists that for the adult Christian mind Christianity must be expressed by reflection as the paradoxical religiousness, yet he insists also that the substratum of it all is "immediacy," the element in which all religion, including Christianity, lives and moves and has its being; and he represents that in giving up the "first immediacy" the Christian attains "immediacy after reflection."

I am reminded rather tardily that "Humanism" is the name often assumed today by the most blatant opponents of Christianity. It must be clear enough that in what was said above I did not have this use of the word in mind. I resent fiercely this misuse. For what has this all-too-human Humanism to do with the Classical culture of Greece of which its exponents are commonly ignorant? It has only this resemblance, that it is paganism—but paganism, be it noted, without religion and without the search for God. The paganism of Greece, as exemplified by its tragedians and its philosophers, represents man's utmost reach after the divine, independent of revelation. This Humanism of Athens was innocent, St. Paul affirmed: "The times of this ignorance God winked at, but now commandeth all men everywhere to repent." No longer was it innocent when it ceased to "seek after God" and rejected the Gospel as "foolishness." I would jealously guard against the misapprehension that S.K., even in his rebellious youth, was a Humanist in this sense, that he was ever a man in full rebellion against God. But he came so near to the brink of the abyss that he could effectively give warning of the danger. This humanism was precisely what he depicted in his aesthetical works, what he branded as demoniacal, what he clearly envisaged as despair, leading to perdition, and out of which, as brands from the burning, he sought to allure men by the promise of the peace of the Gospel, even the peace of suffering. One of his most striking sayings applies here: "Why is it so difficult to believe? Because it is so difficult to obey."

INDEX

A

Aarsleff, Carl, 4
Adler, case of, 126, 192, 210
aesthetic works, 144*ff.*
Ahsverus, 95
allowance, 110
Andersen, H. C., 7, 15, 111, 133, 182
Anger, Pastor, 40
Anti-Climacus, 200*ff.*, 217
Antigone, 76*ff.*
Apostle, 194
"Armed neutrality," 210
attack, open, 239*ff.*

B

background, 3*ff.*
Balle's Lesson Book, 44
Barfod, H. P., 31, 35*f.*, 71
Barth, Karl, 173
becoming a Christian, 125, 174
Berlin, 15, 144*ff.*, 157*ff.*, 186, 203
Boesen, Emil, 8, 120, 144, 157, 254*f.*
Brandes, Georg, 198, 220
Brandt, Prof. Frithiof, 7, 34, 106*f.*, 111
breaking a leg, 98
Brøchner, Prof. Hans, 6
brothers and sisters, 22*f.*, 64
burial, 255*f.*

C

cafés, 58
Captain, the, 231*f.*
Carpocratians, 94
carriage drives, 15, 191
childhood, 25*ff.*, 31*ff.*, 37*ff.*

choice, 174
choice of profession, 82*f.*
Christian Discourses, 197
Climacus, Johannes, 45, 55*ff.*, 166*f.*
Climacus reviews S.K.'s works, 169
Concept of Dread, 93, 163
Concept of Irony, 149
Concluding Postscript, 168*f.*
Copenhagen, 3*ff.*, 9*ff.*, 15
Corsair, The, 7, 176*ff.*, 193
counsels of perfection, 220*f.*
country parish, 169, 185, 190
cramp, 126
crazy upbringing, 50*f.*
cross roads, 79*ff.*
Crucifixion, picture of, 49*ff.*
Cry, the Midnight, 242*f.*
curse, the father's, 71*f.*
Cycle of Essays, 210

D

De omnibus dubitandum est, 166
death, S.K.'s, 253*ff.*
debts, 96
Declaration, First and Last, 169*f.*
dedication to his father, 162
defiance, 97
definite message, 225
demon of wit, 112
Denmark, 3*ff.*, 12*f.*
despair, 97
Diapsalmata, 92, 149
"Diary of the Seducer," 149*f.*
Don Juan, 94*ff.*
Don Juan, 93*f.*
doubt, 122
dramatic instinct, 57
dread, 101*f.*
Dru, Alexander, 84, 90, 136, 203, 207
drunkenness, 99, 114